Chemistry for Beginners

poetry

CHEMISTRY FOR BEGINNERS:

DESIGNED FOR

COMMON SCHOOLS,

AND THE

YOUNGER PUPILS

OF

HIGHER SCHOOLS AND ACADEMIES.

WITH ENGRAVINGS.

BY MRS. A. H. LINCOLN PHELPS,

Author of Familiar Lectures on Botany, Botany for Beginners, Female Student, &c.

NEW YORK:
PUBLISHED BY HUNTINGTON AND SAVAGE,
216 PEARL STREET.
CINCINNATI:—H. W. DERBY & CO.
1850.

ENTERED,
According to Act of Congress, in the year 1834, by
F. J. HUNTINGTON,
in the Clerk's Office of the District Court of Connecticut.

STEREOTYPED BY FRANCIS F. RIPLEY,
NEW YORK.

PREFACE.

THE design of this work is to teach Chemistry to beginners. The author has sought to present the elements of the science in a popular and attractive form, without offending the scholar by marring its classical beauty and proportions. It is difficult for the profound chemist, to whom the *abstruse doctrines* of the science are far more familiar than its *first steps*, to bear in mind, that, to the beginner, chemical terms are as the words of an unknown tongue; and that it is not *principles* alone which he must be taught, but the very *language* in which these principles are expressed. The remark has often been made by experienced teachers, that they had never taught so well as when learning themselves; they were then most sensible of the difficulties which the beginner must encounter, and best able to assist him in overcoming them. A scientific professor once said to a lady, in a sarcastic tone—" and so *you* are going to attempt to teach Chemistry?" " Yes," said she, good-naturedly, " as fast as I can learn it myself." The same professor was afterwards engaged to lecture, and perform experiments before the lady's class, but her pupils complained that his language was so little adapted to their attainments, that they could not understand his lectures until explained to them in the familiar language of their teacher.

A brilliant course of experiments is often of as little use to the beginner as the sight of an exhibition of fire-works, or the ascension of a balloon. They show, indeed, the skill and knowledge of the experimenter, but rather confuse, than assist the ignorant pupil. Thus it is that many a college student graduates, without having profited by the elaborate and elegant lectures with which he may have been favoured, because he was ignorant of the language and first principles of the science. These should have been acquired before. Professors in colleges and universities ought not to be expected to devote their time to teaching the *a b c* of Chemistry; those can do this as well who are not as capable of being useful in the higher walks of science. We trust no learned Professor will be provoked to say to us, in the spirit of the gentleman just quoted—" and so *you* have attempted to write a book on Chemistry;" for we humbly acknowledge that all we have aspired to is, to prepare those who may be privileged to

attend upon his instructions to understand them, without subjecting him
to the necessity of explaining terms and first principles.

There is another class, too, and that probably the most numerous, whose
interests we have had in view in the preparation of this work; it is those
pupils who may not have future opportunities to pursue the study, except
as they are led to make researches by private reading and observation.
To give such a taste for chemical pursuits, (without expecting in this little
volume to make them chemists,) has been the writer's aim; and especially
has she wished to manifest to the young, that every step in the science
throws new light upon the economy of nature, and the wisdom of its
great Author.

The engravings in this book are in many cases from original designs;
some are copied from the works of Hare and Silliman, with the consent
of these gentlemen. Besides the important aid of these works, the author
has availed herself of assistance from Webster's Chemistry, and has derived valuable hints from Eaton's Chemical Instructor. To Professor
Hare she feels greatly obliged for his polite and encouraging attentions in
forwarding to her some recent publications of his own, containing draw
.ngs of newly invented, and highly useful apparatus.

TO TEACHERS.

It is desirable that teachers should be able to make some experiments, let them be ever so simple; but some who use this book, will probably be so situated as to render it very difficult. They must hear lessons in the bustle of the school-room, with neither space nor time for experiments. In view of this, I have endeavoured to make the work plain and simple, and to give such drawings as might compensate, as far as possible, for the want of experiments. Where the classes who use this book can hear lectures, the order of the subjects should be varied to suit that of the lecturer. If your pupils are to hear a lecture on affinity, it would be well that they should previously study upon this subject, and afterwards be examined upon the matter of the lecture as well as the book. In the Female Seminary at Troy, where for several years I had the charge of the chemical department, the pupils were required to perform experiments, and to give lectures before the class on given subjects. In public examinations, each one had a subject assigned her, and was directed to suitable books where she might read and investigate for herself. The labour of thus directing them to search for principles, facts, and illustrations, was, indeed, in some cases, greater than to have written the lecture; but it was often richly rewarded by its beneficial effect on the mind of the pupil.

From a paper before me containing an arrangement of subjects for these lectures of the pupils in 1829, the following is extracted as an example of the method:

Subjects.

Miss *Lucy*   Applications of Chemistry to domestic economy
Miss *Emma*   Applications of Chemistry to medicine.
Miss *Martha*   Supporters of combustion.
Miss *Susan*   Combustible subtances.
Miss *Sarah*   Oxygen.
Miss *Mary*   Charcoal.
Miss *Clarinda*   Chemical principles involved in the making of bread.

Should this little volume lighten in some degree the arduous task of teachers, and assist them in imparting to their pupils a desire for knowledge, the author will feel that she has not laboured in vain.

1*

CONTENTS.

CHEMISTRY FOR BEGINNERS.

CHAPTER I.

INTRODUCTION.

Of the Nature and Importance of Chemistr .

1. To you, who are now commencing the study of Chemistry, it may be proper to give some reason why this is deemed a Science worthy of your attention: the object of this introductory chapter will, therefore, be, to explain what Chemistry is, and why it should be studied by young persons.

2. The knowledge of any science is desirable, because knowledge is in itself good, and it tends to make mankind better, as well as happier.

3. In former ages, knowledge was confined to a few, who, regarded by the ignorant world around them with superstitious dread, ruled over the minds of their fellow beings with the most despotic sway: indeed it was thought that men must be kept in ignorance in order that they might be governed.

4. It is now found to be the case, that the most enlightened people are the most willing to submit to such laws as are necessary for the public good; thus in every school, we find the best and wisest pupils most willing to submit to rules. Since, therefore, knowledge makes us better members of a community and happier in ourselves, it is our duty to learn. We live, too, in a world that God has made, and as his children, we should desire a knowledge of his works.

5. If you should go into a workshop containing many curious things, you would be likely to ask, what those things *were made of,* and *how they were put together.*

1. Of what does the introductory chapter treat ?
2. Why is knowledge desirable ?
3. Has knowledge always been made common ?
4. Why is it our duty to learn ?
5. What inquiries should you be likely to make if you were to go into a workshop ?

6. Wherever you look around, *you behold God's workman-
ship;* and should you not like to know, *what the objects in
nature are made of, and how they are put together?* This
knowledge is called Chemistry.

7. But, perhaps, you will be ready to ask, "since Zoology
tells us about animals, Botany about plants, and Mineralogy
about minerals, what is there left in nature for Chemistry to
explain?" These sciences, indeed, teach you how to class
animals, vegetables, and minerals, according to their *outward*
appearances, but Chemistry shows you *what they are made
of, and how they are put together;*

8. Here is a piece of *salt,* (I mean of that kind which is
used with our food, for there are many other kinds of salt, as
Chemistry will teach you;) this being a mineral, it is classed
among such substances by the mineralogist, who looks chiefly
to *external* characters, such as the *shape of crystals, colour,
lustre, hardness,* &c.

9. The chemist examines salt by a method which he calls
analysis; he finds that it consists of an *acid,* called *muriatic,*
and an *alkali,* called *soda,* and therefore he calls salt *muriate
of soda.**

10. By another method, called *synthesis,* the chemist proves
his analysis to have been correct; that is, he puts muriatic
acid and soda together, and finds that the result of this union
is *muriate of soda,* or common salt.

11. Here is a piece of *chalk;*—the chemist is able, by
means of analysis, to obtain from it a kind of air, called *carbonic acid gas,* and a solid substance called *lime;* thus he
calls chalk, *carbonate of lime.* On bringing lime water into
contact with carbonic acid gas, the lime and gas unite, and a
solid substance is gradually formed;—this substance is *carbonate of lime,* or chalk; and its composition has been proved
by synthesis.

* We are met by a difficulty upon the threshold of the science; since
common salt is of late considered as a *chloride of sodium.* But we are
attempting to divest science of technicalities as much as possible; we
must therefore use such terms as are most generally received, without attempting to reconcile opposing theories.

6. What knowledge is called Chemistry?
7. How does Chemistry differ from Zoology, Botany, and Mineralogy?
8. By what circumstances would a mineralogist class salt?
9. Why would a chemist call salt, muriate of soda?
10. How can the chemist prove the truth of his analysis?
11. By what two methods does the chemist prove that chalk is a carbonate of lime?

12. Having endeavoured to explain, in a familiar manner, what Chemistry is, we will now give you a more scientific definition of it ;—Chemistry teaches to examine the elements of substances, and their laws of combination.

13. The beginner in this study must not expect at once to understand all the terms which will be used; for instance, "the elements of substances" is an expression which may not be understood by the young beginner in Chemistry; and what is meant by " their laws of combination" will not be fully comprehended.

14. But patient application to study will be rewarded by a gradual enlightening of the mind, so that what at first seemed obscure and difficult to learn, will appear plain and simple.

15. We have remarked how Chemistry differs from Natural History, (as the three sciences Zoology, Botany, and Mineralogy are called,) we will now consider how it differs from Natural Philosophy. The latter science treats of the action of large bodies upon each other, as the attraction of the earth and the planetary bodies; it shows what are the laws of motion, and the principles which regulate and govern mechanical operations; while Chemistry, entering within the various substances formed by art, or existing in nature, shows us their internal structure and composition.

16. Natural History, Natural Philosophy, and Chemistry, are all necessary in order to give a complete view of objects; the first explains their outward appearance; the second their mechanical properties; and the third their constitution.

17. There is no science so intimately connected with the very life of man as Chemistry. Almost all kinds of cooking depend on chemical principles; as also the preparation of medicine, the detection of poisons, the arts of bleaching, and pottery, of making glass, ink, and leather, of dyeing, burning lime, working metals, &c. The invention of the steam engine is owing to an application of chemical principles.

18. A science connected with so many kinds of business cannot but be highly interesting to all, especially the young,

---

12. Give a scientific definition of Chemistry.
13. Is the beginner expected to understand all the terms which he will meet with?
14. What will be the effect of patient application to study?
15. How does Chemistry differ from Natural Philosophy?
16. What are the different provinces of Natural History, Natural Philosophy, and Chemistry?
17. Why is Chemistry a useful science, and what are some of the arts which depend upon its principles and discoveries?

who know not what their future condition in life may be, or what kind of knowledge may be most useful to them.) In most of the mechanical arts, and in some of the professions, those who understand Chemistry, have a great advantage over those who do not. In the cultivation of the earth, this science has also its important uses, since it teaches the farmer how to analyze different kinds of soil, and what land is best fitted for particular crops.

19. This science (bears an important relation to housekeeping in a variety of ways, as in the making of gravies, soups, jellies, and preserves, bread, butter, and cheese, in the washing of clothes, making soap, and the economy of heat in cooking, and in warming rooms :—To females, then, some knowledge of Chemistry must be very desirable. They may indeed learn to perform household operations without understanding any thing of their philosophy; but it is natural to the human mind to search into the *causes of things*, and it is thus that improvements are made.

20. We are not to suppose the domestic arts have yet arrived to that perfection of which they are capable; for as chemists are not housekeepers, nor housekeepers chemists, there has been little opportunity for the study of domestic economy in its relation to Chemistry.) Young ladies who attend to this study should therefore pay strict attention to all those facts in housekeeping which may be explained upon chemical principles, such as the action of yeast upon flour, and of pearlash upon sour dough, the change of cider into vinegar, the advantage of keeping a vessel covered in order to hasten the boiling of water, &c.; they should, in short, endeavour to gain that insight into the philosophy of common things which will aid them to perform, in the best possible manner, the duties and business of ordinary life.

21. No young man should be entirely ignorant of Chemistry; and few Americans are denied the means of instruction It is a mistaken idea that professional men only should study the sciences. (A leather-dresser or a shoemaker) should understand the chemical process by which the skins of animals are rendered hard, and tough, and impervious to water. A potter or glassmaker) ought to know why, in order to melt

18. Why is a knowledge of this science important to all, and especially to the young?
19. What relation does Chemistry bear to housekeeping?
20. Why have the domestic arts not yet received great improvement from Chemistry?
21. With what trades is Chemistry more especially connected?

certain kinds of clay and sand, he must unite with them soda, or some other article. The dyer and calico printer should understand the chemical principles connected with the combination of dye-stuffs with silk and woollen, cotton, and flax. The type maker, bell founder, and painter, are daily performing operations which chemists alone can explain. This science has taught men to form, of useless substances, compounds of great value, and to extract from unproductive compounds useful materials.

22. It should be considered by every young person, that the object in studying Chemistry is not merely to *appear* learned, and make a display by talking about *caloric, oxygen,* &c., but in reality to become wiser, and better fitted for usefulness in the world.

23. There is one view in which the science of Chemistry produces in the mind thoughts of a deep and solemn kind, and calculated to humble the pride of man. When we learn that our own bodies are composed of a few elements of the same nature as those which form the very worm that crawls, and that at death the union which subsisted between these elements being dissolved, they will be separated and pass into the substance of the weeds that may spring up from their remains ; we must feel with him, who, in his humiliation, exclaimed, " I have said to corruption, thou art my father, and to the worm, thou art my mother and my sister."* But there is a portion of ourselves which is beyond the scope of chemical science, which cannot be analyzed, because it is incapable of being separated into parts. It is that within us which thinks and feels, which knows good from evil, which is destined to an immortal existence, and which at death passes from its prison of clay to the world of spirits.

All then that is done for the improvement of the mind either in knowledge or virtue, will be permanent, while the labour bestowed upon the care and decoration of the body will perish with that frail and decaying substance.

24. In the beautiful language of one of the most distinguished men of the age,† "the mind of the enlightened and

* Job xvii. 14.   † Sir Humphrey Davy.

---

22. What should be the object of every young person who studies Chemistry ?
23. In what view of the subject does Chemistry produce solemn reflections ?
24. What effect does Sir Humphrey Davy think the study of nature ought to have on the mind ?

pious student of nature will always be awake to devotional feeling, and in contemplating the variety and beauty of the external world, and developing its scientific wonders, he will always refer to that infinite wisdom, through whose beneficence he is permitted to enjoy knowledge; and, in becoming wiser, he will become better—he will rise at once in the scale of intellectual and moral existence; and in proportion as the veil becomes thinner through which he sees the causes of things, he will admire more the brightness of the divine light by which they are rendered visible."

CHAPTER II.

Different kinds of Attraction. Simple Affinity. Elective Affinity. Double Elective Affinity.

25. BEFORE proceeding to consider the *substances* which Chemistry examines, we shall investigate the operation of a *power* by which the *simple elements* of nature are combined and kept together, thus forming all the variety of objects which our earth presents. This power is called *chemical attraction,* or *affinity.*

26. By the term attraction, in its most extended sense, is meant *the tendency of bodies to approach each other.* *Gravitation* is that kind of attraction which exists between distant bodies; it is this which causes a stone to fall to the earth. *Cohesion* is that kind of attraction which holds together similar particles of bodies, as in a lump of salt. *Affinity,* or chemical attraction, is that force which unites different substances into one compound substance; thus, salt is composed of *muriatic acid* and *soda* by chemical affinity. Besides these modes of attraction are reckoned those of Electricity and Magnetism; although chemical affinity may be occasioned by electricity, and magnetism is thought to be connected with it.

27. *The attraction of gravitation* is the power which retains the planets in their orbits. This power is such, that if two bodies of equal size were placed at ever so great a dis-

25. Of what power are we now to investigate the operations?
26. What is meant by attraction; and what are the different kinds of this power?
27. Give a more particular account of the attraction of gravitation?

tance from one another, and if there were no other bodies in
the universe to attract them in different directions, they
would rush towards one another, and meet in a point equally
distant from the one whence they started. The force of gravitation depends upon the size of a body and its distance;—
thus the smaller body will overcome the attraction of a larger
one at a greater distance. The moon is smaller than the
earth; but supposing that body should advance very near
to the earth, so that a stone thrown upwards would approach
much nearer to the moon, the stone, instead of falling downwards from the force of the earth's attraction, would fly off
to the moon. A leaden plummet suspended by a line from
the top of a mountain is attracted towards its *side*, the near-
ness of the mountain overcoming the earth's attraction, which
tends to draw it *downward*.

28. *Experiments.*—Several simple experiments may be
made to show the power of attraction, as, I. Place two globules of mercury or quicksilver on a piece of dry glass, and
push them slowly towards each other; when within a certain
distance, they will rush together.

II. If two pieces of cork or wood be placed in a dish of
water near the centre, they will approach each other with a
rapidity of motion proportioned to their size.

29. The *attraction of cohesion* differs from that of gravitation, because it operates only upon small particles of bodies
which are in contact. A piece of marble shows that it is
composed of a collection of very small particles; these are
held together by cohesion. This attraction may be overcome
by mechanical force, as pounding, grinding, &c., but the elements of which marble is composed, that is, *carbonic acid*
and *lime*, can only be separated by means of chemical analysis, or by fire.

30. Chemical attraction, or *affinity*, holds together the elements of bodies. It is necessary to understand this subject, in
order to comprehend most of the changes which are produced by means of chemical operations. It is introduced in the
beginning of your study that you may be prepared to comprehend what will follow.

31. It is necessary here to make you acquainted with some
terms of frequent use in Chemistry. A *simple* or *elementary*

28. What experiments show the power of attraction?
29. How does the attraction of cohesion differ from that of gravitation?
30. Why should Chemical attraction be introduced in the commencement of the study?
31. What is a simple or elementary substance?
2

substance is one which cannot be separated or decomposed by any chemical process.

32. These simple substances, or elements, are about fifty in number; as you are yet unacquainted even with the names of many of them, it would be of little use to give them to you to learn. We shall bring them before you separately, and when you have learned something of their peculiar characters, we will teach you how they are classed by chemists.

33. A *compound body* is one which consists of two or more simple bodies or elements; thus common salt is a compound body, consisting of soda and muriatic acid, which are united by means of chemical affinity.

34. *Decomposition*—this means a separation of the elements of compound bodies;—thus, to break salt into pieces, would not be to decompose it, but to separate it mechanically;—but in order to decompose salt, the elements must be disengaged from the union in which they are held.

35. *Analysis*—this is a very important operation in chemistry, and consists in the decomposition of a substance, in order to ascertain the elements which compose it.

36. *Synthesis*—this consists in forming a compound by putting together two or more substances.

37. The constituent parts of bodies may be ascertained either by analysis or synthesis. Thus, water is found by analysis to consist of two kinds of gas, called *Oxygen* and *Hydrogen*; and by synthesis, or the union of these two gases, water is formed. The correctness of analysis is proved by synthesis. The former process is sometimes called *decomposition*, the latter *composition*.

38. Substances exist under three forms, viz.: as *solids, liquids*, and *gases*. A solid body has its particles more closely united by cohesion than a liquid, whose particles can be moved about easily. For this reason a liquid is more penetrable than a solid.

39. A *gas* is a substance in which the particles are still less governed by cohesive attraction than in a liquid. When you

---

32. How many simple substances or elements are there?
33. What is a compound body?
34. What is meant by decomposition?
35. What is analysis?
36. What is synthesis?
37. By what two methods may the constituent parts of bodies be ascertained?
38. What is the difference between a solid and a liquid?
39. What is a gas?

burn sulphur, a yellowish vapour of a disagreeable odour rises; this is *sulphureous acid gas.*

40. The atmosphere around us, or the *air*, is a gas. But simple as it seems, the chemist can analyze it into two gases of very different properties. In the one, substances burn with vividness; in the other, burning bodies are immediately extinguished. Thus we say that the former supports combustion, while the latter does not. In the former it is found that animals can breathe freely; while in the latter they instantly die. The gas which supports combustion and life, is sometimes called *vital* air, but being found in most of the acids, it has been named Oxygen, or the *acid-maker*. The gas which extinguishes flame, and destroys life, was at first called *azote*, a *destroyer*, but afterwards, from being found in *nitric acid*, (or aqua-fortis) it was called *nitrogen.* These two gases are *mixed* together in the air, in a certain proportion; this proportion is exactly that which is necessary for the wants of animal and vegetable existence. The oxygen undiluted, would be too powerful an agent; iron stoves would consume in it, and the circulation of the blood would be too rapid for the powers of life. We shall hereafter consider these gases more fully.

41. Some kinds of matter are capable of existing either in a solid, liquid, or gaseous state. Thus ice, water, and steam are the same substances in different forms. Ice becomes water when acted upon by heat; that is, the cohesive power which held it in the solid state is overcome by heat. A greater degree of heat causes the particles of water to expand, and forms steam or vapour, which is the gaseous state. Cohesion may be so far overcome by heat as to change a solid metal into a gas.

42. There are two more terms which it is important you should understand: *homogeneous* means all of one kind; thus when salt is pounded, all the particles are found to be of the same nature. Cohesive attraction operates upon particles which are homogeneous. *Heterogeneous* means mixed; chemical attraction can only take place between heterogeneous particles; it is generally strongest between those substances which are most unlike.

43. There are *three* important particulars to be remember-

40. Is the air a simple gas?
41. What changes in the state of bodies can be effected by heat?
42. Define the terms homogeneous and heterogeneous.
43. What are three important particulars respecting the nature of Chemical affinity?

ed respecting the nature of Chemical Affinity:—*it is exerted at insensible distances ; between particles only ; and those particles are always heterogeneous.*

SIMPLE AFFINITY.

44. *Simple Affinity is that force which causes the particles of substances to unite, and produce a new compound.*

45. *Experiment.*—Take a wine glass containing a little water, and pour into it some sweet oil ; you will perceive they do not unite, but the oil floats upon the surface. Add a small bit of pearlash, and stir the mixture. You now perceive that a union of the three substances is produced, and that a new compound, soap, is formed.

· *Explanation.*—Between water and oil there is no affinity, and therefore they remain without uniting; until the pearlash, having an affinity for both, serves as a bond of union between them.

46. Pearlash contains a large portion of potash, which belongs to a class of substances for which oil and fat of all kinds have a strong affinity. These substances are called by the general name of *alkalies ;* they include lime, soda, potash, &c. We shall consider their nature as we advance in our study ; at present it may be sufficient to observe that they have a peculiar caustic property, that they change vegetable blue to a green colour, and have a strong affinity for *acids.*

47. Acids are of various kinds ; their properties, in general, are a sour taste, changing blue vegetable colours red, and an affinity for alkalies. Thus, if a small portion of a strong acid should be added to the soap, formed by the preceding experiment, the potash would leave the combination with the oil and water, and unite with the acid; this would be an instance of *elective affinity.*

48. We have shown you, by the experiment with water, oil, and pearlash, an instance of simple affinity. The making of soap on a large scale is conducted on exactly the same principles as is here illustrated. · Every economical family save all the bits of fat which are unfit for cooking, in order to use for making soap. The ashes which are collected daily from the fireplaces and stoves, are saved for the same pur-

---

44. What is simple affinity?
45. What experiment illustrates simple affinity ?
46. What is said of alkalies?
47. Of acids ?
48. Describe the process of making soap, as practised on a large scale.

pose. When the soap is to be made, the ashes are put into a
large cask, called a *leach,* and wet with water until they are
saturated, that is, until they have taken up as much water as
they will contain; after this, water being added gradually,
the *ley* runs off through holes near the bottom of the cask.—
This ley contains the strength of the ashes, or potash in solution; it is therefore highly *alkaline.* The materials which
have been collected for the purpose, usually called soap-
grease, are then thrown into a large iron kettle with the ley,
where they are boiled together.* A chemical union takes
place between the alkali and the grease, and soap is the com
pound which results from this combination.

49. By adding grease to cold ley, soap will gradually be
formed. This is called by housekeepers *cold* soap; but heat
causes the action of affinity to be more rapid, and for this reason most chemical operations are performed by the aid of
heat.

50. Hard soap is made with soda instead of potash. The
finer kinds of hard soap are made of olive, or sweet oil, water,
and soda.

51. The volatile liniment, so useful for burns and sore
throats, is made of ammonia, (hartshorn,) sweet oil, and
water, and any person can mix these three substances.

ELECTIVE AFFINITY.

52. *The force of affinity is different between different
bodies.*

53. *Elective affinity signifies that preference which one
substance has for another, by which a third substance is
excluded.*

54. *Experiment.*—Pour a few spoonfuls of camphor which
has been previously dissolved in spirits, into a tumbler, add a
small portion of water, and the camphor will collect in little
scales. It is then said to be *precipitated.*

55. *Explanation.*—The camphor and spirits were united
by the force of *simple affinity,* and formed a clear solution;
on adding the water, the spirits having a stronger affinity for

* In cities it is generally thought economical to dispose of the ashes and
grease to the soap manufacturer, and receive soap in return. In the country it is necessary for every family to make their own soap.

49. How is cold soap made?
50. How is hard soap made?
51. How is volatile liniment made?
52. Is the force of affinity equal between all bodies?
53. What does elective affinity signify?
54. By what experiment is elective affinity shown?
2*

that than for the camphor, united with it and excluded the camphor, which again appears as a white and solid substance.

56. In the next experiment, we shall speak of *sulphuric acid;** as it is a substance of great importance in many chemical operations, we will inform you that its common name is *oil of vitriol,* and that it is made by the union of *sulphur* with a gas called *oxygen,* with which you will soon be made acquainted. The union of sulphur and oxygen is an instance of *simple affinity.*

57. We shall also in our next experiment speak of *muriatic acid gas.* This will be a *new term,* but it is impossible, let us begin where we will in Chemistry, not to be obliged to introduce terms that cannot at first be familiar to the beginner. We shall now propose to you another method of illustrating *elective affinity.*

58. *Experiment.*—Put into a wine glass a teaspoon full of fine salt,† and pour upon it the same quantity of sulphuric acid. You see a white vapour rise from the mixture, and may perceive that the substance in the wine glass is of a different nature from either of those which were used for the experiment.

59. *Explanation.*—Common salt is a compound substance consisting of *soda* and *muriatic acid.* The soda having a greater affinity for the new acid which is added, *elects* it, and excludes the muriatic acid, which escapes in

---

* Those pupils who are provided with a Dictionary of Chemistry will do well to refer to it when any new substance is named. It is impossible to explain every *term,* while we attempt to proceed systematically in the development of the science, as this must be continually taking us from the main path. The use of a Dictionary of terms renders such irregularity unnecessary. No systematic work can be sufficiently full in explanation to preclude the importance of having at hand a Dictionary.

† When we speak of salt without specifying any particular kind, the pupil will understand that we mean the common table-salt. There are a great variety of substances which in Chemistry are known as salts.

---

55. How is it explained?
56. What is said of sulphuric acid?
57. What is said of the use of new terms before their explanations?
58. What experiment illustrates elective affinity?

the form of a *gas.*, But the muriatic acid gas would be invisible, except for its strong affinity for water, of which there is always more or less in the air.—The cloud which is seen rising above the glass, is formed by the union of the gas with particles of water. Near the surface of the glass (as appears in the cut) there is no appearance of vapour; this is because the gas there has not yet combined with particles of water in any considerable quantity.

60. The substance which remains in the glass, is the *soda* united to its *new friend* the *sulphuric acid;* this compound is the *sulphate of soda,* commonly called *Glauber's Salts,* from the person who first introduced it into medicine.

61. *Experiment* 2.—Into a solution of liquid *muriate of lime* let fall a few drops of *sulphuric acid.* The muriate of lime will be decomposed, sulphate of lime will be formed, and the muriatic acid being set free, will pass off in the state of a gas.

62. *Explanation.*—The lime has a greater affinity for sulphuric acid than for muriatic, it therefore *elects* the former, and the latter is excluded.

63. It is by means of *elective* affinity, that the chemist is able to decompose substances which otherwise could never be separated. For you perceive that chemical decomposition is quite different from mechanical separation. By no other means than elective affinity, could the muriatic acid and soda which compose salt, be separated; for let the salt be pounded or ground into the smallest possible particles, every particle would consist of muriatic acid and soda.

DOUBLE ELECTIVE AFFINITY.

64. There is still another form of affinity, more wonderful in its effects than those we have already considered. This is called *double elective affinity, for by its means two compounds, each consisting of two ingredients, are decomposed, forming two new compounds.*

65. In many cases one *single compound,* consisting of two ingredients, cannot be decomposed by any *single element,* as

59. Explain this experiment.
60. What is the substance remaining in the glass?
61. What is the second experiment to illustrate elective affinity?
62. Why does the lime unite with sulphuric acid?
63. Could the elements which compose salt be separated in any other way than by elective affinity?
64. What is double elective affinity?
65. Can the sulphate of soda be decomposed either by lime or muriatic acid?

sulphate of soda cannot be decomposed by lime, because sulphuric acid attracts soda more strongly than it does lime. Neither can the sulphate of soda be decomposed by *muriatic acid*, because the sulphuric acid attracts soda more strongly than the muriatic acid does.

66. But though neither lime nor muriatic acid, singly, can decompose the sulphate of soda, the *muriate* of lime, which is a compound of both, will effect this.

67. *Experiment.*—Take muriate of lime and sulphate of soda, and dissolve them in separate tumblers, then mix them, and a solid substance, the *sulphate of lime*, will settle at the bottom of the glass, while a solution of the *muriate of soda* will be above it.

68. *Explanation.*—Although neither muriatic acid nor lime, singly, could separate the two substances which com pose the sulphate of soda, yet by their mutual action at the same instant, they cause the sulphuric acid to unite itself to the lime, and the soda to the muriatic acid; thus there is a mutual exchange of partners. Lime is attracted strongly by *sulphuric acid*, soda is attracted by *muriatic acid*; and, as if by general consent, the old connexions are broken up and new ones formed.

69. The following diagram may illustrate this subject:—

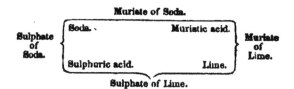

On the outside of the brackets are the original compounds, (sulphate of soda and muriate of lime;) above and below the horizontal lines are the new compounds, (muriate of soda and sulphate of lime;) the turning down of the lower line shows that the sulphate of lime is *precipitated*, and the straight upper line that the muriate of soda is in *solution*.

70. What we mean by *solution* is this:—the combination of a solid with a liquid in such a manner that it will not sepa-

66. What will decompose the sulphate of soda?
67. By what experiment is double elective affinity illustrated?
68. Explain this experiment.
69. Draw a figure to illustrate this subject.
70. What is meant by solution?

rate except by chemical analysis, or by evaporation.) Common salt dissolved in water, sugar and water, and camphor and spirits, are familiar examples of solution. A *mechanical mixture* like earth and water separates on being suffered to stand undisturbed.

71. A *precipitate* is the formation of a new body, which is insoluble in the liquor in which its elements were dissolved.) Thus when lime unites with sulphuric acid, (as in the preceding experiment,) an insoluble compound, the sulphate of lime, is formed, and this remains in a solid state. But the muriate of soda, (common salt,) which was one of the products of the double decomposition, is dissolved by water, which being present, holds that substance in solution:—and because it is lighter than the solid, it holds the upper place in the glass. All precipitates do not sink. Pour water into spirits of camphor, and the camphor precipitated floats in the spirits and water.

It may be difficult for the beginner to understand the complicated process of double decomposition; should it perplex you, it will be best to pass on to what you can the more easily comprehend; and then when you take up this subject again it will seem more intelligible.

72. We have in this chapter considered the nature of attraction in general, its different kinds, and especially the different kinds of chemical attraction or affinity) these were *simple, elective,* and *double elective.*

73. There are few compound substances in which the chemist has not been able to overcome the resistance of affinity. The means of doing this are various and often very complicated; many forces may be made to act upon a substance, which seldom effectually resists when the decomposing forces are judiciously employed.

74. "*All the processes which may be resorted to in the treatment of different substances, can only be known by a knowledge of the action which bodies exercise upon each other, of the changes which accompany this action, and of the compounds which result from it;) it is this knowledge which constitutes Chemistry.*" *

* Dictionary of Chemistry.

71. What is a precipitate?
72. What have we in this chapter considered?
73. Are there many compound substances which the chemist has been unable to decompose?
74. What knowledge is said to constitute Chemistry?

CHAPTER III.

Chemical Affinity.   Definite Proportions.   Laws of Affinity.

75. As the subject of chemical affinity is one which the student should well understand, we will devote a little more time to the consideration of some of its phenomena. By *phenomena*, you are to understand *changes* and *appearances*. It is a convenient term to express an idea which would, otherwise, require several words. By the *phenomena* of chemical affinity, we mean those *changes* which it produces on bodies, and the *appearances* which accompany these changes.

76. We have seen by experiments already made, that the change produced by chemical affinity is very great; so much so as, in many cases, wholly to alter the nature of substances.

77. *Sulphuric acid* and *potash* in a separate state, are distinguished by qualities essentially different : potash is a solid alkali, which, on being added to blue vegetable infusions, changes their colour green. Sulphuric acid is a liquid which changes blue vegetable colours red. The two substances are also distinguished by their peculiar caustic taste, and their different action on other bodies. But let us add sulphuric acid to potash, in small quantities, we shall, at length, attain a certain point, at which the compound will exhibit neither acid nor alkaline properties, will be insipid to the taste, and produce no effect on blue vegetable colours. This compound is called a *neutral salt*. The acid and alkali appear to have destroyed the properties of each other, and therefore this union is called *neutralization*. Here we see two of the most powerful and corrosive substances with which we are acquainted, producing a third which may be handled or swallowed without danger. The third substance is *sulphate of potash*, ranked in Chemistry among the *salts*, an important class of substances formed by the union of acids and alkalies.

78. When opposing properties are thus destroyed by chemical combination, the two substances are said to *saturate* each other, and the exact point at which this change is accomplished is called *saturation*.

---

75. What is meant by the expression, the phenomena of chemical affinity ?
76. What is said of the change often produced by chemical affinity ?
77. Give an example of this change.
78. What is meant by saturation ?

· 79. *Experiment.*—Put into each of two wine glasses half a teaspoon full of *muriatic acid*—weigh two equal parts of *carbonate of soda*—put gradually small quantities of these parcels into the two glasses of acid;—at first there will be a violent action, accompanied by a hissing noise; this is called *effervescence:* when the acid is saturated, or has taken up all the alkali with which it can unite, the effervescence ceases. On weighing what remains of the carbonate of soda, you·will find the two portions equal, that is, if you have been careful not to add to either glass after the effervescence ceased. On examining the contents of the wine glasses, you will find them to be a solution of common salt.

80. *Explanation.*—Carbonate of soda is composed of carbonic acid and soda—but soda has a stronger affinity for muriatic acid than for carbonic; it therefore unites with the former and expels the latter, forming the *muriate of soda,*) (common salt.) The effervescence was caused by the escape of the carbonic acid gas.

81. But what we are chiefly to illustrate by this experiment is the law of *definite proportions*, viz.: that when two substances have united up to a certain point which nature has fixed, there can no longer be any combination between them.) Should you continue to drop into the acid pieces of the carbonate of soda after it had received its definite proportion, there would be no union, but the surplus carbonate of soda would fall to the bottom of the glass, and remain unchanged in its nature. It can easily be tested whether the exact point of neutralization has been obtained, by dipping into the solution paper stained with the juice of the petals of blue violets, or with any other vegetable blue. If the alkali predominates, the colour will be greenish; if the acid prevails, the colour will be of a red tint; where the compound is *neutral*, the colour will remain unchanged.

82. Water will unite with common salt until it becomes incapable of dissolving more.) In making brine for salting meat, (especially pork, which requires a strong brine,) it is best to have some salt at the bottom of the barrel; this will always be the case when more is put into the water than that can hold in solution. When some salt remains undissolved,

79. What experiment shows the effect of saturation?
80. Explain the changes which take place in this experiment?
81. What is meant by definite proportions?
82. Is there a point beyond which water will not unite with common salt?

the proof is certain that the brine is as strong as it can be, or that the water is saturated with salt.

83. In the instance of brine, the common salt (muriate of soda) does not (as in the last experiment was the case with the carbonate of soda) change its nature by parting with one of its elements, but unites with water, (without suffering any decomposition.) But in the one case there is a great change of properties, and indeed the formation of an entirely new substance, while in the other, the qualities which belonged to the original substances remain in part the same; that is, the taste and other properties of brine are like that of salt.

84. When the carbonate of soda and muriatic acid united, a violent action was seen to take place among the combining particles; but in the union of common salt with water, as nothing is excluded, the operation goes on in a quiet manner, unattended by any remarkable phenomena. It is a general law, (that chemical action takes place when the *new substance which results from a chemical combination possesses properties unlike those of its constituent parts;*) on the contrary, when the new compound partakes in part of the properties of the substances from which it is formed, little or no visible action takes place among the combining particles.

85. By affinity, some substances unite in *indefinite proportions,* while their properties are not essentially altered. If you mix sulphuric acid and water, or alcohol and water, their properties will remain the same, although the particles being diffused among the water, there will be less in a given space.

LAWS OF CHEMICAL AFFINITY.*

86. 1st. *Affinity takes place only between bodies of a different nature,* as between an acid and an alkali: the attraction between particles of a similar nature being that of cohesion, or, as it is sometimes called, of *aggregation.*

87. 2d. *Affinity takes place only between the most minute particles of bodies;* therefore the more substances are divided by pounding, grinding, or by solution, the more read-

* The complicated nature of chemical equivalents is not here discussed, as it might perplex the beginner at the commencement of his course.

83. Does muriate of soda change its nature by uniting with water?
84. In what cases do the appearances attending chemical combinations differ? and what is a general law with respect to such combinations?
85. Do some substances unite in indefinite proportions?
86. What is the first law of chemical affinity?
87. What is the second law of chemical affinity?

ily they act upon each other; thus, if a lump of sulphur is thrown into alcohol, no action will take place; but if sulphur be finely divided and then put into alcohol, the two substances will unite, and form a transparent solution.

88. 3d. *The union produced by affinity is permanent, and cannot be destroyed by mechanical means;* solutions of salt and sugar are not decomposed by standing for any length of time, but a mixture of powdered chalk or coal having no affinity, would in time exhibit a separation, the solid part settling at the bottom, and the water appearing clear.

89. 4th. *Bodies having no affinity, are sometimes brought to unite by a third body;* thus an alkali unites oil and water.

90. 5th. *The force of affinity is different between different bodies;* this was illustrated in the decomposition of common salt by sulphuric acid; where the affinity of soda was found to be greater for sulphuric, than for muriatic acid.

91. 6th. *A change of temperature often takes place at the moment of combination;* this is very apparent in the case of adding sulphuric acid to water, when the heat becomes so great that it is impossible to hold the glass containing the mixture in the hand.

92. 7th. It is one of the most important of all the laws of affinity that, *bodies combine in certain proportions only.* Thus water is always constituted of one part, by weight, of hydrogen, to eight parts of oxygen. A salt called *sulphate of barytes*, always consists of seventy-eight parts of barytes to forty parts of sulphuric acid, and whether this salt is found native, or formed by art, these proportions are always the same. Sometimes the same substances combine in several different proportions, in which case compounds of a very different nature are produced. Sulphuric acid, for example, unites with potash to form two salts; the one, sulphate of potash, consists of forty-eight parts of potash, to forty of sulphuric acid; the other, the bi*-*sulphate* of potash, consists of forty parts of potash to eighty parts of sulphuric acid. Thus, where substances unite in more than one proportion, one of the ingredients is double, treble, or some multiple of the lowest combining numbers. We shall hereafter consider this subject more minutely.

---

* From bis, two, signifying that there is a double quantity of acid.

---

88. What is the third law of chemical affinity?
89. What is the fourth law of chemical affinity?
90. What is the fifth law of chemical affinity?
91. What is the sixth law of chemical affinity? -
92. What is one of the most important of the laws of affinity?

CHAPTER IV.

Matter.   Light—its Effects—its laws of Motion.   Rays of Light.   Colour.

93. WE are now prepared to commence an examination of *matter*, since we have considered that great law which chemically unites or brings together the *elements* out of which are formed the various natural and artificial substances which exist upon the earth.

94. What is matter? It is something which possesses qualities that are in some way manifested to our senses. Your book is matter, so is your table, the trees and stones, the bodies of animals, and your own body ; all these are *solid* matter.   The water, and all kinds of *liquids*, are another kind of matter.

95. Is the *air* matter ? When you look from the place you now sit, across the room, you see some space which *seems* to be empty, but it is not so in reality, it is filled with air. Move your hand rapidly, and you will feel the air ; its motion will be attended with a sensation of coolness.   What you can discern by any one of your senses is matter. Feeling or *touch* is a sense ; air is perceived by it, therefore air is matter.   It is a *gas*.

96. There are substances which chemists consider to be matter, that appear under a form different in many respects from our ideas of material substances ; these are *light* and *heat, electricity* and *magnetism ;* they are manifested to us only as they act upon other substances.

97. Light is not what we see, but it is that, which, by falling upon other substances, and then coming to us, seems to tell us of their existence.   If you enter a room in the dark, you do not perceive what furniture it contains, but enter the same apartment in the light of day, and your eyes at once inform your mind of the existence of chairs, tables, carpets, &c.   The picture made upon the eye is the effect of light. Its touch is so gentle, that unless the light is very strong, it gives no pain to that delicate organ, the eye ; but unless it

93. What preparation have we made towards commencing the examination of matter.
94. Give some account of matter.
95. How do you know that air is matter ?
96. Are light, heat, electricity, and magnetism, matter ?
97. Do we see light ?   What produces the picture upon the eye when images are there formed of external objects ?

touched the eye, how could it there form an image of the furniture of a room, of the landscape abroad, and the expanse of
the heavens ?

98. Light is a most wonderful agent, and the organ on
which it produces its effect is no less wonderful. When you
look upon the heavens in a clear starlight, and behold its
countless millions of suns and worlds, separated from each
other by distances beyond the power of numbers to compute,
(you see all this in a picture)not more than an inch in diameter.
Your eye does not go to the stars to learn their places and
arrangement, but light travelling in every direction, comes to
your eyes, and imprints there, that which your mind con-
templates. So that it is not the heavens which you actually
see, but a picture of them upon that part of the eye called the
retina.

99. The study of the phenomena of light, as it is connected
with sight or vision, belongs to Natural Philosophy, and is
called (*optics.*)

Light, however, as (one of the substances in nature, and as
causing some chemical changes,) claims the notice of the student in Chemistry.

100. Although light is classed among *material* substances,
(it cannot be weighed,) because neither our balances nor organs of sense are sufficiently delicate. It is therefore called
imponderable.*

101. Light proceeds *directly* from the (sun and the fixed
stars, and from the moon and the planets) by *reflection;* this
is called (*celestial* light) it also accompanies heat in fire, and
in other cases of chemical combination, and this is called *ter-
restrial light.*) We say other cases of combination, because
fire itself, or the combustion which produces it, is supposed to
be caused by chemical affinity.†

102. Light moves with astonishing *velocity ;* it is computed

---

* The word *pondus* in Latin signifies weight, from whence comes *ponderable,* having weight, and *imponderable,* having no weight.

† Combustion, by some of the most distinguished chemists of the present day, is supposed to depend on the union of opposite electricities, the
oxygen of the air furnishing the negative, and the combustible substance,
the positive electricity.

, 98. When we look abroad, do we see objects themselves, or pictures of
them ?

99. What is the study of the phenomena of light, as connected with
seeing, called ? Why is the subject of light treated of in Chemistry ?

100. Why is it called *imponderable ?*

101. What are the sources of light, and what are its different kinds
called ?

that it travels at the rate of *two hundred thousand miles in a second.* A ray of light is supposed to pass from the sun to the earth in about *seven minutes.*

103. Light moves in *right lines,* never in curves; when turned at all out of its course, it is always at an angle.

104. When light falls upon polished surfaces, it is thrown back or *reflected.* A person standing directly before a mirror sees his image as if it were fronting him; but if he stand a little on one side, his image will appear just as far upon the other.

105. The rays falling from the person upon the mirror are called *incident rays,* those which are thrown back are called *reflected rays ;* the angles which they make are always equal. Thus, two persons at opposite angles of a plane or flat mirror, see each other's images, although they cannot see their own.

106. Nothing can appear less like a compound substance than light, and yet it is found to consist of seven colours, which are separated by means of a prism. Sir Isaac Newton, observing that drops of rain exhibited a variety of colours when the sun shone upon them, and also that the arrangement of the colours of the rainbow was always the same, was led to conclude that these colours resulted from the decomposition of light. He proved this to be the case by the following experiment:—He caused a window shutter to be closed, and placing before a hole in the shutter a three-cornered piece of glass called a prism, the light which issued through the aperture was *refracted,* or bent out of its course towards the ground, and thrown upwards upon the opposite wall. Here the circular beam of light was oblong, and arranged in seven colours; the uppermost part, or the most refracted

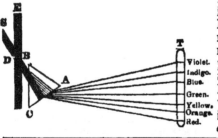

ray, was the violet, then indigo, blue, green, yellow, orange, and lastly red, which was the least refracted. The figure represents the *Solar Spectrum,* as the decomposed light is called. E is the window shutter; D a hole in the shutter ; S rays of light from the sun,

102. What is said of the velocity of light ?
103. In what lines does light move ?
104. What effect is produced when light falls upon polished surfaces ?
105. What are *incident* and what *reflected* rays ?
106. How did Newton prove that light is a compound substance ?

passing through and falling on the glass prism, B A C, which preventing the rays of light from going straight on in a downward course, bend them so that they leave the prism at A C. T is the light on the opposite wall spread from a circle; B, an oblong, and representing the refracted rays; it will be seen that the violet ray is most turned out of its course, and the red ray the least bent.

108. The violet ray is the most *refrangible,* and the red the least refrangible of the seven primary rays.

The rays also differ in their *illuminating* power;—the yellow ray is the brightest, next to this is the green ray; the violet is thought to be most deficient in this property.

The *heating* power also varies; the red ray producing most, and the violet ray least.

Certain *chemical* effects, such as separating oxygen from its combination with metals, are observable in some rays; the blue and violet seem to possess this power in the greatest degree.

To the violet ray, and those nearest it, is ascribed a *magnetic* power, decreasing with refrangibility.

A prism may be supported on a frame for more convenient use, though the glass, simply, will serve all necessary purposes.

109. You may see in a rainbow exactly the same effect produced by the separation of the rays of light as that exhibited by the prism. The drops of water, or falling rain, through which the sun's rays pass, act as the prism to separate and reflect them according to their different degrees of refrangibility.

110. By mixing the seven primary colours, in due proportions, white is produced.

111. Colours are not in bodies themselves. The rose, which you call red, is so constituted as to absorb all the other

107. Describe the solar spectrum.
108. In what properties do the primary colours differ ?
109. What produces the colours of the rainbow ?
110. What is the effect of mixing the seven primary colours ?
111. Do colours belong to bodies, and if not, how are they produced ?
     3*

rays, and reflect the red ray.) The leaves absorb all except the green ray. In the dark, neither the rose nor its leaves has any colour.

112. White bodies reflect all the rays, black ones absorb all, and therefore reflect none; for this reason, white and black are not considered colours.

113. It will at first appear to you a very strange idea that the colour of different substances is not in themselves, but is caused by the manner in which they reflect light to our eyes. We cannot explain why some bodies appear red, others green, &c., except by saying that it is because their particles have an affinity for the other rays of light, and reflect the red, or green, or whatever colour they may appear to us to have. For you must understand that the colour which an object appears to have, is, in reality, that which it *has not*, or that which it rejects or throws off.

114. It follows, from what has been said, that *colour depends on the capacity which the particles of bodies possess of absorbing or reflecting the different rays of light.*

115. *Experiment.*—Soak in water some leaves of purple cabbage, the roots of radishes, or flowers of blue violets, and you may thus obtain a vegetable blue colour. Pour into this a few drops of *sulphuric acid*, and the colour is changed to red.)

Explanation.—Since sulphuric acid is a colourless liquid, it cannot be that mixing it with the blue liquid, should change its colour in the same way as by mixing red and yellow paint together you produce an orange, an intermediate colour, partaking of the nature of both. We infer, then, that by the union of the blue infusion with the sulphuric acid, a new arrangement of the particles took place, which caused a different coloured ray of light, viz. the red, to be reflected.

116. Thus, by mixing solutions of corrosive sublimate and pearlash, both colourless substances, we are presented with an orange colour. By mixing a solution of pearlash with blue vegetable colours, we have green. An infusion of nut-galls mixed with one of copperas, produces black, by pour-

---

112. Why are white and black not considered as colours ?
113. Is that colour which an object seems to have, the one for which its particles have an affinity ?
114. What does colour depend on ?
115. What experiment proves that colour depends on the arrangement of particles ?
116. Give some other examples of the changes which are produced upon colours by the mixing of different substances.

ing in a small proportion of sulphuric acid, the black changes to white. That is, from a state in which the particles reflected all the rays of light, they are thrown into one in which they absorb all, and reflect none.

117. These are effects produced by chemical combinations. You can perceive, then, how important it is to those who mix colours either for dyeing or painting, to understand, as far as possible, what may be done with different substances in the way of producing variety and beauty of colours by means of such combinations.

118. Light is contained in all bodies, though in many cases it remains in a state invisible to us. You have seen sparks of fire produced by two pieces of iron, or other hard bodies being brought forcibly and suddenly in contact; the fire was made manifest by means of the light which accompanied it.

119. Light and heat are not always connected; the light of the moon, called *lunar** light, is unaccompanied by heat.

120. Some animals emit light, as the glow-worm, and several species of fire-fly. This is called phosphorescence; it is not accompanied by heat. Those who sail upon salt water often observe a luminous path seeming to follow the vessel; this is owing to animal matter dissolved in sea water, or to collections of living animals so small and unformed as to exhibit no other appearance than a jelly-like mass. Putrid fish, rotten wood, and many other substances emit phosphorescent light. Phosphorus derives its name from this property of bearing light without heat.

121. The importance of light to the growth of vegetables is well known—if they grow at all in the dark, they usually exhibit a sickly appearance, and are destitute of colour and fragrance. Healthy green vegetables, by the action of light, yield oxygen, which is needed to supply what is constantly consumed by the breathing of animals.

122. Both plants and animals exposed to a strong light usually exhibit richer and more lively colours than those which live deprived of light, or where it is feeble; thus, the

* From luna, the Moon.

---

117. What is important for those who mix colours for dyeing or painting?
118. Does light exist in any bodies in an invisible state?
119. Are light and heat always connected?
120. What is phosphorescent light?
121. Do plants grow without light?
122. Why are the animals and vegetables of the torrid zone of a richer and deeper colour than in other portions of the earth?

birds, insects, and flowers of the torrid zone surpass those of the other parts of the world, in the brilliancy and beauty of their colour. In the torrid zone only, are black people found, except it be among their descendants who have been carried to other parts of the globe.

CHAPTER V.

Heat, or Caloric.

123. We could not explain to one who had never felt the *sensation of heat* what it is, any more than we could make a blind person understand the nature of colours, or a deaf one the nature of sounds. This is the case with all our *sensations ;* that of taste, for example, can be explained but by reference to the sensation itself; there are various kinds of sweets, as that of honey, of sugar, and of many fruits which all differ from each other, in a manner which could never be explained to one who had not tasted them.

124. But the *sensation*, or feeling of heat, is as different from the *cause* of heat, as the sensation we call sweet is from the sugar which produces it.

125. The *feeling* of *heat* is caused by a substance called *caloric* from the Latin *calor*, heat.

126. Caloric, like light, is an imponderable body, or one that has no known weight.

127. Caloric and light are intimately connected ; the one being generally accompanied by the other. But they are proved to be two distinct substances; and as we have shown that light sometimes appears without caloric, we shall also find that caloric may be perceived when there is no evidence of light.

128. Iron may be made so hot that you cannot bear your hand upon it, and yet it will exhibit no light. Here is an instance of caloric without light.

---

123. Could we explain our sensations to one who had never experienced them ?
124. Does the feeling of heat resemble its cause ?
125. What causes the feeling of heat ?
126. Is caloric known to have weight ?
127. Are caloric and light the same substance?
128. Give an example of caloric existing without light.

129. Caloric and light may be distinguished by the different sensations they produce. Light is only perceived by the eyes, it produces *vision* or *sight*. Caloric may be perceived by its effects on every part of our body, which is one general organ of *touch:* the sensation it produces is that of *heat.*

130. Caloric exists in two different states, *free* and *combined.*

131. Free caloric comprehends all the sources of heat which are manifest to our senses, as that which comes from the sun, from the fire, and from heated bodies.

132. Combined caloric exists in a concealed state in all bodies. It is called latent, or hidden caloric, and in this form exists even in ice itself.

133. You will doubtless find it somewhat difficult to believe that to be a real existence which has never been seen; but yet there is something which causes heat, which produces flame, which is active in the vegetable and animal creation, and which has never been seen by us;—though its *effects* are around us on every side, it is itself invisible.

134. Light and caloric seem to be, in many respects, the representatives and types of Him who created them, and since we cannot deny that there is something which, though itself unseen, produces vision, and reveals to us the forms of bodies, and that there is something which produces the sensation of heat which is also invisible, can we but acknowledge that there may be, around and about us, one great and pervading Spirit, the source of mind, the Creator of matter, and the Director of all things visible or invisible?

135. When we speak of caloric, you will, therefore, understand that we mean a something which actually exists, and not a mere property or quality of matter;—divisibility is a property of matter denoting that it is capable of being divided; but divisibility is not itself a substance, any more than high or low, hard or soft, are substances.

136. Caloric passes from one substance to another; *it is only when in motion* that we perceive its existence. When it is entering our bodies, we feel warm or hot: when it is leav-

---

129. How may caloric and light be distinguished?
130. In what different states does caloric exist?
131. What is meant by free caloric?
132. How does combined caloric exist?
133. Do we perceive caloric itself, or only its effects?
134. How do light and caloric represent their Creator?
135. Is caloric an actual existence, or a mere property of matter?
136. When is it that we perceive the existence of caloric?

ing them we feel cool or cold according to the degree of caloric we receive or lose.

137. All our senses are affected by *motion*.

The motion of light produces vision.
That of air hearing.
That of odoriferous particles smelling.
That of sapid substances tasting.
That of bodies which touch us feeling.

138. Since there is a something which produces heat, it would be natural to suppose that when this enters bodies it would increase their size; this is found to be the case; from whence this principle is established, that *caloric expands all bodies*.

1st. Caloric expands *solids*.

a   b   c

139. *Exp.*—Take an iron rod *a* fitted in length to the space *b*, and in diameter to pass through the circular aperture at *c*; heat the rod to redness, and it will be found too long to fill the one space, and too thick for the other. On cooling, the rod will again in length, and diameter, fill the same spaces as at first.

140. *Explanation.*—The caloric which enters into the iron, crowds itself between the particles of metal, and separates them at a little distance; thus increasing the size of the rod.

141. On putting the heated rod into cold water, the caloric leaves it, and passes into the colder substances; (the rod is of the same dimensions as at first.) It would cool in the common air, but not so soon as in cold water.

142. Thus you see that caloric is the antagonist power to attraction, since one of its most obvious effects is the expansion of bodies, by lessening the cohesion of their particles.

143. An instrument called a *pyrometer*, from the Greek *pur*, fire, and *metron*, measure, has been invented to show the degrees of expansibility of different metals by heat. The

---

137. In what manner are our senses affected by motion of different bodies?
138. How does caloric enlarge the size of bodies?
139. By what experiment is the expansion of solids illustrated?
140. How is this explained?
141. When the rod is again cooled, is its size affected?
142. To what is caloric opposed?
143. What is a pyrometer?

figure shows a rod of metal, A, A, resting horizontally upon supporters.

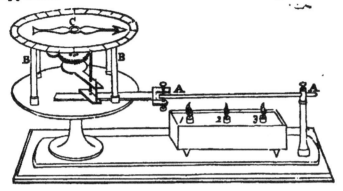

One end of the rod touches the wheelwork B, B, which is so connected with the index C, that a slight motion of the wheels causes a considerable movement in the index. The rod of metal being heated by the lamps 1, 2, 3, presses against the wheelwork, which communicates motion to the index. The expansibility of the metal is denoted by degrees marked on the plate.

144. The pendulum of a clock, in order to vibrate seconds, must always be of a given length; but as metals expand with heat, the pendulum is liable to shorten in winter, and lengthen in summer:—it follows, that the clock will be faster in winter than in summer. By lengthening or shortening the pendulum, this evil is remedied. About thirty-nine inches is found to be the length necessary for a pendulum to vibrate seconds. The pupil will readily understand why a short pendulum should vibrate faster than a long one, when he considers, that in both cases, the pendulum is as the *radius* of a circle, which circle is larger or smaller, according to the length of the radius. Thus, suppose A and B to be two pendulums, of which B is the longer. B must describe the arc c d of a circle, while A is moving from e to f.

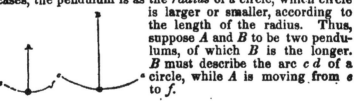

144. Why does a clock go faster in winter than in summer?

145. A piano or harp that has been tuned in a cold room, will often be out of tune when the room is warmed; this is because the strings are expanded by heat.

146. Glass stoppers sometimes get fitted into the necks of decanters, so that it is difficult to take them out; if the bottle is plunged into hot water up to the neck, or a sponge containing hot water is applied to it, the glass will expand, and the stopper become loosened.

147. The thinner any solid body is, the more readily it expands by heat; thus, thin glass is not so liable to be cracked by hot water as that which is thick; cut glass being very thick, is easily cracked, either by sudden expansion or condensation. A very careful housekeeper, who knew well the effect of sudden heat upon glass, broke an elegant cut glass dish by putting into it a quantity of ice-cream in a hot day. The frozen mixture, by abstracting caloric suddenly, caused the particles of the glass in contact with it to condense before the other parts of the dish were affected—this produced an unequal strain upon the glass.

148. The cause of the cracking of glass and china when put into hot water, is their sudden expansion; thus they are more liable to crack in cold than in warm weather, when the difference in the temperature of the atmosphere and that of the hot water is not so great. When a china teapot is used in cold weather, lukewarm water should be put into it before boiling water. Glass tumblers and china cups should not have boiling water poured upon them in frosty weather.

149. 2d. Caloric expands *liquids.*

Liquids expand more readily than solids, as the cohesive attraction in the former class of bodies is less strong, and caloric can pass more freely among their particles.

150. Some liquids are more expansive than others.

---

145. Why does a piano or harp appear out of tune in a warm room?
146. How can a glass stopper, fitting tight in the neck of a decanter, be taken out?
147. Why is thin glass less liable to be cracked by expansion or condensation than that which is thick?
148. Why does glass and china sometimes crack when put into hot water?
149. Why do liquids expand more readily than solids?
150. What experiment shows that different liquids have different degrees of expansibility?

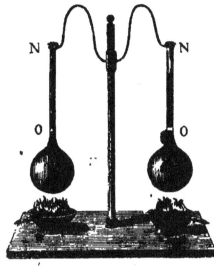

Exp.—Fill two globular glass vessels as far as to *o, o,* the one with alcohol, the other with water; place under each a pan of burning charcoal. Both liquids will rise into the necks of the bottles, but the alcohol will rise higher than the water. The same principle may be illustrated by immersing two glass bulbs, the one containing water, and the other alcohol, into a vessel of hot water.

151. Molasses, wines, and other fluids, being expanded by heat, the same quantity will occupy more space in summer than in winter; thus it is more economical to buy them in winter.

3d. Caloric expands *gases.*

152. As the particles of gases are very little influenced by cohesive attraction, caloric easily insinuates itself among them.

153. When a fire is made in a stove or fireplace, the air of the room immediately begins to grow warmer; it expands also, and becomes lighter. The warm air escapes in all directions through cracks in the doors, windows, &c., and cold air rushes in to supply its place.

154. Children who are fond of roasting eggs learn that it is necessary to crack the shells lightly, or it will burst with an explosion; this is in consequence of the expanding of the

---

151. Why is it more economical to buy articles which are fluid in winter than in summer?

152. Why are gases much affected by caloric?

153. What changes take place with respect to the air when a fire is made in a room?

154. Why are the shells of eggs cracked before they are put into a fire to roast?

vapour within, which escapes when it can find vent; but if confined, bursts the shell by the expansive power of heat.

155. Another amusement in which children sometimes indulge, is that of observing the expansion of the air in bladders; this is a chemical experiment. If a bladder be tied tight at the neck, although it should contain so little air as scarcely to swell it, yet when held to the fire it will expand until it bursts; when withdrawn from the heat, it contracts. The addition of caloric expanded the air, the loss of it reduces its bulk, by condensing the particles, that is, by bringing them into closer contact.

156. *Exp.*—Let the tube of a glass bulb, having in it a small quantity of water, be inverted in a vessel of water. Apply the heat of a lamp to the bulb, caloric will pass into it and expand the air, and this forces the water down the tube. Remove the lamp, and as the air contracts, the water rushes back into the bulb.

157. The expansion of air is eight times greater than that of water, and that of water 45 times greater than that of iron.

158. We have learned that solids, liquids, and gases, are expanded or enlarged in bulk by the addition of caloric, and that they shrink, or are condensed by the loss of caloric.

159. There is one remarkable exception to this law of nature—water, though it expands by heat until it becomes a mere vapour, which we call steam, does not condense by the loss of heat beyond a certain point. On the contrary, when water freezes, its bulk is found to be increased, as many a housewife has known to her sorrow, when she has found her

---

155. What is the effect of heat upon bladders containing a small portion of air?
156. By what experiment is the expansion of air shown?
157. How does the expansion of air compare with that of water, and the expansion of water with that of iron?
158. What have you now learned respecting solids, liquids, and gases?
159. What exception is there to this law of nature?

earthen pitchers or glass tumblers cracked, by being suffered to stand full of water, exposed to a freezing atmosphere. You can very easily satisfy yourselves that water expands in freezing, by filling with it a tin basin, and letting it stand exposed to the cold of a winter night; you will see the ice swelled out considerably above the surface of the basin.

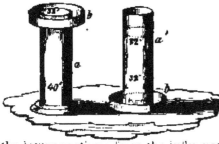

160. The effect of this expansion of water at a certain degree of cold is, to make its specific gravity less, (that is, to make it lighter,) and thus the frozen water remains on the surface of lakes and other large bodies of water, protecting the lower portions from the influence of a cold atmosphere. Suppose a a to represent two vessels filled with water at the temperature of about 60°, which is neither cold nor hot; b b are tin trays surrounding the upper part of one vessel, and the under part of the other, and filled with a freezing mixture, (viz. ice and salt.) The first effect of the cold is to reduce the temperature of the whole mass of water to 40°, at which point water is of its greatest density. After this, the cooling process in the vessel a will be limited to the surface, where the thermometer will gradually fall to 32°, at which point the water will freeze; for the ice-cold water being lighter than the water below, it will remain on the surface. This is what takes place in lakes and large bodies of water. In the vessel a, where the cold is applied, at the bottom, the effect is very different; for the cooled water below 40° becomes lighter, and rises, and the warmer, or heavier portions descend, in their turn become cooled, and again rising, other successive portions follow the same course, until the whole being reduced to 32°, or the freezing point, hardens into one solid body of ice. The process described in the vessel a, is that which goes on in nature; that in the vessel a', is what would take place did not water, unlike all other known substances, become lighter before it freezes, so that a stratum, or layer of ice cold water (at 32°) lies over a mass of warmer water (at 40°.) It appears a wonderful provision of the Almighty

160. What is the effect of this expansion of water at a certain degree of cold ?

water, the mercury will rise to 212°; if plunged into meltin:
snow or ice, it will fall to 32°. What was said with respect
to the expansion of bodies by heat, will help you to understand the cause of the rising and falling of the mercury in the
thermometer.

165. The thermometer is of great use, not only to scientific men in their experiments, but for many common purposes. The apartments of the sick should always be of the
same temperature; and to regulate this, a thermometer is
necessary. It is needed by gardeners to regulate the temperature of their green-houses. It assists the navigator, by
informing him, by means of the increased coldness of the
water, when he is approaching land, soundings, or shoals;
especially warning him against the icebergs so common in
northern latitudes; on the contrary, when approaching the
Gulf Stream, the water becomes warmer.

166. There is another kind of
thermometer, which we will now
describe; it is called an *air thermometer*, because it operates by
means of the expansion of air.
The figure represents the air thermometer of Sanctorius, an Italian
physician of the seventeenth century; this was the first of the kind
which was invented. This is
merely a tube with a thin bulb at
the upper end, and dipping at the
lower, and open extremity, into a
cup containing a coloured liquid;
on applying the warm hand to the
bulb, the air expands, and a portion
escapes; as the bulb cools, the air
becomes again more condensed,
(that is, the particles are in closer contact, and occupy less
space,) and a portion of the liquor rises into the tube to fill
the vacuum. The air thermometer is now ready for use.
Heat, by expanding the air in the bulb, drives the liquor
downwards; and cold, by condensing the air, causes it to
rise.

---

165. What are some of the practical uses of the thermometer?
166. Describe the air thermometer of Sanctorius.

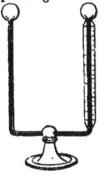

167. Thus air thermometers are useful in determining those slight differences of temperature, which would not materially affect the mercurial thermometer; for you will recollect that gases are more expansible than any other bodies, therefore air will be sooner affected by heat than mercury.

168. Another kind of air thermometer consists of a glass bottle, containing a small quantity of coloured liquid, and so closely corked that the air within cannot escape; a very small glass tube is fitted into the cork, and extends down so as to pass into the fluid. On applying heat, the air in the bottle being expanded, presses upon the liquid beneath it, and forces a portion up the tube. The height of the fluid shows the expansion of the air, or the degree of heat to which the air thermometer has been subjected.

169. The pupil will here observe, that though the two air thermometers are differently affected by heat and cold, the cause of the liquid rising or falling is the same in both, viz: *the expansion of air.* In the one case, the air in the ball above, by its expansive force, presses the liquid down; in the other case, the air is in the bottle below the tube, but above the liquid in the lower part of the bottle; its expansive force, by pressing on the liquid, will therefore force it upward.

170. There is still another kind of thermometer; it is called the *differential* thermometer, because it is used to determine the *difference* of temperature in any two bodies, or places. It has two bulbs; its tube is partly filled with a coloured liquid, while the remainder is filled with air. When both bulbs are exposed to an *equal* temperature, the fluid in the tube remains unmoved, but if one bulb is exposed to more heat than the other, the expansion of the air will force the liquid upward towards the opposite bulb.

---

167. For what are air thermometers useful ?
168. Describe an air thermometer of a different construction ?
169. Why does the liquid in the air thermometer of Sanctorius fall in the tube by heat, while, in the other air thermometers, the same cause makes it rise ?
170. Describe the differential thermometer.

171. The *barometer* is used for ascertaining the weight of the atmosphere; the mercury in that instrument rises when the pressure of the air is greatest, and falls when it is least; it is never lower than about *twenty-seven* inches, nor higher than about thirty-three inches. A column of air forty-five miles high, is supposed to be of equal weight to a column of mercury thirty inches high, and a column of water thirty-three feet high.

CONDUCTORS OF HEAT OR OF CALORIC.

172. *Caloric has a constant tendency to pass from one body to another*, that is, to go from a substance containing more, to one that has less, until both shall be of an equal temperature, or as chemists would say, until an *equilibrium* between the two is produced. Suppose that one person having very cold hands takes the warm hand of another person—you can imagine the very different sensations which each would experience. The one says, "how cold your hand is," the other, "how warm." Caloric leaves the warm hand to go to the colder one in contact with it; this causes the sensation of cold to the person who loses caloric, while the one who gains it, feels the sensation of warmth.

173. But let a healthy person having a warm hand, take the burning hand of one in a fever, and the latter will seem hot, while to the sick person, the hand of the other will appear cool.

174. If the door of a warm apartment be opened into a colder one, the warm air rushes out, and the cold enters, until the two apartments are of an equal temperature.

175. Some substances *conduct* heat much more readily than others. *Experiment.*—Take a pipe-stem and an iron wire of equal size and length, and stick to one end of each, balls of beeswax, of equal size: place these in such a situation that the ends opposite the wax will receive an equal degree of heat from burning coals. The wax on the iron rod will

171. For what is the barometer used, and what causes the mercury in that instrument to rise?

172. What is the constant tendency of caloric?

173. How does the hand of a person in a fever appear to the warm hand of a healthy person?

174. What is the effect of opening the door of a warm room into a cold one?

175. What experiment shows the difference in substances, as to their power of conducting heat?

soon melt, while that on the pipe-stem will scarcely be affected by heat.

Explanation.—Both rods receive caloric, which passes from one particle to another, but is transmitted with much greater rapidity by the particles of iron than those of the clay.

176. *Exp.*—Take four small rods of metal, wood, glass, and whalebone, and cement one end of each to a ball of sealing wax; then let the opposite ends be equally exposed to heat; the metal will soon become so hot as to melt the sealing wax, the wood and whalebone will burn near the wax without melting it, and the glass may be heated so that it may be bent, without affecting the wax.

177. If you hold one end of a pin or needle in the flame of a candle, it almost instantly becomes so much heated at the other end, as to burn the fingers. The end of a glass rod of equal size may be held in the flame until it melts with heat, and yet the other end seems little affected by it. A piece of charcoal, while burning at one end, may be held in the hand at the other end. You will now perceive why a silver or tin coffee-pot should have a wooden handle, rather than a metallic one.

178. Such substances as feel coldest to the touch, are generally the best conductors, while those that in their ordinary state feel warmest, are the poorest conductors. Thus metals are good conductors; while feathers, wool, and hair, are poor conductors.

179. Bodies conduct heat with less facility when their parts are spongy and divided; thus iron filings are poorer conductors than an iron bar of the same weight; this is supposed to be owing to the existence of air between these parts, and air is a poor conductor.

180. Stones are not as good conductors of caloric as metals

---

176. What is the second experiment to prove that bodies differ in their power of conducting heat?

177. What other examples can you give?

178. What substances are generally the best, and what the poorest conductors?

179. Why are iron filings poorer conductors of heat than an iron bar?

190. What is said of stones and bricks as conductors of caloric?

—bricks are poor conductors, and for this reason, when heated and wrapped in a cloth, they are useful for keeping the feet warm in cold weather; but a heated piece of plank is still better, because wood conducts, or loses caloric less easily than brick.

181. Wool, hair, and fur, are poor conductors of caloric. Thus we find that the animals of cold countries are protected against the severities of their climate by their various coverings. These are not warm in themselves, but they keep the animal heat from escaping into the cold atmosphere.

182. We speak of particular garments being warm; but this is incorrect. The less readily substances conduct heat, the warmer they keep our bodies, by preventing their caloric from passing off. The looser the materials of which garments are made, the warmer they will be; thus, quilted under-garments containing a slight quantity of cotton, are much warmer than the same weight of cloth of firmer texture. Our good grandmothers used to labour hard to manufacture thick and heavy woollen blankets and coverlets; but we have learned that two thicknesses of calico, quilted with a few pounds of cotton between, make a bed covering much warmer, lighter, and cheaper, than the carpet-like blankets of former days.

183. The finer the fibres of substances are, the less do they serve as conductors of caloric; thus, the animals of cold countries are furnished by their Creator with finer and softer feathers, wool, and fur, than those of warm countries. When the animals of warm countries are removed to cold regions, He who gives them their covering, makes it to grow softer and finer, that they may be protected from the cold.

184. Ice and snow are bad conductors of caloric; thus, the ice in rivers and lakes protects the water below from freezing; snow is of great use in protecting vegetation from frosts and severe cold. When the snow comes early in the season, and remains late, the farmer expects a good crop of grain; but when there is not snow to protect it, it is often *winter killed.*

---

181. Of what use are the wool and fur of animals in cold countries?
182. Are some garments really warmer than others, and if not, why are our bodies warmer when clad with them than others?
183. Why is it that the animals of cold countries are furnished with softer feathers, wool, and fur, than in hot countries?
184. What advantages arise from the circumstance that ice and snow are bad conductors of caloric?

185. *Liquids are not as good conductors of caloric as solids;* in the latter the particles are fixed, and transmit caloric from one to the other; when liquids are heating, the particles themselves are in motion, and carry caloric with them.

186. When a kettle of water is placed over the fire, the particles of the fluid at the bottom of the kettle first receive caloric—they expand, become lighter, and rise to the top; the colder particles sink, and are in their turn heated, and rise. This process continues until the whole is heated. The figure shows the heated particles rising, and giving place to colder ones.

187. You will perceive, from the manner in which water becomes heated, that if a vessel of this liquid were placed *under*, instead of *over*, a fire, the lower portions of the water would not be heated, because the warm particles, being lighter, would still remain at the top.

188. This principle may be illustrated (as in the figure) by inserting into the bottom of a vessel of water an air thermometer, and burning ether or alcohol upon the surface of the water. The bulb of the thermometer, although within half an inch of the flame, will be unaffected by heat. This experiment may be made, by pouring spirits of any kind upon water, and inflaming them with a lighted taper, or a burning pine stick; the spirits being lighter than water, will remain on the surface, if not agitated. Any young person making this experiment, must be cautious, in inflaming the spirits, not to burn himself, as, from the combustible nature of alcohol, it springs suddenly into a blaze on the application of heat.

---

185. What is the difference in the conducting power of liquids and solids?
186. What process goes on when water is heated?
187. What would be the effect of placing liquids under a fire instead of over it?
188. How may this principle be illustrated?

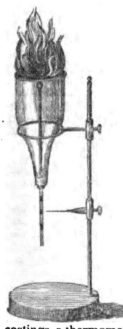

189. *Gases are poorer conductors of caloric than liquids or solids*

190. The common air stops the progress of caloric more than any other substance. Why do people use a fan in warm weather? Because, when the air is set in *motion*, the warmer particles are driven away, and cooler ones take their place.— These are pleasant and refreshing for the moment; but that they do not take away heat from us is evident, from the fact, that the instant we cease to fan ourselves, we feel as warm as at first.

If, instead of cool air, we had been bathed with cool water, we should have felt our bodies sensibly cooled.

191. Metals are painful to the touch when heated to 120°.* Water scalds when heated to 150°; but air may be heated to nearly 300°, without giving painful sensations. In a certain manufactory, where a large oven is kept heated for the purpose of drying the moulds of plaster of Paris used for castings, a thermometer hanging in the oven usually stands at 300°, almost one hundred degrees above the heat of boiling water. Now the workmen are in the habit of going into this oven when thus heated, and remaining in it for several minutes at a time. It would be unsafe to touch any good conductor of heat, in such an oven. One gentleman, wishing to try the experiment of breathing in such an atmosphere, entered the oven with his silver mounted spectacles on, and, as might be expected, had his nose burned.

192. *When air is heated, currents are produced.* In a room where there is a fire, the air in the upper part is warmer

* The young pupil will observe that the sign °, placed as above, signifies degrees.

189. Are gases good conductors of caloric?
190. What is the use of a fan in warm weather?
191. What fact is stated to show that heated air does not easily communicate caloric?
192. What produces currents of air?

than that in the lower part, because the particles which are warmed, instantly rise, are cooled as they ascend, and then fall again; thus, in a warm room there is always an ascending and a descending current of air. If the door of a warm room be opened, hot air rushes out at the upper part, while cold air blows in below. This may be proved by holding the flame of a lamp at an open door; at the upper part the flame will be blown outwardly—at the lower part inwardly, while midway, the flame will remain in its usual perpendicular position.

193. When a bonfire is burning in a calm day, you may observe a rushing wind moving towards the fire from all quarters. This is because the air near the fire being constantly made lighter by heat, rises into higher regions of the atmosphere, and colder air rushes in to fill the vacuum.

194. You can now understand the *causes of winds*, which are only currents of air; thus, warm air, being lighter, rises upwards, while cold air, being heavier, presses downwards. In geography, you read of the *monsoons* of India, or of winds which blow six months from the south, and six months from the north; the cause of them is this: the sun is six months in going from the equator to the northern tropic and returning to the equator; during this time the surface of the earth north of the equator is heated; the warm air rises, and cold air from the southern hemisphere rushes in to supply its place; this a southerly monsoon; the northerly monsoon is in like manner produced when the sun is in the southern hemisphere.

195. The constant circulation, both in the air and waters of the globe, is of vast importance to the comfort of man. In this way the hot air of the equatorial regions, is tempered by winds from cooler countries, and the heated waters of one portion of the earth, mingle with the cooler currents from the other.

EVAPORATION.

196. When you leave a small quantity of water in a tea-saucer, or any open, shallow vessel, in a short time you perceive the dish is dry. Did you ever think what becomes of

---

193. What makes winds to blow in all directions towards a bonfire ?
194. What causes the monsoons of India ?
195. How does the circulation in the air and waters of the globe tend to the comfort of man ?
196. What do you understand by evaporation ?

the liquid in this case? It passes into the air in fine particles, called *vapour*; thus, we say it has *evaporated*.

197. Caloric is the great agent in evaporation; the warmer the weather is, the faster the process of evaporation is carried on. In very hot weather a floor that has been sprinkled with water will soon be dried, that is, the water will have evaporated, and the air having parted with caloric, will appear cooler.

198. In cities, during hot weather, persons are employed to go about the streets with large casks of water, which, by an apparatus contrived for the purpose, is sprinkled over the path, as the cart which contains it moves slowly along. This not only prevents the dust from rising, but has a very sensible effect upon the atmosphere, from which the water, in evaporating, withdraws a portion of caloric.

199. Physicians sometimes order their patients to be bathed with cold water, by means of a wet sponge applied to the face, chest, and limbs. In a few minutes, a large basin of cold water, thus applied to a person in a high fever, will become warm from the caloric which it has gained. Such a process, as you might naturally suppose, has a tendency to abate inflammation; and though it may not remove the cause, it affords a temporary and refreshing alleviation.

200. The air always contains more or less moisture, some degree of which is necessary to respiration: when the air is unusually dry, we feel as if our lungs were parched, and we desire to drink often.

201. That the air contains moisture, is shown by the appearance of a tumbler of cold water in a hot day. It will be covered by moisture or even drops of liquid; this cannot proceed from within, since the water does not penetrate the glass; it is caused by the condensing of the fine vapour of the air by the coldness of the tumbler.

202. You will now perceive that Chemistry is a vast science. Though yet in its infancy, how many phenomena has it explained to the understanding of man, which were once either regarded with superstitious terror, or passed without

---

197. What is the great agent in evaporation?
198. Why are the streets in cities sprinkled with water during the hot weather?
199. Why do physicians sometimes order their patients to be bathed in cold water?
200. Is moisture in the air necessary?
201. What shows that the air contains moisture?
202. How does science prevent superstition?

observation! But while science teaches us not to regard the changes of nature with superstitious dread, as though they were effects of some unknown mysterious agent, it should inspire us with reverence for that infinite wisdom which governs the universe by laws, so simple, that even a child may comprehend them.

203. Society is now rapidly improving, and inventions by means of scientific principles and discoveries are continually succeeding each other. Much of the labour which was once performed by men, is now carried on by machinery; this gives more leisure for *observations* and *experiments*, which are the means of making farther discoveries.

204. When we examine the names of those who have benefited the world by their discoveries, we find that practical mechanicians, those who have at the same time worked and studied, have done as much, even for science, as those who have been wholly devoted to the learned professions. This should teach the student respect for the labouring man. How often indeed is the labouring man the true student of nature, while he who enjoys facilities for learning, never opens his eyes, or his ears, to see the beauties, or to hear the music of nature!

CHAPTER VII.

Radiation of Caloric. Reflection and Absorption of Caloric. Freezing. Boiling. Sources of Heat.

205. We have seen that caloric is conducted from one particle of a substance to another, and that bodies differ in their conducting power. We are now to consider caloric as passing directly from one body to another by means of a power which enables it to dart forward without assistance from any intermediate substance. This is called *radiated* heat, because it passes off in rays, in the same manner as light is radiated.

---

203. What is said of scientific improvements?
204. Who have most benefited the world by their discoveries?
205. What is meant by radiated heat?

206. *Heat radiates from bodies in right lines, and is susceptible of reflection like light.*

Exp.—Let two concave mirrors of polished tin, or any other
bright metal, be placed directly opposite upon a table, at the
distance of a few feet; and let a red hot iron ball or a flask of
boiling water be placed in the *focus** of one mirror, and a
thermometer in the focus of the other. The thermometer
will soon be affected by the heat radiated.

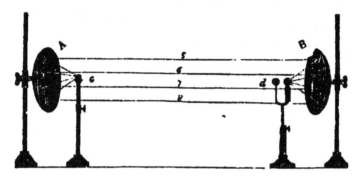

A and B concave mirrors fixed on stands. *c* a heated iron
ball placed in the focus of the mirror A. *d* a differential thermometer in the focus of the mirror B. 1, 2, 3, 4 rays of caloric, radiating from the iron ball, and falling on the mirror A.
5, 6, 7, 8 the same rays reflected from the mirror A to the
mirror B. 9, 10, 11, 12 the same rays reflected from the mirror B to the thermometer.

207. *Explanation.*—Caloric is radiated from the heated
body in every direction; those rays which are intercepted by
the mirror, are reflected back in right lines, until reaching the
other mirror, they are then reflected in a collected form, upon
the bulb of the air thermometer standing in its focus. " It is
a property of *concave* mirrors to render *parallel* the *diver-
gent* rays received from its *focus ;* and to cause the *parallel*

* By the *focus* is meant that point before the mirror where all the reflected rays meet. This point can be ascertained by holding a lighted
candle before a concave mirror, and observing at what distance from the
mirror the reflected rays meet.

---

206. How is the radiation of heat proved ?
207. How do you explain this experiment ?

rays which it intercepts to become *convergent*, so as to meet in its *focus*." •

208. To prove that the thermometer is not affected merely from its being near the heated body, let a sheet of pasteboard be held between the mirror B and the thermometer; the latter will immediately indicate the absence of a portion of heat it before received, though the source of this heat is as near the bulb as before, and there is no interposing substance between them. If we even advance the heated ball a little out of the focus of the mirror A, and bring it nearer the thermometer, the latter will show a diminution of heat, in consequence of the arrangement for reflection being disturbed.

209. Surfaces which reflect light most perfectly, are not always best for the reflection of heat; a glass mirror placed before a heated ball would absorb the rays of caloric, and become warm itself, without reflecting the rays. Glasses are used to protect the eyes from the effects of intense heat during some chemical experiments.

210. If, instead of a heated iron ball, a mass of ice were placed in the focus of one of the mirrors, the air thermometer in the focus of the opposite mirror, would show a diminution of temperature, or that it had lost caloric. You might, from this, suppose that cold was radiated like caloric, but in this case the radiation is from the thermometer itself, which is the hotter body, and parts with some of its caloric to the ice.

211. *There is no such thing as cold.* Cold water contains some caloric, the loss of a portion of which changes it to ice ; ice contains some caloric, for there are colder substances than this, as freezing mixtures of various kinds. Cold is a term denoting the absence of heat, though no substance is known to exist without some caloric in combination.

212. Polished, or light-coloured surfaces, do not radiate heat as well as those which are rough and dark-coloured.

---

208. How can you prove that the thermometer is not affected by being near the heated body instead of radiated heat ?

209. Are surfaces which reflect light most perfectly, the best for the reflection of heat ?

210. What would be the effect if a mass of ice were placed in the focus of one of the mirrors, and an air thermometer in the focus of the other ?

211. Is cold a real existence ?

212. How is it proved that polished and light-coloured substances do not reflect heat as well as those which are rough, or dark-coloured ?

Exp.—The figure represents a square glass bottle placed opposite a concave metallic mirror. You are to suppose one side of the bottle to have been smoked with the flame of a lamp, until completely blackened, and another side covered with tin. In the focus of the mirror is placed the bulb of a thermometer, having before it a circular screen, to prevent any rays of heat from the bottle falling directly upon the thermometer. The bottle being filled with boiling water, the different sides, viz., the blackened, the tin, and the glass sides, are successively turned towards the reflector; the thermometer indicates the greatest increase of temperature by the blackened side, and the least by the tin side, while the effect of the glass is greater than the one, and less than the other.

Explanation.—Rays of caloric from the bottle of hot water were thrown upon the mirror, which reflected them in a concentrated form upon the air thermometer placed in its focus. The blackened side parted with heat faster than the other sides; of course the thermometer denoted the greatest increase of caloric when that side was presented. The tinned side being bright and polished, did not admit the rays of heat to pass freely through it, and thus, when that was presented, the thermometer showed a lower degree of caloric. The glass side transmitted heat better than the polished tin, but not so well as the blackened and rough side; of course it affected the thermometer more than the one, and less than the other.

213. An experiment, illustrating the same principle, may be performed in a more simple manner, by holding a thermometer successively before the sides of a tin canister, one of which has been scratched and blackened with lamp smoke, while the other sides remain bright and smooth. The thermometer will be more affected by the direct rays of caloric, than in the other experiment by the reflected rays.

---

213. How may the same principle be illustrated in a more simple manner?

214. The following statement shows the different proportions in which heat was radiated from a cubical tin vessel, one of whose sides was blackened, another papered, and another glazed:—

The thermometer was raised by the

blackened	side	100 degrees
papered	"	98°
glazed	"	90°
bright metallic	"	12°

215. (Those bodies which *absorb heat most readily*, radiate it most powerfully, that is, their *absorbing* and *radiating* powers are equal; a piece of iron heats soon, and parts with its heat readily; a brick neither heats as soon, nor so quickly parts with caloric. Before men were as wise as they now are, they supposed that such substances as *received* heat most readily, must *retain* it longest; philosophers, therefore, in reference to this theory, thought that housekeepers should make their tea in earthen or porcelain teapots, rather than in metallic ones; but tea-makers insisted that they found by *experience*, that tea would "*draw best*" in bright silver or pewter teapots. The latter opinion is now proved by philosophy to be correct, since water retains its heat much longer in the polished metallic vessel, and by this means extracts more fully the peculiar virtues of the tea-leaves.

216. (*Radiation* and *reflection* are found to be in an *inverse* proportion; that is, those bodies that *radiate* caloric most powerfully, *reflect* it least; thus, the reflecting mirror did not radiate heat which came from its own substance, but threw back the rays which fell upon it, as a hard substance causes the rebounding of a ball.

217. Some colours absorb caloric more readily than others. This may be shown by a very simple experiment. Take a piece of black woollen cloth, and another of the same size and quality of white, or light-coloured woollen cloth, and lay them upon the snow, when the sun is shining. In a few hours the black will be found to have sunk considerably below the surface of the snow, while the white will remain on the surface. From this we infer, that the black cloth *absorbed* caloric from the sun, and gave it off in sufficient quantity to melt

214. In what proportions are different surfaces found to radiate heat?
215. What bodies radiate heat most powerfully? and why is a metallic teapot to be preferred to an earthen one?
216. How do radiation and reflection differ?
217. What is said of the difference in colours, with respect to absorbing caloric?

the snow beneath, while the white did not absorb caloric.
You will recollect that black bodies absorb all the rays of
light, while white ones reflect them all.   But in the case of
caloric, black substances not only absorb, but reflect it, while
with respect to light, black does not reflect any of its rays.—
You can now see why a white beaver hat is better for summer than a black one; and why lighter coloured clothes are
worn in summer more than in winter.

FREEZING.

218. We have already remarked, that there is, in reality,
no such thing as cold; what we call cold being merely the
absence of heat.   When we put our hand upon a piece of
marble, or ice, we say, "it is cold"—we feel what we call a
sensation of cold; but the sensation is caused by the loss of
caloric which our hand experiences on coming in contact
with a colder substance.) You will remember the property of
caloric to produce an *equilibrium*, and that a body which contains more heat, always communicates it to another which
has less, when the two are brought together.

When *solids* become *liquids, caloric is absorbed from surrounding bodies.*) You may easily prove this by putting
your hand into a vessel of common salt and water; the salt,
in dissolving, (that is, in passing from a solid to a liquid
state,) absorbs caloric from the water, and renders it so cold
as to be painful to the hand.

220. Ice-creams, which it was formerly thought could only
be obtained at a confectioner's, may be easily prepared in any
family by the following simple process:—put the cream, suit-
ably prepared with sugar, &c., into a tin vessel, with a tight
cover, and place this in a larger pail or tub, surrounded with
pounded ice and fine salt; the edges of the cream will soon
freeze; a spoon should then be introduced into the vessel of
cream, to remove the frozen part into the centre, and in the
course of a few hours the whole will be frozen. The process
should be carried on in a cool room, and the vessel of ice
kept covered, to protect it from the caloric of the air.*)

* It must be remembered, that the vessel, containing the cream, should
be perfectly tight, or the same accident will occur which happened to a
lady, who, having prepared some ice-cream for a party, had the mortifi-
cation to find it quite too salt to be palatable.

218. What causes a sensation of cold when we put our hand upon ice?
219. What is the effect upon surrounding bodies when solids become
liquids?
220. How may ice-cream be prepared?

221. You will scarcely need to have this experiment explained, since you understand that solids, in becoming liquids, take caloric from surrounding bodies. Ice alone would make the cream very cold, (but would not, in melting, take away sufficient caloric to freeze it; but by adding another solid, viz. salt, which, having a great affinity for water, assists in bringing it into a liquid state, and is thus itself dissolved, more caloric is taken from the cream, so that its temperature is reduced below the freezing point; of course it becomes solid.

222. We have seen that solids in becoming liquids absorb caloric, and you must also have thought, from the example of the cream becoming ice in consequence of parting with caloric, that freezing is a process by which heat is given off; this is the case, (freezing is a *warming process*, and melting is a *cooling process*.)

223. (Our winters would be much colder were it not for the freezing which is going on, and which, in changing liquids to solids, gives out caloric into the atmosphere.)

224. The cold, chilly winds that are so common in the spring in our climate, (are caused by the melting of ice and snow.)

225. The caloric which exists in cold water is called *latent*, (from *lateo*, concealed,) because it is not perceptible to our senses.)

226. *When liquids become solids, heat is given out.*

227. (This may be illustrated by the slaking of lime ; the water unites with the lime in a solid state, and much heat is pressed out ; buildings have taken fire in consequence of water having accidentally been brought in contact with lime.— As more caloric is necessary to keep a body in a liquid than a solid state, you can perceive the reason for the fact stated.

228. The same principle may also be illustrated, by adding to a small quantity of muriate of lime in a wine glass, a little sulphuric acid ; both the substances are liquid, but they unite and form a solid sulphate of lime ; so great a quantity of latent caloric is pressed out, that the glass becomes almost too hot to be held in the hand.

---

221. Why is ice alone not sufficient to freeze the cream ?
222. What are the different effects of warming, and freezing, upon surrounding bodies ?
223. What prevents our winters from being colder than they now are ?
224. What causes the cold winds of spring ?
225. Why is the caloric in cold water, called *latent* caloric ?
226. What takes place when liquids become solids ?
227. How may this be illustrated ?
228. In what other way may the same principle be illustrated ?

229. (As ice becomes water by gaining caloric,) water becomes steam or vapour by the same process. Put a piece of ice on a fire shovel and hold it over the fire, the addition of heat to the solid, soon changes it to a liquid ; continue to hold the shovel over the fire, and the liquid soon disappears ; it has gained sufficient caloric to change it to steam. The steam, by losing caloric, is condensed and becomes water ; and water, by losing still more caloric, becomes ice again.

BOILING.

230. When liquids are united to a certain degree of heat, they are converted into steam or vapour ; this process is usually attended with a bubbling noise and an agitation of the fluid, called *boiling*.

231. We have shown under caloric, (see page 47,) that when a kettle of water is placed over the fire, the heat soon causes particles of the fluid to rise, by rendering them lighter, while, a he same time, there is a descending current of the colder particles ; this process continues until the whole mass is heated to 212 degrees ; a new operation then begins.— The heated water at the bottom, now receives more caloric, and becomes steam, or vapour, which passes off into the atmosphere. The water in the kettle is not raised above the 212°, but remains at this point until the very last drop has been changed to vapour.

232. Steam is *invisible*, though we usually think of it as having a smoky appearance, as in the cut. But observe a boiling tea-kettle, and you will see nothing issue from the spout, though just above it, there is a dense cloud or smoke. This is owing to the condensation of the steam by the atmosphere. The heat is most intense at the spout of the kettle, or where the steam is unmixed with air.

229. How is ice affected by gaining caloric, and how may steam be changed to ice ?
230. What is boiling ?
231. Describe the process by which water is converted into steam.
232. Is steam visible ?

233. Vapour or steam is of the same temperature with the boiling liquid, so far as indicated by the thermometer; which stands at 212° in boiling water, and the same in the steam which issues from it; but yet there exists in steam a much greater quantity of caloric, although in a latent state. As a large quantity of latent caloric is combined with water, a still greater portion is necessary to hold water in the gaseous state.

234. A celebrated chemist computed the heat of steam in the following manner: he noted the time necessary to raise a certain quantity of water to the boiling point, or 212°; he then kept up the same heat until the whole was evaporated, and marked the time consumed by the process. Allowing the increase of heat to continue in the same ratio, he estimated that the steam contained 810° of latent heat, or that this quantity was necessary towards keeping water in a state of vapour; this, added to the 212° of heat apparent by the thermometer, would make the actual caloric existing in steam, 1022°.

235. When steam is condensed, or when vapours return to their liquid state, their latent heat is rendered sensible; a small quantity of steam gives off a great portion of caloric.

236. The powerful heat of steam is experienced by those who accidentally hold their hands for a moment near the spout of a boiling tea-kettle. The pain which ensues is very acute. Children have been known to die from inhaling into their lungs the least portion of steam, from the spout of a teapot of hot water. If such be the effects of the very least quantity of steam in contact with any portion of our limbs or our lungs, how awful must be the condition of those unfortunate persons, who, in the bursting of the boiler of a steamboat, are not only enveloped in an atmosphere of this powerful and dreadful vapour, but obliged at every breath to inhale it into their lungs!

---

233. Is there more caloric in steam th n in boiling water?
234. How did a celebrated chemist coi pute the heat of steam?
235. What takes place when steam is condensed?
236. What is remarked of the powerful effects of the heat of steam in contact with our bodies?

237. This figure is intended to give you some idea of the expansive force of steam, which is so powerful as to carry forward the railroad car on the land, and the steamboat on the water, with astonishing rapidity. But this force, so useful to man when properly regulated, may, by carelessness, prove a dreadful agent of destruction. You are to suppose the little glass bulb, suspended over the lamp, to contain a very small quantity of water, and its tube to be hermetically sealed. The heat of the lamp converts the water into steam, the expansive power of which is so great, that the glass bulb would soon burst with a violent explosion, if the heat were continued. Where there is any vent, or way of escape for the steam, it will pass off without bursting the vessel. The boilers of steamboats are usually of copper, and furnished with a valve, or little door, which can be opened as occasion requires, for the purpose of letting off the steam.

238. The degrees of steam are marked in such a way that the engineer can know what force is employed, and understanding the power of his steam engine, if he use due care, accidents will seldom happen, for when he finds the steam increasing too fast, he lets it off by means of the safety-valve.— But should the engineer neglect this, and suffer more steam to be formed in the boiler than it can contain, you can at once perceive, by the experiment with the glass bulb, that the boiler must burst.

239. At the temperature of about 400°, the force with which

237. What does the figure represent ?
238. What is the cause of the bursting of steamboat boilers ?

steam presses against the vessel containing it, is equal to 14,700 pounds on a square inch; such a pressure as this, few vessels can resist. : Those who have heard the noise made by letting off steam in a steamboat, can form some idea of its expansive force.   People are often alarmed when they hear this noise, lest the boiler should burst, but there is, usually, then the least danger, because the steam has vent.

THE EFFECT OF ATMOSPHERIC PRESSURE UPON BOILING.

240. We are surrounded on all sides by the atmosphere, or air; it is supposed to be about 45 miles in height; that is, that this distance on every side of our globe is occupied by this invisible and elastic substance.   Thin and light as air is, yet it has weight; and it has been proved that a column of air 45 miles high, is equal in weight to a column of water thirty-three feet high, and a column of mercury thirty inches high.

241. As you will learn many particulars respecting this in Natural Philosophy, we shall only consider the weight or pressure of the air as it respects boiling of different substances.

242. Although we are not sensible of the fact, yet the air is pressing upon us, and upon all bodies on the earth, at the rate of about fifteen pounds for every square inch.

243. When liquids boil, steam in ascending has this weight of the air to overcome. When the atmospheric pressure is less than common, water boils at less heat than 212°, which is what is usually required.

244. As we ascend mountains the pressure of the air is less. At Mont Blanc, and upon the Andes, water was made to boil at a heat of about 180°.   It is said that for every five hundred and thirty feet of elevation, the boiling point is lowered one degree of Fahrenheit's thermometer.

245. *Exp.*—The following is a curious illustration of the effect of pressure in opposing the boiling process. You are to suppose a glass vessel which is half filled with water and clo

---

239. What is the force of the pressure of steam ?
240. By what is our globe surrounded ?
241. What are we now to consider with respect to the air?
242. What is said of the pressure of the air upon all bodies?
243. What is to be overcome before liquids can be made to boil?
244. What is said of the pressure of the air upon mountains?'
245. What experiment illustrates the effect of atmospheric pressure to opposing the boiling process?

sed perfectly tight, to be heated until it is entirely filled with steam; the boiling now ceases, but let the vessel be taken from the fire, and apply a sponge wet with cold water, the liquid within will begin to boil again. The process may be repeated; when the vessel is over the fire, boiling will cease, and will continue to be renewed upon the application of a cold substance.

246. *Explanation.*—The vessel being filled with steam, its pressure prevented the farther boiling of the water. If it were to be kept for a short time in this situation, the increase of steam would burst the glass. On taking the vessel from the fire, and applying the cold sponge, the steam was condensed, and the pressure being thus removed, the boiling began again. This experiment shows that a lower temperature, or less heat, is required for boiling liquids when the pressure of the atmosphere is taken off.

247. The figure shows a vessel of boiling water under a glass vessel, called a bell-glass. You are to suppose the air has been all exhausted from the receiver by means of an *air pump*. The water, heated to the boiling point, being withdrawn from the fire, the boiling ceases; on placing it under the exhausted receiver, the boiling again takes place, and will continue for some time.

248. The explanation of this phenomenon is in one respect the same as given for the last experiment, viz. *pressure* is removed; in this case, it was the pressure of the atmosphere; in the other experiment, the pressure removed was that of steam, which, when condensed, left a vacuum.

---

246. Explain this experiment.
247. What does the figure represent ?
248. What is the explanation of the phenomenon here observed ?

249. *If pressure be greater than that of the atmosphere, more than 212° of heat will be required to boil water.*—

Suppose a matrass, partly filled with water, and placed over a lamp, as represented in the figure. If the mouth of the vessel is closed with the thumb, the water, though heated to 212°, will not boil, but the vapour created will press upwards until its force renders it difficult to keep the thumb over it. On removing the matrass from the lamp, and lifting the thumb from its mouth, boiling commences. This experiment shows that if the pressure of the atmosphere were greater than it is, a proportional increase of heat would be necessary in order to overcome this pressure sufficiently to boil liquids.

SOURCES OF HEAT.

250. The *Sun* is the great source of heat as well as of light. It radiates caloric in all directions; these rays may be collected by mirrors of a peculiar kind. In the focus of these mirrors a powerful heat may be obtained, sufficient to inflame combustible substances.

251. *Combustion, or the burning* of different materials, is the most important source of heat, next to the sun. It is by means of this, that cooking of most kinds is performed, and that we are made warm and comfortable in winter, and are furnished with lights in its long evenings.

252. Did you ever think, as you looked at the fire, and felt the warmth from it, what it is which creates the heat? Suppose that in a cold room some dry wood is laid in the fire-place, and a spark of fire struck from a tinder box, makes a blaze; very soon the fire burns brightly, and you begin to feel warmth. Yet the wood was cold, every thing in the room was cold, but now there is warmth.

---

249. What will be the effect when there is a greater pressure than that of the atmosphere?
250. What is the great source of heat?
251. What is said of combustion?
252. What takes place when a fire is made in a cold room?

253. We will explain this. By striking two pieces of flint violently together, caloric, which was latent in them, is brought into a free and active state; this, meeting with the dry, combustible substance, unites with it, and produces flame. The air furnishes caloric, which exists in it in a latent state but is pressed out by the process of combustion, and become *sensible* warmth.

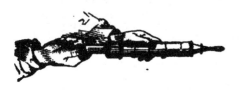

254. That the air does contain *latent heat*, may be proved by the use of a little instrument, called a fire syringe, which is very convenient for lighting a fire.— This consists of a small metallic tube, to which is fitted a rod and piston, as seen in the figure. A piece of *tinder* is fastened to the end of the piston; the rod is forcibly pushed to the bottom of the tube, and the tinder is set on fire. *Explanation.*—The tube was filled with air; on being compressed by the piston, the particles of air were brought so closely in contact as to force out caloric.

255. The *flame* which accompanies the burning of wood, oil, &c., is a subject about which chemists have entertained various opinions, and which seems still to be doubtful. It has been defined *luminous, gaseous matter*, and its heat is often very intense, where the light is but feeble.*

256. Combustion may proceed without flame; this is the case when any substance burns without being exposed to the air. Thus, the timbers of a house beneath a brick fireplace, have been known to become so much heated as to burn to a coal without the fire being perceived; had a column of air been admitted to the timbers thus consuming, a powerful flame must have been the consequence.

* As in the combustion of hydrogen gas, where the flame is so feeble as scarcely to be visible by daylight, but where the heat is so intense as to melt, or burn metals.

---

253. How do you account for the warmth which is produced by combustion?

254. How can it be proved that air contains latent heat?

255. What is flame?

256. Can combustion proceed without flame?

257. *Heat is often the result of chemical affinity.* The figure represents a tube, containing coloured alcohol, placed within a shorter and larger tube, partly filled with water; on adding to this water a quantity of sulphuric acid, the heat produced by the union of the two substances will be so great as to cause the alcohol in the inner tube to boil violently. Alcohol boils with less heat than water, but the experiment proves that a large portion of caloric is pressed out by the combination which takes place between the water and sulphuric acid.

258. *Combustion results from chemical affinity.* Put some of the *chlorate of potash* upon a deep plate containing alcohol, and set the plate in a larger vessel. Then pour a little sulphuric acid upon the two substances in the plate, and flame of a beautiful colour will burst forth. The glass containing the sulphuric acid is fastened to the end of a rod, because there is some danger from the explosion which

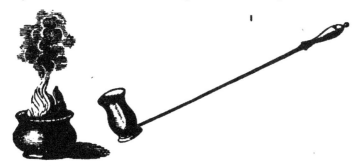

takes place. The combustion which takes place, is in consequence of the action among the particles of the different bodies, and the new combinations which take place.

---

257. By what experiment is it shown that chemical affinity produces heat?

258. How is it proved that combustion results from chemical affinity?

6*

259. Besides the *sun, combustion*, and *chemical affinity*, there are other sources of caloric, as *electricity*, whose phenomena appear on a grand scale in a thunder storm, *percussion*, or the violent striking of hard bodies against each other, and *friction*, or the rubbing of substances. By *percussion*, fire is struck from flint by steel; and carriage wheels, when in violent motion, strike fire from the stones in the path. By the *friction* of dry leaves, or other dry combustibles, the Indians are said to obtain fire in the forests.

260. We have said nothing of the cause of *animal heat;* indeed, the greatest philosophers find much difficulty in explaining the wonderful operations which are carried on in the complicated machinery of living bodies. Although chemists are able to learn the composition of salts, minerals, gases, &c., they yet remain ignorant of what constitutes the principle of *life* in a plant, an insect, or a man.

261. Hitherto, we have treated of subjects which, from their nature, were somewhat abstruse, and, in some respects, calculated to confuse the mind. You will recollect that *Affinity* is not a *substance*, but a *power;* and a power on which the science of Chemistry chiefly depends for its operations. *Light* and *Caloric* are *supposed* to be *substances;* they are called *imponderable*, because they are too delicate to be weighed by any balances which we have; indeed we cannot perceive them by any of our senses, not even by that of sight. Light, like our eyes, enables us to see other bodies, although it is itself invisible. Caloric is only visible by its *effects;* the flame which we see, is produced by the union of caloric with a combustible substance, aided by a certain substance (oxygen) which exists in the air. The heat which we feel, is only the effect of caloric entering our bodies.

CHAPTER VIII.

Electricity. Galvanism. Magnetism.

262. ELECTRICITY is an imponderable fluid, which we know only by its effects. The term was derived from the Greek,

259. What other sources of caloric are there, besides those which have been mentioned?
260. What is said of animal heat, and of *life?*
261. What general remarks conclude the chapter?
262. What is electricity? and what is this term derived from?

electron signifying amber, because it was in this substance that electricity, or a power of attracting light substances, was discovered.

263. The electric fluid is supposed to be diffused throughout the earth as extensively as caloric; and like caloric, it seems to exist in a latent state, except when its equilibrium is disturbed.

264. You may observe, on rubbing the back of a cat in the night, that sparks as if of fire appear, accompanied by slight crackling noises, and a prickling sensation in the hand; these effects are produced by electricity. Fur is one of those substances called *non-conductors* of electricity, because, instead of conducting off the electric fluid, it is capable of accumulating it, and becomes *electrically excited*. In this situation it gives off electricity, which is manifested by the *sparks*, by the *light*, *noise*, and prickling sensation.

265. Another familiar example of the effect of the electrical fluid may have been noticed by you. When taking off clothing of silk or woollen, which has been worn near the skin, sparks are often seen to come from it, accompanied by a crackling noise. The garment having collected electricity from the body, gives it off when exposed to the air. The hair often appears as if electrified, especially in cold weather; this is manifested by its standing erect, and appearing to fly back when the hand is placed near it.

266. But the grandest of all the appearances caused by electricity, is that which is witnessed in a thunder storm.— The state of the atmosphere, from some unknown cause, becomes, at times, especially during hot and sultry weather, such as to disturb the equilibrium of the electric fluid; clouds are formed, some of which contain more electricity than others. When such clouds, containing different degrees of electricity, meet, the one which contains most, discharges the fluid. This discharge produces both the thunder and lightning; the latter is seen, before the former is heard, because light travels faster than sound.

267. We are able to estimate the distance of thunder by the

---

263. Is the electric fluid extensively diffused?
264. What causes sparks to appear on rubbing the back of a cat in the night?
265. What other familiar example of the effect of electricity is mentioned?
266. What causes the discharge of the electric fluid in a storm?
267. How are we able to judge of the distance of thunder from us?

time which intervenes between the flash and report. Light
moves with such velocity that the discharge of the electric
fluid, and the appearance of the lightning are almost instanta-
neous, while sound is supposed to move only at the rate of a
little over twelve miles in a minute, or about one mile in five
seconds. When we count slowly, we may consider one, two
three, &c., as standing for so many seconds; therefore, if,
when we see the lightning, we count slowly until we hear the
report, the number counted may be considered as so many
seconds of time between the flash and the report. Suppose
this number to be 20: on dividing it by 5, (the number of seconds which pass while sound travels one mile,) the quotient
will be 4. We may then suppose the storm to be within four
miles. We sometimes hear a single clap of thunder, at other
times a rumbling, irregular sound, like successive discharges

of cannon, is heard. Suppose the observer to be at *a*, while
b marks the direction of the lightning, (or the course of the
electric fluid,) he will hear but one report; the sound will
reach him first from the nearest point, and die away with
increasing distance. But lightning is usually less regular in
its progress, as in the line *c*; supposing the spectator to stand
at *a*, the sound will first come to him from the nearest point,
and will then seem to recede, and again to approach, rumbling
irregularly as the sound arrives from the different portions of
traversed air, some nearer and some further from him. When
the report follows the flash almost at the same moment, we

may know that the storm is very near us. When persons are struck with lightning, the cloud, being directly over their heads, the thunder and lightning appear at the same instant.

CONDUCTORS AND NON-CONDUCTORS OF ELECTRICITY.

268. It is of importance to learn what are *conductors* and what *non-conductors* of electricity, that we may take proper care in thunder storms not to expose ourselves unnecessarily. The *metals* are conductors—for this reason it is unsafe during a thunder storm which is very near, for people to wear spectacles with gold or silver bows, watches, thimbles, buckles in shoes, or indeed any metallic substance, about the person—for when a house is struck with lightning, the *electric fluid* is usually conducted by the air down a chimney, or by the beams or walls into different apartments, and will dart out of its way if a bright metallic substance offers itself as a conductor.

269. Feathers and hair are *non-conductors*—for this reason a feather bed or mattress is a safe position in a thunder storm. A seat upon a sofa or chair drawn out from the wall, with both the feet placed upon a stool, is also one of the most secure against the approach of the electric fluid. An object is said

268. Why is it unsafe for people in a thunder storm to have metallic substances about their persons?
269. What are t1e most safe positions in a thunder storm?

to be *insulated* when surrounded by non-conductors of electricity.

270. *Glass being a non-conductor,* it is safer to have windows closed in a thunder storm, than open.

But after all our care, we must ever reflect that life is in the hands of Him who gave it. He can call up storms when we are travelling in the open sky, with no means of escape; and He can even cause the very laws which He has established over nature, to vary whenever it is His will to take the life of man in a peculiar way. Thus, at times, the most skilful physicians find their usual remedies powerless, or producing con trary effects from what they have in other cases observed.— This shows us that it is God, and not *nature,* who governs the universe; since nature herself is made to bend to His will.

271. Buildings may generally be secured from the effects of the electric fluid, by means of what are called *lightning rods.* These are long rods of iron, pointed at the upper end, while the lower end is placed in the earth. The lightning rod should be higher than the building; then if there be a discharge of the electric fluid from a cloud near the building, the metallic points attract it, and the rod conducts it downwards into the earth.

In general the conductors and non-conductors of caloric correspond to those of electricity.

Our own countryman, Dr. Franklin, was the first who proved that lightning and electricity were the same. It had before been suggested by some philosophers, but he first dared to bring down lightning from the clouds, that he might ascertain its nature. This he did by means of a common kite, which he raised on the approach of a thunder storm, being in the fields, accompanied only by a young lad, his grandson.— "A considerable time elapsed without any appearance of success, and a promising cloud passed over the kite with no effect, when, just as he was beginning to despair, he observed some loose threads upon the string of the kite begin to diverge and to stand erect; upon this, he fastened a key to the string, and on presenting his knuckle to it, was gratified by the first electric spark that had ever been thus drawn from the clouds; others succeeded, and when the string had become wet with the falling rain, a copious stream of electric fire passed from the conductor to his hand. It is said that

---

270. Why is it more safe to have windows closed in a thunder storm than open?

271. How may buildings be secured from the effects of electricity?

such were Franklin's emotions when he saw the fibres of the string diverge, and the sparks glitter, that he uttered a deep sigh, and expressed himself ready to die. He knew that his name would be immortalized by the discovery."

POSITIVE AND NEGATIVE ELECTRICITY.

272. When a body contains more than the usual quantity of the electric fluid, it is said to be in a *positive state*, when less, in a *negative state*. These two states are sometimes expressed by the terms *plus*, more, and *minus*, less.

273. *Opposite* electricities *attract*, while *similar electricities repel* each other; that is, a body in a *positive state attracts a body in a negative state;* while two bodies, both in a positive, or both in a negative state, *repel* each other.

274. A stick of sealing wax, or a glass tube, rubbed with a silk handkerchief, are in a different state of electricity from the surrounding bodies, and will attract light substances, if presented to them. If some little balls of pith, suspended by a fine thread of silk, be presented to a body which is *electrically* excited, the balls will at first be attracted towards it. If one ball be brought in contact with the excited substance, and the attempt made to suspend it by the side of the other balls,

272. When is a body, with regard to electricity, said to be in a positive, and when in a negative state?
273 What is said with respect to attraction and repulsion ?
274. Give some examples of attraction and repulsion.

it will be repelled. The cause of this is, that the one ball acquiring from the excited electric, a new portion of electricity, communicates a portion of it to the ball which it touches, and thus they are both excited, and, like two persons under the influence of angry feelings, mutually repel each other. But if one of the balls in this situation be touched with the finger, it will give off its electricity, and return quietly to its companions.

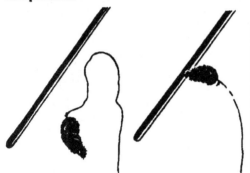

A light feather, suspended by a thread of white sewing silk, shows to advantage the effect of electrical excitement. The figure represents the appearance of the feather attracted by the excited tube, and the same feather repelled after having received electricity from the glass by direct contact. In the one case, we see, by the feather clinging to the glass, that bodies in *opposite* states of electricity *attract* each other; in the other case, we see that bodies *similarly electrified repel* each other

THE ELECTRICAL MACHINE.

The ancients had some idea of the existence of electricity, as it was early observed that certain substances, such as amber, sulphur, and some stones, (especially the mineral called *tourmaline*,) when rubbed, had the property of attracting and repelling light bodies. Thales, a philosopher who lived six centuries before the Christian era, was so struck with the discovery of these properties in amber, that he imagined it animated. Darwin, a philosophical poet of modern times, says,—

> " Bright *amber* shines on his electric throne,
> And adds ethereal lustre to his own."

After the subject of electricity began to be studied, a supply of the electric fluid for experiments was obtained by rubbing a glass tube with the dry hand, or with dry silk. It was then said to be *electrically excited,* and was in a state to *attract* light bodies, such as feathers, hair, or fine silk thread ; these having been drawn towards the excited tube by some invisible agent, no sooner touched the tube than they were thrown back with force, and again alternately attracted and repelled. At length, the electrical machine was invented, by means of which a larger quantity of the electric fluid can be accumulated. This machine is of various forms; one of which is here represented. The principal parts are the *glass cylinder*

A. The *cushion* to the *chain* C, and the *conductor* B. The cushion is usually stuffed with hair, and covered with an amalgam of tin and zinc; on turning the cylinder, this cushion, partly by friction, and partly by the effect of the metals, causes an accumulation of electricity; which passes from the glass cylinder to the *conductor*, where it is collected. The chain communicates with the earth, and is supposed to convey from thence to the cushion new supplies of electricity, which are imparted by the cushion to the glass cylinder, and by that to the conductor. The conductor is then said to be *charged*. In a dry atmosphere, and with an electrical machine in good order, when the cylinder is turned a crackling noise is heard, and sparks of light are seen upon the glass, passing from the cushion to the conductor. If the knuckle be held within a few inches of the conductor, sparks will pass from it, and a shock be received by the person.

7

GALVANIC ELCTRICITY.—*Its Discovery.*

275. There is a mode in which electrical phenomena may be produced, called *Galvanism.* This is so named from Galvani, an Italian, who, near the close of the last century, discovered that the muscles and nerves of dead animals may be excited by the electric fluid; or, rather, this is said to have been the discovery of Madame Galvani, who, being in her husband's laboratory, accidentally observed convulsions in a dead frog, which chanced to lie near the electrical machine, when in action.

276. On examination by the professor, it appeared that a knife near the machine, had touched one of the nerves in the limb of the frog; and that when any other metallic substance, in contact with a nerve of the animal, was brought within the action of the electrical machine, there followed a twitching of the limb.

277. Since then, many discoveries have been made of the astonishing effects of galvanic electricity. Some philosophers were so enthusiastic as to believe that the dead might be restored to life, by its power. Various experiments have been made upon the dead bodies of criminals; and although terrible and appalling contortions of the frame, and frightful changes of countenance were produced, still it had not the power to restore life, for as soon as the galvanic action ceased, its effects disappeared.

278. When two metals are connected by some substance capable of exciting their different electricities, galvanic effects may be observed. For instance, take a piece of silver and a piece of zinc, place the silver upon, and the zinc under the tongue, and bring their edges together at the tip of the tongue; you will instantly perceive a singular metallic taste, a slight twitching of the nerves of the tongue, and a flash of light. Place upon a piece of zinc a bit of silver, and lay a worm on the silver, there is no appearance of galvanic action; but if the worm be brought in contact with the zinc and silver at the same time, it will writhe as if in distress.

279. Acids of various kinds, and also water, are found use-

275. What can you say of the discovery of galvanism?
276. What had formed a communication between the nerves of the frog and the electrical machine?
277. What is said of experiments which have since been made?
278. When do metals produce galvanic effects?
279. What substances are found useful in promoting the development of electricity in metals?

ful in promoting the development of electricity in metals; thus, the moisture in the tongue, in the limbs of the skinned frog, and in the substance of the worm, were essential in producing the galvanic effects which have been described.

GALVANIC CIRCLES.

280. The cut represents a vessel containing an acid, much diluted with water, and two plates, the one of zinc, the other  of copper, as shown by the letters *z* and *c;* to each plate is soldered a piece of wire, which meet in the centre, opposite the place of insertion. This is called a *simple galvanic circle.* It is supposed that when in operation, there is, in such a circle, a continual current of electricity, flowing in the direction of the *arrows,* from the zinc to the fluid, from the fluid to the copper, and from the copper back to the zinc. When the wires do not communicate with each other, the galvanic circle is said to be broken;—the wire attached to the copper plate is *negative,* and that attached to the zinc plate *positive.* The wires are also called *poles;* thus we say the copper is the *negative pole,* and the zinc the *positive pole.*

281. A *compound galvanic circle* consists of many *simple circles,* by means of which a more powerful action is produced.

282. The *Voltaic pile* is so named from an Italian chemist, Volta. This is made by placing pairs of zinc and copper plates, one above another. Here we have a series of simple circles; between each pair of plates is placed a piece of flannel, wet with a weak acid. The figure shows you a *Voltaic*  *pile,* commencing with zinc *z,* and ending with copper *c.* The wires which meet in the centre are the two *poles.* The arrows show, by their points, the direction of the electric current.

In constructing the Voltaic pile, from thirty to fifty plates of copper, and as many of zinc, are generally used; these are placed in regular order—each pair of plates being separated by a piece of flannel of the same size; thus, a regular succes-

---

280. What is meant by a simple galvanic circle?
281. What is a compound galvanic circle?
282. How is the Voltaic pile composed?

sion of copper, zinc, flannel, copper, zinc; flannel, is kept up
through the whole series.

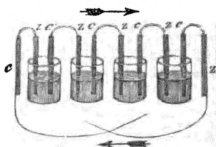

283. The *couronne de
tasses** is a galvanic circle in which the acid so-
lution is contained in
separate cups. Each cup
zcontains a pair of plates,
and each zinc plate is
attached, by a wire, to
the copper of the next
pair. These cups, by
being multiplied or di
minished in number, in-
crease or lessen the action of the galvanic fluid.

284. Dr. Hare, of Philadelphia, who has done much for the
honor of American science, has invented an apparatus called
a *calorimoter*, which means, *mover of caloric*. It is very
powerful in exciting heat, though its electrical power is comparatively small. Another and more important invention of
Dr. Hare, is his *deflagrator*, or an instrument exceeding all
others in its power to burn metals, and those substances which
resist all the ordinary effects of heat.

285. It has recently been maintained by chemists, that
electricity was the great agent in all cases of chemical affinity, and combination. You will recollect, in considering the
subject of affinity, we found that substances most unlike, unite
the most readily, as in the case of an acid and alkali. Now
we find these substances to have opposite electricities, and
that opposite electricities do attract one another; therefore,
the inference is in favor of electricity, as being the great con-
necting link in the chain of the material creation.

MAGNETISM.

286. There is a form in which electricity appears, called
magnetism. The power of the *magnet* to *attract* and *repel*
bodies, appeared mysterious, until discoveries in electricity
suggested the idea, that this fluid was the agent in the phe-

* Pronounced couron-de-tas; meaning *crown of cups.*

283. Describe the Couronne de Tasses.
284. What is said of the calorimoter and deflagrator of Dr. Hare?
285. What is said of the connexion of electricity with Chemistry?
286. To what is magnetism attributed?

nomena of magnetism. Electricity when accumulated produces certain effects, many of which have been already laid before you. But the new appearances which magnetism exhibits, are supposed to be owing to the electrical fluid *moving in currents* around the magnet.

287. It is not known with certainty who first discovered the properties of the magnet. A native of Naples, several centuries ago, is said to have observed that pieces of iron were attracted towards masses of a certain kind of iron ore; and that this ore communicated to other substances, containing iron and steel, the same property of attraction. This person is also said to have travelled for the purpose of ascertaining whether this singular effect was peculiar to his own country, or was a general law of nature.

History relates that a trial of the magnetic power on water was first made in the following manner. "A ship was moored out at sea, in a direction agreeing with that indicated by a magnet turning freely on its centre; and a boat having a magnet similarly mounted was sent out at night to the ship. The boat was steered exactly in the direction of the magnet, and arrived close to the vessel stationed at sea. This was a successful experiment; and the magnet was, in process of time, formed into an instrument called the *mariner's compass.*"

288. The following are among the most important properties of the magnet:—1. It attracts iron and steel. 2. When allowed to move freely, it points towards the poles of the earth, and the same end always points to the same pole.— 3. The natural magnet has the power of imparting its properties to other bodies. 4. All magnets have a *north* and *south* pole.

289. The attractive power of the magnet for steel, may be shown by the following recent fact. A young man engaged in some mechanical operation, had a small sharp bit of steel fix itself in his eyeball. The pain which it produced was distressing; no relief could be obtained, and it was determined that he must submit to the operation of having his eyeball taken out in order to save his life. Some person suggested the use of the magnet—a powerful one being applied to the eye, the bit of steel left it and fastened itself to the magnet.

290. A steel needle rubbed with a magnet is an *artificial*

---

287. What is said of the discovery of magnetism?
288. What are some of the most important properties of the magnet?
289. What fact shows the attraction of the magnet for steel?

7*

magnet, possessing all the properties of a natural one. When left to move freely, a *magnetic* needle always points to the north and south poles; this is called its *directive* property. By means of it the navigator, when out of sight of land, directs his course through the trackless ocean. Until the discovery of the magnet, and its application to the *mariner's compass*, navigation was confined to mere coasting voyages ; for if the sailor went out of sight of land, he had no means of finding his way back to port. Without the mariner's compass, Columbus would never have adventured into the broad ocean, in search of a new world.

291. The origin of the name *magnet* is no less doubtful than the period of its discovery. By some the name is supposed to be derived from *Magnesia*, a province in Macedonia, where it was anciently found in large quantities; others say it was very anciently discovered by one *Magnes*, and named from him. In chemistry the magnet is known as the *oxide of iron*. The common name of the magnet is the *loadstone*, or leading stone. Its colour is dark gray; it is heavy, and has a metallic lustre.

292. *Exp.*—Many interesting experiments may be performed with a magnet, either natural or artificial. A knife, by touching a magnet, becomes itself magnetic, and when a needle is presented to it, will pick it up and hold it attached to its edge. If two corks, having small magnets lying upon them, are placed in a basin of water, they will be seen to move towards each other, or from each other, according as opposite or similar poles are presented. For *opposite* poles *attract*, while *similar* poles *repel*. That is, a *south pole* or end repels a south pole and attracts a north pole, and a *north pole* repels a north pole, but attracts a south pole. An amusing experiment may be made by placing magnets in the mouths of small figures representing ducks, and placing them in a basin of water. They will either advance, or swim away from each other, according as the poles of the magnet present themselves.

293. It has been discovered that the conducting wires of the

---

290. To what use is the directive property of the magnet applied ?
291. What is said of the origin of the name magnet? and what are its chemical and common names ?
292. What experiments may be performed with a magnet ?
293. What seems to confirm the theory that magnetism is the same thing as electricity ?

galvanic circle communicate to some metals magnetic attraction; this seems to confirm the theory that magnetism is but a modification of the electric fluid.

294. If the imponderable agents, *light, caloric, electricity,* and *magnetism,* are not all essentially the same substance, appearing under different modes, they must be connected by some common tie, since they so closely attend upon and follow the steps of each other.) Whatever these imponderable substances may be in their nature, or whatever bond of union may exist between them, we feel that they are mysterious and powerful agents operating within our own bodies, around us on every side; constituting the soul of material things, and keeping in action the elements of nature—and yet, after all, these are passive instruments in His hand who created them, and gave them laws.

---

† **CHAPTER IX.**

Alphabet of Chemistry.   Gases.   Mode of collecting Gases Oxygen.

295. You will recollect that the great object of Chemistry is to ascertain what bodies are made of, and how they are put together—we ought also to add another part of the office of Chemistry, which is to show what are the properties of bodies; that is, what *changes they are susceptible of themselves, and what changes they can produce in other bodies.*

296. The teacher of Chemistry must proceed with his pupil, like one who teaches a child to read. We should expect he would first teach the alphabet of letters, out of which words and sentences are made. The pupil in Chemistry must be taught his alphabet, before he can learn the nature of the compounds which are formed with it.

297. The alphabet of Chemistry consists of about *fifty simple* substances, called *elements.*

---

294. What general remark is made respecting imponderable agents ?
295. What are the two important objects of Chemistry ?
296. How ought the teacher in Chemistry to proceed?
297. What does the alphabet of Chemistry consist of?

298. The ancients considered that there were but four simple elements, viz.: fire, air, earth, and water. The three latter are now known to be compounds; while the list of simple elements is increased by substances, of which the ancients knew not even the existence, and by others, which they considered as compounds.

299. Among the substances unknown to the ancients, are *gases*, which do not exist in nature in a separate form, but are obtained, by being disunited from their combinations, through chemical agencies. Among the simple elements supposed by the ancients to be compound, are the metals.

300. By the *alchymists* of former days, a set of men, who, with some vague ideas of Chemistry, were wholly ignorant of its true principles, it was thought that the less valuable metals, such as iron, lead, &c., might be so reduced and purified as to produce gold.

301. We have now learned something of *chemical affinity*, or that *power* which unites substances of different kinds;— we have considered *light* in some of its chemical relations; and examined the nature and properties of *caloric*, and the various forms of *electricity*, as manifested, not only in electrical phenomena, but in *galvanism* and *magnetism*. We do not include the imponderable agents in our alphabet of Chemistry, because they seem, in a greater or less degree, to pervade all matter, and in some form of combination to exist in all substances.

302. The elements which we are now to consider, are of a less subtle nature than the imponderables; and we are better able to understand what they are, and how they operate. We call them *ponderable* substances, because they are all known to have weight. As two or more letters put together form words, so two or more of these elements form compounds.

298. What was the opinion of the ancients in respect to *elements*?
299. What substances were unknown to the ancients? and what simple substances did they consider compound?
300. What is said of the alchymists?
301. What subjects have been considered?
302. What do we call the substances which are known to have weight?

ALPHABET OF CHEMISTRY:
OR, TABLE OF ELEMENTARY SUBSTANCES.

I. GASES.

1. Oxygen.
2. Hydrogen.
3. Nitrogen.
4. Chlorine.

II. SOLID SUBSTANCES *not Metallic.*

5. Carbon.
6. Sulphur.
7. Selenium.
8. Phosphorus.
9. Boron.
10. Fluorine.
11. Iodine.
12. Silicon.
13. Bromine.

III. METALS.

14. Potassium.
15. Sodium.
16. Lithium.
17. Barium.
18. Strontium.
19. Calcium.
20. Magnesium.
21. Aluminum.
22. Glucinum.
23. Yttrium.
24. Zirconium.
25. Thorium.
26. Cerium.
27. Tellurium.
28. Arsenic.
29. Antimony.
30. Chromium.
31. Vanadium.
32. Uranium.
33. Molybdenum.
34. Tungsten.
35. Columbium.
36. Titanium.
37. Iron.
38. Manganese.
39. Nickel.
40. Cobalt.
41. Zinc.
42. Cadmium.
43. Lead.
44. Tin.
45. Copper.
46. Bismuth.
47. Mercury.
48. Silver.
49. Gold.
50. Platinum.
51. Palladium.
52. Rhodium.
53. Iridium.
54. Osmium.

On examining this list of simple substances, you meet with some which are common and familiar, as sulphur, iron, silver, &c., but most of these names are new to you. You are

303. How many of the elementary substances are *gases ?* how many are solid *non-metallic* substances? and how many are metals?

not expected to commit to memory these names; but as you separately study the different properties of the simple substances, the names of each will become familiar to you. Some of these elements are very abundant in nature, either existing alone, or in combination with other substances, while others are found in small quantities, and in few situations.

304. By the various combinations of these fifty-four substances, all known bodies upon the earth, beneath its surface, and within its atmosphere, are formed, as all the words of our language are formed by various combinations of the letters of the alphabet.

GASES.

305. Gas is a word derived from the German *geist*, and signifies *spirit*, or air. Four of the simple substances are gases, and besides these, there are several compound gases. The number in all is about thirty. The common air, though an aeriform body, is not reckoned among the gases. Some gases are lighter, others heavier than the air. Some promote combustion, others extinguish it. Some are red or green, others are white, and some invisible. Some are destitute of smell, while others throw off offensive or suffocating odours.

PNEUMATIC CISTERN.

306. Gases are collected by various processes; the most common is by means of the *pneumatic cistern.* (The word pneumatic is from the Greek, *pneuma*, wind, or air.) As most gases pass through water without mixing with it, and being lighter than water, rise above its surface; this fluid is found convenient for collecting them in a pure and unmixed

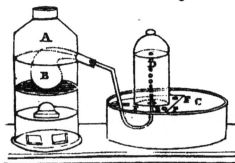

form. A represents a furnace; B a retort, containing the substance which furnishes the gas: C the water-tub or cistern; D the bell glass to receive the gas; E F a shelf so fixed that the water rises a few inches above it, and having holes to per-

304. Of what are all known substances composed ?
305. What can you say respecting gases ?
306. Describe the pneumatic cistern.

mit the ascent of the gas. The receiver D, being filled with water, is placed upon the shelf with its mouth downward, but as the shelf is below the water in the tub, the water in the receiver does not run out in consequence of this vessel being turned downward. The gas, issuing from the retort, passes through the tube, and is conducted by it to the mouth of the receiver, and being lighter than the water, rises up in little bubbles, and displaces the water which descends into the tub, as the gas fills the receiver. Common air may be introduced into the receiver, if a vessel containing it (that is, in common language, an *empty vessel*) be inverted under the shelf in such a manner that the bubbles of air will ascend into the receiver; as the air rises, the water in the receiver lowers. The water in the receiver is necessary in collecting a gas, because if this vessel contained common air, the gas introduced would mix with the air and become impure. Those of you who can have access to a pneumatic cistern, should not fail to exercise yourselves in transferring common air from one vessel into another, and of collecting gases where an opportunity presents. Any person can put a piece of board over a tub, and with water and two tumblers, may learn by practice (the best of all methods) how to collect gases.

Two things in this process may seem at first unaccountable to you; the manner in which the water remains in the inverted vessels, and the displacing of the water by the air which is introduced below. The water remains in the vessels, because the pressure of the atmosphere on all sides supports it; and it would support an unbroken column of water thirty-two feet high, as in the case of pumps. The air or gas rises through the water, because it is lighter; if oil were introduced below the mouth of the vessel of water, it would rise in the same manner, for that is lighter than water.*

OXYGEN GAS.

307. Oxygen gas always exists in nature in combination with other substances, and can only be obtained by separating it from them. This gas is an important part of air and water. It is the great *souring* principle; that is, a certain proportion

---

* *Note to teachers.* It is often difficult to explain, in words, very simple processes. The experienced teacher will always supply, by explanations and illustrations, any deficiency of the text-book. The gas apparatus may be exhibited in a small cheap way, and it is an important lesson in natural philosophy to observe the suspension of a liquid, the ascent of air, and the consequent displacing of the liquid.

---

307. In what substances does oxygen exist?

of it combined with a substance produces an *acid.* United to sulphur, it forms *sulphuric acid,* and cider by being combined with it becomes vinegar.

308. The name of *oxygen* is so called from the Greek *oxus,* acid, added to *gennao,* to produce, because it produces acids; the German name for oxygen is *sauerstoff,* which in English means sour stuff. Other names have been at different times given, such as *fire air,* because it is important in combustion, and *respirable air,* because it is a part of the atmosphere necessary to the support of animal life.

309. Oxygen may be obtained in various methods; that which is most common is, by heating a substance called the *peroxide of manganese;* this is usually found in connexion with iron ore, to which it bears a resemblance.

310. An *oxide* signifies a union of a substance with a small proportion of oxygen; a *deutoxide,* denotes a greater proportion of oxygen; and a *peroxide,* the highest proportion of oxygen with which a substance can unite, without being an *acid.*

311. The *peroxide of manganese* is a substance composed of a metal called manganese, united to oxygen in the proportion of one hundred parts of the former, to fifty-six parts of the latter. On the application of heat, caloric unites with the oxygen of the metal, and carries it off in a gas: so that oxygen gas is, in reality, composed of oxygen united to caloric.

MODE OF OBTAINING OXYGEN.

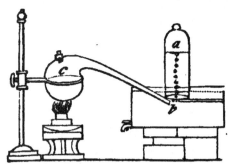

312. Suppose the retort *c* to contain a portion of pulverized peroxide of manganese; *b* is the pneumatic cistern filled with water; *a* is a bell glass receiver filled with water, and inverted over the shelf of the cistern. The retort being heated to a red heat by the lamp, oxygen gas begins to

308. From what is the name derived? and what other names have been given to it?

309. How is oxygen obtained?

310. What do you understand by the terms oxide, deutoxide, and peroxide?

311. What is the peroxide of manganese, and what is the effect of heat upon it?

312. Explain the process of obtaining oxygen gas?

pass through the neck of the retort; at first, it is impure, being mixed with the air which was in the retort; therefore the first gas that comes over should not be collected in the receiver. In a short time, all the atmospheric air being expelled, pure oxygen will appear. The neck of the retort being then placed in a suitable position, large bubbles of the gas will pass rapidly up and displace the water in the receiver. When the gas ceases to issue from the retort, the manganese has parted with all the oxygen that may be expected. One pound of the peroxide of manganese, if good, will furnish from four to five gallons of oxygen gas. Red lead, which is a *deutoxide of lead*, is often used for collecting oxygen gas in the manner we have described.

313. Vegetables give off oxygen when acted upon by light. This may be proved by putting a sprig of green mint into a large vial filled with water; then inverting the vial in a basin of water, and leaving it for a short time exposed to the action of the sun's rays, small bubbles will begin to appear on the surface of the leaves. These are bubbles of oxygen, which, rising into the upper part of the vial, will, in a few days, afford a sufficient quantity of the pure gas for the purpose of experiment.

314. Having obtained oxygen gas, a variety of beautiful and interesting experiments may be made with it;—these experiments show us the nature and properties of this wonderful substance. We say substance, because, although we can neither see, smell, nor taste it, it is one of the most powerful and active agents in nature.

315. Like common air, oxygen gas is invisible, elastic, and inodorous. It is heavier than air, and not absorbed by water.

316. We shall now consider the peculiar properties of oxygen gas. 1st. *Oxygen is the great supporter of combustion;* that is, its presence and aid are necessary to the burning of substances.

Exp.—We will suppose the glass vessel represented in this figure, standing upon the shelf in the pneumatic cistern, and filled with oxygen gas. Its purity is tested by introducing into the vessel a lighted taper; if it burn with increased brilliancy, it is pure oxygen gas. A piece of fine iron wire having been

313. How may it be proved that vegetables give off oxygen?
314. What is said of experiments that may be made with oxygen?
315. How does oxygen resemble common air?
316. How is it proved that oxygen is a supporter of combustion?

prepared into a coil, by winding around a larger wire, has at the end a bit of thread covered with sulphur. Having been inflamed by holding it for an instant in the flame of a lamp, the coil of wire is then plunged into the vessel of oxygen; a beautiful and splendid appearance is now presented by the burning of the metal, which throws off sparks glittering like the most brilliant stars. If there were sufficient oxygen, the metal would continue to burn, until the whole wire was consumed. The product of this combustion is a little ball of melted iron, which falls into the water at the bottom of the vessel.

317. *Explanation.*—Oxygen, being a powerful supporter of combustion, is capable of igniting metals, surrounded by it, with some increase of temperature at first. The thread, dipped in sulphur and inflamed, gave the first impulse to combustion, and the oxygen gas supported, and gave it the force and power which this experiment manifests. In this process, the caloric which existed in combination with oxygen gas, is pressed out by the union of oxygen with the iron wire. The little ball of iron, found at the bottom of the vessel after the combustion, is an *oxide of iron.* On being weighed, this is found to be heavier than the wire before it was burned. This shows that it has gained something. Now as there was only iron and oxygen gas in the vessel, besides the caloric necessary to hold oxygen in the state of a gas—and this has been seen to come out from its latent to a free state—we must, as the oxygen has disappeared, conclude that it united with the iron, which conclusion is confirmed by the fact, that the iron has actually acquired something which adds to its weight.

318. We see from this experiment, that if the air were pure oxygen, every thing would be consumed. On attempting to kindle a fire in an iron stove, the stove itself would begin to burn. The brass tube of the bellows with which we blow the

---

317. How do you explain the appearances exhibited in this experiment?
318. What consequences would ensue if the air were pure oxygen?

fire, would burst into an intense blaze ; and the blacksmith, in attempting to pursue his labours, would see his hammer and anvil kindling into a flame. But the Author of nature designed not this element as an agent of destruction. He therefore so tempered it, by mixing with other elements, as to sustain the lives and conduce to the comfort of his creatures.— He united it with one element to form air, with another to form water, and we meet with it in an almost infinite variety of most useful combinations. He gave to the air that proportion of oxygen which promotes the combustion of wood, oil, and coal, sufficiently for all the purposes of human life. Less oxygen would be insufficient to afford us the necessary fire and light; more oxygen would render combustion dangerous and destructive.

319. It is important that you should consider attentively what takes place in burning or combustion. You have, in the burning of metal, understood that though there is a change of state in the two substances, oxygen gas and iron, yet neither of them are destroyed or lost. This is the case with every thing that burns ; (nothing is destroyed,)but substances in burning change their state or condition. Some portion passes off in smoke or vapour, another remains in the form of coal, ashes, or soot. Philosophers say, and the assertion appears to be proved by all the experiments which have yet been made upon material substances, that no portion of matter has ever been destroyed. Thus we find that not even in burning, which seems the most destructive of all processes, is any particle lost. Who then would dare to say, since God thus saves every material atom that he has created, that he will annihilate the noblest of his works, the human soul?

320. The union of any substance with oxygen is called *oxidation,* which term is, by some chemists, considered as meaning the same thing as *combustion.* We have seen in the case of burning iron wire in oxygen gas, that combustion was the consequence of this gas uniting with another substance. The flame and heat are not always perceptible, because in ordinary cases the process of oxidation is more gradual.

321. Iron *rust* is an instance of *slow* combustion ; it is an *oxide of iron.* Any iron vessel or utensil which stands long exposed to the weather, will become rusted. Iron has such an affinity for oxygen, that it attracts it from the air, and from

319. Are substances destroyed by burning?
320. What is oxidation ?
321. What causes iron to rust so easily

the moisture which is in the air ; if the vessel is left with a little water in it, the oxygen from the water hastens the process of oxidation.

322. A *burnt* and an *oxidated substance* mean the same thing. All bodies which will unite with oxygen are therefore called *combustible*; the metals, gases, and indeed all the simple elements, unite with oxygen in a greater or less degree.

323. There are various degrees of oxidation; the lowest is called an *oxide*, the highest an *acid*. Some substances unite with oxygen but in one proportion, others in four. The lowest proportion in which oxygen unites with any substance is 8; therefore this is considered the representative number of oxygen; a second proportion of oxygen would be 16, a third 24, and so on, each being some multiple of 8.

Oxygen important to Animal Life.

2d. *Oxygen supports respiration*, or *breathing*.

324. A little girl caught a beautiful humming bird, and to secure it till she could obtain a cage, put it under a large bowl. In a little time, going to look at her bird, she found to her sorrow that it was dead. Had she understood Chemistry, she would have known that the bird, small as it was, would soon, in breathing, consume all the oxygen contained in a bowl full of air, and then nothing would be left but *nitrogen*, which cannot support life, and another gas thrown off in breathing, viz. *carbonic acid*, which is destructive to life.

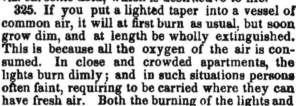

325. If you put a lighted taper into a vessel of common air, it will at first burn as usual, but soon grow dim, and at length be wholly extinguished. This is because all the oxygen of the air is consumed. In close and crowded apartments, the lights burn dimly; and in such situations persons often faint, requiring to be carried where they can have fresh air. Both the burning of the lights and the breathing of the people, exhaust the air of its oxygen, and although there is no ordinary room but admits some air, still, under such circumstances, the main body of the air must be

---

322. What substances are called combustible ?
323. What is said of different degrees of oxidation ?
324. What anecdote is related to prove that oxygen is essential to respiration ?
325. What may we infer respecting the quality of air, when a candle will not burn freely in it ? and why does the air in a crowded room, and with many lights, become bad ?

(unwholesome.) No animal can live in air that will not support combustion. But besides the want of oxygen, there are other circumstances which render the air in certain situations destructive to life and combustion. We shall consider this more particularly when we treat of carbonic acid gas.

Oxygen the great Acidifying principle.

326. 3d. *Oxygen produces acids.* It was long considered as the only *maker of acids* which exists, and is now supposed to be of much greater importance in this respect than any other substance, though some other acidifying principles are now known to exist.

327. *Exp.*—The figure represents the burning of a substance called *phosphorus*, in oxygen gas. The phosphorus is contained in a bent spoon, which is introduced into the jar of oxygen gas. On inflaming the phosphorus, it burns with great brilliancy. A white, flaky substance soon appears on the sides of the vessel; if this is rinsed off into water, the liquid will be sour to the taste, and will also exhibit another property of acids, viz. that of reddening blue vegetable colours.

Explanation.—The jar contained only water, oxygen gas, and phosphorus; nothing now remains of these three substances but the sour liquid, therefore we infer that the union of oxygen with the phosphorus has made it acid; this is called *phosphoric acid.*

328. In making vinegar of cider or wine, the vessels containing the liquid should be unstopped, and left exposed to the ai·, which furnishes oxygen. The vessel should be but partly filled, that a large surface of liquid may come in contact with the air. Frequent agitation promotes the acidifying process, by successively exposing different portions of the liquid to the air. (As light has an influence in promoting the union of oxygen with other substances, it is well to place the vinegar barrel in the sun.

326. Is oxygen the only acidifying substance?
327. What does the figure represent? How do you explain this experiment?
328. Why should a vinegar barrel be exposed to air and light?

8*

Discovery of Oxygen.

329. This gas was discovered about the year 1774, by Dr Priestly, an English chemist, though Scheele, of Sweden, and Lavoisier, of France, are supposed to have made a similar discovery about the same time. Dr. Priestly observed, that "by heating certain metals, a kind of air was obtained, much purer than the atmosphere, and in which combustible substances burnt with great brilliancy;" such was the simple manner in which this wonderful gas was first introduced to the notice of the world. Since that period, the whole science of Chemistry has changed its character, and all has seemed to become subservient to this great agent. "Oxygen," says a celebrated chemist, "may be considered as the central point around which Chemistry revolves." We should not fail to inform you that oxygen gas is thrown off by vegetables, in a proportion about as great as that consumed by animals. Thus the one part of creation made to depend on the other; for the carbonic acid gas exhaled by animals in respiration, is as important to the life of the vegetable, as oxygen gas is to that of the animal.

CHAPTER X

Nitrogen. Atmosphere. Nitric Acid. Law of definite proportions. Nitrous Acid. Nitric Oxide. Nitrous Oxide.

330. WE are now to examine a substance which, though resembling oxygen in being a gas, without either colour or odour, is yet very different in its essential properties. Nitrogen is so called because it exists in *nitre;* it was at first called *azote,* from the Greek *a,* to deprive of, and *zoe,* life, because an animal soon dies when surrounded by this gas. The French still retain the name azote.

331. Nitrogen composes four-fifths of the common air; that is, air consists of four parts of nitrogen to one of oxygen, when reckoned according to the space they occupy; thus four tumblers of the one with one tumbler of the other, would make a compound, resembling the atmospheric air. In esti-

329. When and by whom was oxygen discovered?
330. From whence are the terms nitrogen and azote derived?
331. What proportion of nitrogen exists in common air?

mating by *weight*, the proportions are different, for nitrogen is a little lighter than the air, and oxygen a little heavier; thus *two proportions of nitrogen to one of oxygen*, when reck-oned in weight, make common air. The proportional num ber of nitrogen is 14; two proportions are 28;—the propor-tion of oxygen is 8, therefore these two gases in the atmo sphere are as 28 united to 8.

332. *Exp.*—Nitrogen gas may be obtained in a very simple manner. (Place a bell glass over a vessel containing a little water,

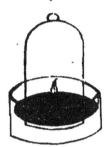

and introduce a lighted taper under it, as you see in the figure. When the taper goes out, you have an evidence that the oxygen of the air has been consumed; the nitrogen does not unite with the burning body, and is left free. As fast as oxygen is absorbed, water rises in the bell glass to fill its place. By this method of obtaining nitrogen, the gas is not left entirely pure, since some vapours from the burning ta-per have mingled with it; but it is suffi-ciently pure to exhibit the most striking properties of this substance.

Nitrogen destroys Combustion.

333. A very elegant and striking experiment may be made to prove that nitrogen destroys combustion, that oxygen sup-ports it, and that a mixture of these two gases in the propor-tion of four parts of nitrogen to one of oxygen, forms a com-pound resembling atmospheric air.)

ca   aa   o   n

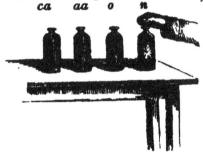

Exp.—Four large vi-als are represented in the cut, which you are to suppose filled as follows: the first *n*, with oxygen, the second *o*, with nitro-gen, the third *aa*, with a mixture of the two, form-ing artificial air, and the fourth *ca*, with common air, or, as we should say in common language, empty. A little wax taper, suspended by a wire, and burning brightly, is first let down into the vial of nitrogen; here it will be immediately extinguished, but while the wick yet remains at a red heat, the taper is plunged into the first vial, containing oxygen; here it is relighted, and burns brilliantly; the taper is then let down into the third vial, containing the artificial air, where it burns less vividly than in the oxygen, and in the fourth, which is filled with common air, it burns exactly in the same manner as in the third.

334. *Explanation.*—Nitrogen affording no aid to the burning process, the flame of the taper expired—oxygen by its energy rekindled it; and the burning of the taper in the two last vials proved that the mixture of nitrogen and oxygen, in the proportions of four to one, formed air resembling that of the atmosphere.

335. Although nitrogen does not support combustion, it does not act as a positive agent, but destroys the flame by preventing the approach of oxygen; in the same manner a burning taper, wholly immersed in oil, would be extinguished.

336. Nitrogen destroys animal life; but as in the case of combustion, it is not an active agent; an animal confined in it, dies for want of oxygen.

337. It possesses the *positive electricity*, as when subjected to the action of the galvanic circle it is attracted to the negative pole; while oxygen, on the contrary, is always attracted to the *positive* pole, and is therefore *electro-negative.*

338. Nitrogen is contained in all *animal substances*, but in few vegetables, except the cruciform plants, such as cabbage, turnip, &c.

339. Nitrogen is not active in its properties, but it forms many important compounds.

340. It was discovered about the same time as oxygen; that is, about the year 1774.)

ATMOSPHERE.

341. We have now examined two *elements*, or two letters of the alphabet of Chemistry: we have found that these combined, form the atmosphere, or air.

---

334. Explain the experiment?
335. Does nitrogen, by its own power, destroy flame?
336. How does nitrogen affect animals?
337. How is nitrogen affected by the galvanic circle?
338. Is nitrogen contained in animals and vegetables?
339. Is nitrogen active in its properties?
340. When was it discovered?
341. Of how many elements is the air composed?

342. This surrounds the globe to an extent not exactly known, but supposed to be about forty-five miles in height.

343. The air was long considered as a simple body, but some chemists had begun to suspect its compound nature, when Lavoisier proved, by a course of experiments, that it was composed of two gases which possessed very different properties; his discoveries were of great use to succeeding chemists, in enabling them to ascertain the nature of these gases, and the proportions in which they exist in nature.

344. If a portion of air were divided into one hundred parts, and the two gases which compose it were separated, there would be found seventy-nine parts of nitrogen, and twenty-one of oxygen. Air also contains aqueous vapour, and a small portion of carbonic acid, probably one part in a thousand. Though other gases may arise from the earth, and mingle with the air, neither they nor carbonic acid are considered as essential parts of it.

345. Carbonic acid gas is diffused through the atmosphere in various ways, chiefly by the burning of vegetable substances, and the breathing of animals. The air would by these means soon become impure, were it not that vegetables, needing carbon to promote their growth, take it from oxygen, with which it is combined in carbonic acid gas; and the oxygen, being disengaged, returns back to purify the air. In countries, as New England, where a low temperature during a part of the year prevents the active growth of vegetation, the winds which agitate the atmosphere, and the mosses and evergreens, maintain an equilibrium in the proportion of oxygen in the atmosphere.

346. Atmospheric air has neither colour nor smell; in these respects it resembles oxygen and nitrogen gas; its weight, or specific gravity, is estimated as 1, the weight of all other aeriform fluids being settled by a comparison with it; thus the specific gravity of oxygen is 1.11, or a fraction more than the weight of air, while that of nitrogen is .9722, or less than a unit.

347. It is not settled among chemists, whether the air is

342. What is the height of the air?
343. What is said of Lavoisier's experiments upon the air?
344. In what proportions are the elements of air combined? and what other substances mingle with these?
345. What prevents carbonic acid from increasing so much as to destroy the purity of the air?
346. What is the specific gravity of air?
347. Is air a *mixture*, or a *chemical combination*?

merely a *mixture* of the two gases, or a *chemical* combination. If it were only a mixture, we should expect the heaviest portion, oxygen, would settle below the other part; but
we do not find in portions of air standing in a vessel undisturbed, that this separation does take place—and yet the experiment of making artificial air, by simply mixing the two
gases, would tend to prove that it is not a chemical combination, or if so, that the affinity is not strong between the gases,
since the union takes place without any agitation.

348. The following are some of the most important properties of air: (it is a *bad conductor of electricity and heat ;* it
supports *combustion ;* by parting with oxygen it causes *acidity* in many liquids; it *oxidizes metals ;* it is *necessary* to
breathing, on account of the oxygen which it contains; it is
heaviest near the earth ; it is coldest in the higher regions ;
it may be compressed by being subjected to a heavy weight ;
and it may be dilated by heat. The two elements which
compose it, possess opposite electricities.

349. When air is decomposed, it is always the oxygen
which unites with other bodies; no substance is known which
will absorb nitrogen from the air.

We shall now observe some other combinations of the two
elements which form the atmosphere ; but instead of a mild
substance like the pure air, we shall first find one of the most
destructive and corroding of all the acids, viz.,

NITRIC ACID.

350. Nitric acid is so called because it was first obtained
from the *nitrate of potash*, (saltpetre ;) it was at first called
the *acid water of nitre*, afterwards *spirits of nitre*, and *aqua
fortis ;** it was called nitric acid in 1782, by the French
chemists.

351. *Exp.*—This acid may be obtained by the following method: some pounded saltpetre, or *nitrate of potash,*

---

* *Aqua fortis* means strong water, being from the Latin *aqua*, water,
and *fortis*, strong ; this is now the common name for nitric acid.

---

348. Mention some of the most important properties of air.
349. When air is decomposed, which of its elements unites with other
substances ?
350. What is said of the different names of nitric acid ?
351. How is nitric acid obtained ?

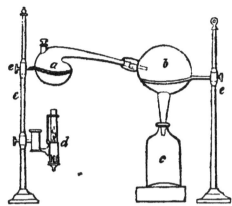

is put into a tubu-
lated retort, (such
as you see in the
figure at *a ;*) upon
this is poured suffi-
cient sulphuric acid
to wet it; on apply-
ing heat to the re-
tort from the lamp
at *d*, the nitric acid
gas will begin to
pass over into the
receiver *b*, from
whence it will pass
into the bottle *c*,
where it will be
absorbed by water, a small portion of which is put into the
bottle for that purpose. Upon examining the water, it will
be found to be weak nitric acid, or aqua fortis.

352. *Explanation.*—The nitrate of potash is composed of
nitric acid and potash; the latter having a stronger affinity
for sulphuric than for nitric acid, unites with it, and the nitric
acid being excluded, passes off in gas. The use of the tubulated retort is to let out the common air when the gas begins
to ascend; and also by the little tube, the sulphuric acid is introduced after the apparatus is fitted in the manner represented by the cut. A glass stopper closes the aperture when
necessary; at *e e* is represented a lamp-furnace and a stand,
which are very important parts of a chemical apparatus.

353. Nitric acid, when combined with water, is called *hydro-nitric acid*, from the Greek *udor*, water; when in a dry
state, or without water, it is called *anhydrous* nitric acid, from
a Greek preposition, signifying without, added to the word
denoting water; but such is the affinity of this acid for water
that it is seldom found entirely free from it.

354. Its *specific gravity*, or weight, compared with water,
is 1.5, that is, one and five-tenths, which is equal to one and a
half.

355. Nitric acid resembles water in having neither colour
nor smell, but it is extremely caustic and corrosive; it acts

352. Explain this process.
353. What are hydro-nitric acid, and anhydrous nitric acid?
354. What is the specific gravity of this acid?
355. What are some of the properties of nitric acid?

strongly upon animal and vegetable substances. A drop of it upon the flesh causes a burning sensation, and produces an ulcer, as if fire had touched the spot. It is actually a *burn*, since the effects are produced by the oxygen, which, leaving the acid, unites to the flesh, or oxidates it; and *oxidation*, you have learned, means the same thing as burning, although there are very feeble degrees of it, which do not produce the effects commonly ascribed to burning.

356. It is because nitric acid readily parts with oxygen, that it produces the effects we have just described. Most combustible substances decompose nitric acid by attracting its oxygen; the quantity of oxygen absorbed, varies according to the affinity of substances for this gas.

ILLUSTRATION OF THE LAW OF DEFINITE PROPORTIONS, OR ATOMS

357. No part of the study of Chemistry illustrates more fully the law of *definite proportions*, than that of nitrogen, considered in reference to its various combinations with oxygen. This law we have already mentioned in several instances. In treating of affinity, we found that sulphuric acid united with soda to form the sulphate of soda; but when the two substances had combined exactly in the proportion to form that salt, their union would proceed no farther.

358. Nitrogen and oxygen unite in several proportions.— You may understand this the more readily if we use the term *atoms*, which some chemists adopt. For instance, 14 being the lowest proportion, in weight, in which nitrogen unites with any substance, this is considered as its *ultimate atom*, or the lowest division of it which can be made. The lowest proportion in which oxygen unites with any substance, is 8, therefore this number is considered as the weight of its ultimate atom. Hydrogen gas unites with oxygen to form water, in the proportion of 1 to 8; the ultimate atom of hydrogen is represented by 1. These atoms may be represented by signs thus:

> *weight.*
> 1—☉ atom of Hydrogen,
> 14—Φ   "   Nitrogen,
> 8—*O*   "   Oxygen.

359. Water, which is compounded of an atom of oxygen

---

356. Does nitric acid part with oxygen readily?
357. What law is illustrated by the combination of nitrogen and oxygen?
358. What numbers express the ultimate atoms of nitrogen, oxygen, and hydrogen, and by what signs are they represented?

and one of hydrogen, may be either represented by the sum of 1 and 8, which is 9, or by the signs, ⊙ *hyd.* *O ox.* Air, which is composed of one atom of oxygen and two of nitrogen, may be either represented by the sum of 8 and 28, which is 36, or by the signs, *O ox.* ΦΦ *nit.*

360. Besides the union of nitrogen with oxygen, forming atmospheric air, these two gases unite to form five different compounds, viz.

Nitrous oxide, one atom Nitrogen 14 to one oxygen 8
Nitric oxide　　 "　　　Φ = 14　　OO　 = 16
Hypo*-nitrous acid "　　Φ = 14　　OOO　 = 24
Nitrous acid　　 "　　　Φ = 14　　OOOO = 32
Nitric acid　　 "　　　Φ = 14　　OOOOO = 40

361. All these combinations formed, it may be seen, are either with the atom 8, or some multiple of it, as twice, three times, four times, and five times 8. The number which represents the compound is the sum of all the atoms; thus the representative number of nitric acid is 54, it being composed of oxygen 40 and nitrogen 14.

NITROUS ACID.

362. Nitrous acid has been long known in Chemistry; indeed the chemists of the last century called all the gases formed by a union of nitrogen and oxygen, by the general name of nitrous acid gas. But as we have already observed, there are now known to be several distinct gaseous compounds of this family.

363. We have found that nitric acid exists in a liquid state. When this substance loses one portion of its oxygen, it exhibits red fumes or vapours, and is changed to *nitrous acid* gas. Nitrous acid may also be obtained by heating in a small retort, the nitrate of lead. It is remarkable for its colour, which at a low temperature is a bright orange. When water absorbs this gas, it first appears green, then blue, and at length orange colour. The liquid, when tested, is found to be acid. ✗

* *Hypo* is a Greek preposition signifying *under;* the term *hypo-nitrous acid* denotes that it is less acid than *nitrous acid.*

359. How may water and air be represented?
360. What other compounds besides air are formed by the union of nitrogen with oxygen?
361. Why is the representative number of nitric acid 54?
362. Has nitrous acid been long known?
363. How may nitrous acid be obtained? and for what is it remarkable?

HYPO-NITROUS ACID.

364. *Hypo-nitrous* acid, (which means a substance containing less oxygen than nitrous acid,) though named and described by chemists, seems to be but little understood by them;) indeed, they seem to be scarcely certain that they have ever obtained it. Since this is the fact, we will not puzzle the beginner with attempting to explain at what exact point, when uniting with more oxygen to form nitrous acid, the *nitric oxide* passes into the state of hypo-nitrous acid.

NITRIC OXIDE.

365. Nitric oxide is also called *nitrous gas,* and the *deutoxide of nitrogen.* It is lower, as respects the proportion of oxygen it contains, than the hypo-nitrous acid, and higher than the nitrous oxide, which being the lowest combination of oxygen with nitrogen, is called a *protoxide.*

366. Nitric oxide may be obtained from nitric acid, by the following process.

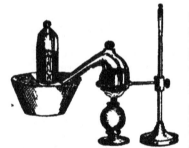

Exp.—Put some small bits of copper or copper filings into a retort, and pour upon them some nitric acid. As soon as this mixture begins to be acted upon by heat, from a lamp beneath the retort, a violent action commences, and a red looking gas begins to pass over; this is *nitrous* acid, which having a great affinity for water, unites with that in the tub; after this a colourless gas appears, which does not unite with the water, but passes through it into the bell glass in little bubbles; as *nitric oxide* gas rises to fill the bell glass, the water is displaced and sinks into the vessel below.

367. *Explanation.*—Nitric acid contains five atoms or proportions of oxygen; three of these unite with the copper, and form an oxide of copper; two atoms of oxygen then being left with the nitrogen, form the gas called nitric oxide, which

364. What is said of hypo-nitrous acid?
365. By what different names is nitric oxide known?
366. Describe the manner of obtaining nitric oxide.
367. How is the experiment for obtaining nitric oxide explained?

passes off through the tube of the retort into the receiver.—But in the retort was a portion of atmospheric air, which furnishing oxygen, changed the nitric oxide into the red, or orange-coloured gas, called nitrous acid, which united with the water of the receiver. As soon as all this was taken up, the pure nitric oxide passed over.

368. Nitric oxide is of use among chemists to determine the proportion of oxygen in the air; for so great is its affinity for this gas, that when mingled with common air, it attracts all the oxygen, and becomes the red nitrous acid, leaving nitrogen free. The nitrous acid which is formed, may be wholly absorbed by water.

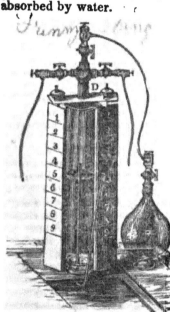

369. In this figure you are presented with a very ingenious instrument, contrived by Dr. Hare, for the analysis of atmospheric air, by means of nitric oxide. It is called a *volumescope*. It consists of a hollow glass cylinder, thirty inches high, and four and a half in diameter; it is placed over the pneumatic cistern. At each side of the cylinder, there are strips of wood, on which are marked degrees. You perceive three tubes; these are of lead, and made flexible, so that they can be bent as may be necessary; the entrance to each of these tubes may be closed by the turning of the stop-cocks which appear near the places of their connexion with the instrument. To one of these tubes is connected a pear-shaped bottle, which Dr. Hare calls a *volumeter*, (a measurer of volumes, or of equal quantities.) This bottle holds just as much air or gas as three degrees of the glass cylinder. Now, supposing part of the air to be exhausted from the cylinder by means of an air pump, to which one of the tubes is made to communicate; the water then rises up to fill the vacuum. The volumeter being filled with

368. What useful application do chemists make of nitric oxide?
369. Explain the use of the volumescope.

nitric oxide, and a communication opened by turning the stop-cocks, gas ascends into the cylinder. The orange red fumes of nitrous acid then appear. By means of an India rubber bag and tube, jets of water are thrown up into this gas, which is soon wholly absorbed by the water. The number of degrees which the water rises, shows the quantity of gas which has been taken up from the air, and as oxygen only unites with the nitric oxide, forming, by its union, the orange, fuming gas, called nitrous acid, the quantity of oxygen which the air contained, is thereby ascertained. That is, the whole portion of air having at first been measured, by observing how much nitrogen remains, we are able to tell the quantity of oxygen which has been absorbed.*

NITROUS OXIDE.

370. You know that the termination in *ous* denotes a lower proportion of oxygen than that in *ic*. Nitrous oxide, therefore, as the name would denote, has less oxygen in combination with it than nitric oxide, which we have just examined. *Nitrous* oxide is sometimes called the *protoxide of nitrogen*, while *nitric* oxide is the *deutoxide*.

371. Nitrous oxide may be obtained from nitric oxide, by the action of substances which will abstract one atom of its oxygen. Nitrous oxide is more like the common air than any of the other combinations of nitrogen with oxygen, since it may be breathed with more safety. It was quite fashionable, a few years ago, for those who attended chemical lectures, to prove the nature of this gas by inhaling it into the lungs. It was at first thought to be harmless; but at length cases occurred in which it produced faintness and distress, and threatened serious injury. The effects of breathing nitrous oxide were in many cases singular, and often highly ludicrous. It was perfectly intoxicating to many. The most serious persons, under its influence would become gay, and vent their feelings by immoderate laughter, capering about the room,

* This somewhat complicated instrument may not be understood by the young pupil; though its object may be clearly comprehended. As Dr. Hare had kindly forwarded to the author some papers containing his recent discoveries and improvements, she was anxious to show to the beginner some of the curious apparatus by which he so happily illustrates some of the most difficult subjects in Chemistry.

370. What does the name *nitrous* oxide denote?
371. How may it be obtained? and what is said of breathing it?

or opening their mouths without being able to close them, although sensible of making a most ridiculous appearance.— Fun-loving urchins, and frolicsome youths, after breathing nitrous oxide, would sometimes suddenly assume the most laughable and incongruous gravity of countenance and demeanour, gazing around, without the power to smile at their own appearance. Sir Humphrey Davy, the first who attempted inhaling it, breathed four quarts of the gas. Some who repeated the experiment after him, declared it must be "the very atmosphere of heaven."

372. It is now acknowledged by chemists, that there must always be some danger in inhaling nitrous oxide, from the difficulty of obtaining it entirely free from some portion of nitric oxide, which is suffocating, and destructive to life.

373. We perceive, from the nature of nitrogen and oxygen, that the proportions which the Almighty has established between these two gases in the atmosphere, are exactly such as the living beings who exist in it need. Less oxygen would not be sufficient to support respiration, more would quicken and stimulate the vital powers to a degree which would soon destroy them; or, as has been said, "as a candle burns brighter in oxygen gas, and is more quickly consumed, so in this gas, the flame of life would be more vivid, but sooner burnt out."

374. We have now seen that with two elements or letters of the alphabet of Chemistry, several substances are formed, viz. air, nitrous oxide, nitric oxide, nitrous acid, and nitric acid.

375. *Nitric acid* forms with various substances, *nitrates*, and *nitrous acid* forms *nitrites.* There are many other important compounds formed with nitrogen, which we shall notice hereafter, when we have learned something about the other elements with which it unites.

---

372. What renders it dangerous to inhale nitrous oxide ?
373. What fact do we perceive respecting the composition of the air, by learning the properties of oxygen and nitrogen ?
374. What substances have we found to be formed by two letters of the alphabet of Chemistry ?
375. What are nitrates and nitrites ?

9*

CHAPTER XI.

Hydrogen. Its properties. Its agency in producing Earth-quakes and Volcanoes. Water. The Compound Blowpipe.

376. WE are now to examine a new element, *hydrogen* the name of which is derived from the Greek *udor*, water added to a word signifying to produce, because, in connexion with oxygen, hydrogen forms water.

377. In studying the gases, we are continually met by new and interesting facts; and the gas now under consideration, furnishes its full proportion of beautiful experiments. But we will first observe the manner in which it is obtained; hydrogen, like oxygen, must always be in a gaseous state, since such is its affinity for caloric, that it can never be condensed to a solid.

Mode of obtaining Hydrogen Gas.

378. Water being composed of hydrogen and oxygen, if the oxygen unites to a metal, the hydrogen will be liberated and pass off in the state of gas.

Exp.—Some iron filings being put into a flask, and weak sulphuric acid poured upon them, a lively effervescence takes place; the hydrogen gas immediately begins to escape, and, by means of the tube which passes under the mouth of the bell glass, is collected through water. Nearly half the water with which the bell glass was filled, has now disappeared, the gas having risen and taken its place.

379. *Explanation.*—The oxygen of the water being strongly attracted by iron, leaves the hydrogen, and unites with the metal; the hydrogen, which existed in a liquid state with oxygen, is no sooner disengaged, than it combines with sufficient caloric to become a gas. The manner in which sulphuric acid aids the process, is not satisfactorily explained by

---

376. What does the word hydrogen signify?
377. In what form is hydrogen always obtained?
378. How can hydrogen be obtained from water?
379. What explanation may be given of the changes which take place in this experiment?

chemists. Professor Silliman says—"It appears to me better to say that we do not understand it, and to wait till we do, before we attempt to explain the fact."* The oxygen of the water uniting to the iron filings, forms an *oxide of iron;* the sulphuric acid is not decomposed, but unites with the newly formed oxide, and forms a *sulphate of iron,* (copperas,) which when allowed to stand for a sufficient time, appears under the form of green crystals. No heat is applied in performing this experiment, but so much caloric is disengaged by the chemical combination of the sulphuric acid and water, as to heat the flask.

380. Iron heated to redness, decomposes the steam from boiling water, by uniting with the oxygen and setting the hydrogen free.

✝ *Properties of Hydrogen.*

381. Having collected hydrogen gas we will proceed to an examination of its properties. 1. It is the *lightest* of all substances which have been weighed, that is, of all *ponderable* substances, being about 14 times lighter than atmospheric air, and 16 times lighter than oxygen.

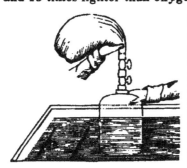

382. *Exp.*—The levity of hydrogen gas is very prettily exhibited by the following experiment. A bladder, furnished with a stop-cock, is first filled with hydrogen gas, as represented in the figure, and then adapted to a common tobacco-pipe. The bowl of the pipe being dipped into a basin of soap lather, and the stop-cock turned so as to allow the hydrogen to issue forth, the

---

* I cannot neglect this opportunity of observing to the pupil, that the most enlightened persons are the least afraid to confess there are things beyond their comprehension. It is the pretender to knowledge, and not the really learned man, who is ashamed to say, "I do not understand." An eminent physician was asked the cause of some particular disease;— he modestly answered, "I do not know; but," said he, "ask my young student here, *he will tell you !*" It is scarcely necessary to add that he intended to convey a reproof to a conceited young man.

---

380. How does hot iron decompose steam ?
381. What is the first property of hydrogen which is mentioned ?
382. By what experiment is the levity of hydrogen illustrated ?

lather is blown into bubbles.—These bubbles, instead of falling, like those blown by children, will rise rapidly into the air.

383. *Explanation.*—The bubbles, being inflated with hydrogen gas, ascend because they are lighter than air. The figure shows a bubble just passing off from the pipe. If the flame of a lighted candle is brought into contact with these bubbles, they are set on fire. If, instead of pure hydrogen, the bubbles were made of a mixture of hydrogen and oxygen, they would explode as well as burn.

384. Balloons ascend on the same principle as these bubbles; they are made of oiled silk, inflated with hydrogen gas. As a large quantity of the gas is needed for this purpose, barrels or other capacious vessels are used for containing the water which is to be decomposed, and the hydrogen is conducted into the balloon by means of long flexible tubes. The *æronaut,* (as the navigator of a balloon is called,) must experience new and sublime emotions, as the car in which he sits, rises aloft into regions of the air which no human being has before penetrated. Owing to the variety of the atmosphere in these upper portions, its power of reflecting light is feeble, and he sees the sun like an orb of fire in the midst of an expanse of blackness, or if it be night, the moon and stars, like orbs of silver upon a ground of black. The presumption of man might lead him to attempt to make these aerial voyages to a much greater extent than has yet been done; he

383. What causes these bubbles to rise?
384. What are balloons filled with?

might even hope to be able to visit distant planets in his earthly body, had not God placed an eternal barrier in his physical constitution, which can endure the rarity and cold of the atmosphere but a few miles above the earth.

385. 2. Hydrogen *is highly combustible, but it does not support combustion.*

386. A lighted candle placed under a jar of this gas, and with its flame immersed in it, is extinguished as you see in the figure. This is because there is no oxygen to support combustion; for in this process, two things are always necessary, a *combustible substance,* and a *supporter of combustion.* Here then we have one, but not the other. When the candle is immersed in oxygen gas, it burns because it is itself combustible, and it is surrounded by a supporter of combustion. The flame at the mouth of the jar is that portion of the hydrogen in contact with the air, which furnished oxygen. In this situation the hydrogen was inflamed by the lighted candle.

387. The annexed figure shows hydrogen itself burning. Some iron filings were put into the flask, and water added. To hasten the decomposition of the water, we pour into the flask a small portion of sulphuric acid—the hydrogen gas immediately begins to rise into the tube, which is fitted to the mouth of the bottle. On applying a lighted candle to the gas, it is inflamed, and burns with a pale flame, but with intense heat. This is called the philosophic candle. To the ignorant it might well have afforded matter for astonish-

---

385. What is a second property of hydrogen?
386. Why will not a lighted candle burn in a vessel of hydrogen?
387. What experiment shows that hydrogen is combustible?

ment to see water burning; and its pale, unearthly looking flame, tended to confirm their superstitious belief that this was the effect of magic. You can understand that the combustible substance, hydrogen, being inflamed by the candle, and furnished with oxygen from the surrounding air, burns as oil would do in the same situation.

388. But what do you think is the product of this combustion of hydrogen? You will perhaps be surprised to learn that it is water. If you hold a bell glass over the flame of burning hydrogen, you may see a moisture upon its sides, occasioned by the union of the hydrogen with the oxygen of the air.

389. This figure presents you with another instance of the burning of hydrogen. You say—"we see nothing here but a common looking lamp, and candle." The burning of lamps and candles is, however, one form of the combustion of hydrogen. This may be proved by holding a tube for some time over the flame; moisture will collect upon the sides of the tube. This moisture is formed by the union of oxygen and hydrogen. The oil and tallow furnish hydrogen; it is this which renders them so combustible; they contain also another combustible substance, carbon; but it is the hydrogen,

388. What is produced by the burning of hydrogen?
389. What causes the flame of lamps and candles?

principally, which causes the flame. The air furnishes the necessary oxygen.

390. 3. Hydrogen, *when mixed with oxygen, or atmospheric air, on being inflamed, explodes like gunpowder.* The firing of the hydrogen gun, in the lecture room of the chemist, often causes both terror and amusement. A vessel of tin being filled with a mixture of one part hydrogen to two of air, a cork is put into the open end. On applying a lighted taper to a small aperture, the gas inflames, and expands so much as to drive out the cork with great force, accompanied by a loud report.

391. From the explosive nature of hydrogen, it is thought that this gas is concerned in producing earthquakes. In the bowels of the earth are vast quantities of iron; water also exists in an equal proportion, filling chasms and fissures in the rocks. You have seen that when water comes in contact with iron, it yields its oxygen to the metal, and the hydrogen becomes a gas. You have also seen that when this gas is mixed with atmospheric air, if it comes in contact with a burning substance, an explosion takes place. Thus we may imagine that in the vast caverns which exist in the earth, hydrogen, mingling with the air, meets with something which inflames it; in the explosion which follows, the ground is thrown up, and in some cases whole cities are buried up in the chasms thus made.

392. 4. *Hydrogen gas does not support respiration.* Like nitrogen, however, it destroys life rather by excluding oxygen, than because it possesses any noxious quality. By a mixture of hydrogen and oxygen, an atmosphere might have been formed that would have supported life. But such a mixture, we have seen, is explosive, and would have been destructive to the most solid portions of the earth. We see, therefore, that He who formed and tempered these elements, knows best how to mingle and proportion them, that they may all perform a part in sustaining, instead of destroying his works.

390. What is the third property of hydrogen ?
391. What reasons are there for supposing that hydrogen may be concerned in producing earthquakes ?
392. What is a fourth property of hydrogen gas?

393. Hydrogen gas exists in almost every compound substance; making a part in most fluids, as water, and every thing which contains water, and in all animal and vegetable substances. In minerals, especially coal, it exists in abundance. The burning wood owes its flame, in part, to hydrogen, usually, however, combined with carbon, a substance yet unknown to you. The pale flame of wood is the hydrogen; it is most abundant in green wood, while carbon is more plentiful in dry wood, and affords a richer and a deeper flame. The sulphur which exists in coal often gives it a bluish flame. Oil and tallow, as we have remarked, contain a great portion of hydrogen, which causes their combustible nature.

Water, or Hydrogen and Oxygen united.

394. Water is composed of 2 parts of hydrogen, and 1 of oxygen; that is, when reckoned by *bulk*; in *weight*, 1 part of hydrogen, and 8 parts of oxygen constitute water. This you can as easily understand, as that a quantity of feathers, occupying double the space of the same quantity of wool, might weigh but 1 pound, while the wool weighed 8 pounds.* The weight of the two elements, hydrogen 1, and oxygen 8, makes 9, which number represents water. The following diagram shows the proportions of hydrogen and oxygen in water, according to the *bulk* of the atoms; the numbers represent the weight of the atoms.

Water, 9.

Hydrogen 1.	Oxygen 8.

Water is the *protoxide* of hydrogen; it is so called, because it consists of hydrogen, and one atom of oxygen.

395. There is a *deutoxide* of hydrogen, sometimes called *oxygenated water*, but it is always the production of art; its properties are very different from those of water; it is corrosive to the skin, and exhibits acid qualities. Here we see that

---

* It is not important that the relative specific gravity of wool and feathers should be here given correctly, but the case is merely stated for illustration?

---

393. Is hydrogen abundant?
394. What are the proportions of oxygen and hydrogen in water?
395. What is said of the *deutoxide* of hydrogen?

one additional proportion of oxygen entirely changes the nature of water.

The union of oxygen and hydrogen may be thus shown.

Water, or the *protoxide of hydrogen.*			Deutoxide of hydrogen.	
1. Hydrogen.	8 Oxygen.		1 Hydrogen.	8 Oxygen.
				8 Oxygen.
Represented by 9.			Represented by 17.	

396. The nature of water may be proved in two ways, (*analysis,* or a separation into its elements, oxygen and hydrogen, and (*synthesis,*) by which these two gases are combined, and form water. A simple *mixture* of the gases does not form water, but for this purpose combustion is necessary; that is, the hydrogen, *while burning,* must unite with the oxygen.

397. Water exists in nature in the form of a transparent, colourless, inodorous liquid, capable of dissolving a great variety of substances.

398. It becomes solid, or ice, at 32°; and assumes a gaseous form at 212°, occupying a volume 1700 times greater than in the liquid form.

399. Freezing is the *crystallization* of water; the crystals are usually confused, but their true form is that of *hexagonal* (six-sided) prisms.

Water is a bad conductor of electricity. It refracts light strongly.

400. Water is seldom found pure in nature; in order to obtain it pure, it must be distilled. The figure shows the manner in which this is done. *a* Represents a boiler of water in a furnace; *b*, the *head* of the still, (or distilling apparatus,) to which belongs a spiral tube, called the *worm.* The water in the boiler being converted into steam, passes

---

396. How may the nature of water be proved?
397. How does water exist in nature?
398. At what temperature is water solid? and at what temperature does it become a vapour?
399. What is freezing?—What is said of water as to its power of conducting electricity, and refracting light?
400. How may water be obtained pure?
10

into the cask *d*, (called the *refrigerator*,) which contains cold water. Here the steam is *condensed* into water, which falls in drops from the end of the spiral tube. This is pure distilled water; it is used for delicate experiments in Chemistry.

401. Water in a solid form constitutes immense glaciers upon the summits of high mountains, and exists in vast quantities in the polar regions. The clouds and vapours of the atmosphere are water in a gaseous form. When condensed by cold, it solidifies, and being then heavier than the air, it falls in the form of hail, snow, or rain.

402. Water was long considered as a simple element—it was not analyzed until the latter part of the eighteenth century.

403. We have now considered the subject of hydrogen gas. Its most important properties are its inflammable nature, and its lightness, or specific levity. Its most important combination is water.

Blowpipe.

404. We ought not to omit the mention of the *compound blowpipe*, in which hydrogen, in connexion with oxygen, is made of great use in Chemistry. But first we will teach you the construction and use of the common *blowpipe*, which you here see represented. It is merely a simple brass pipe, having a bulb in the middle, tapering, and bent at the smaller end; it is used for impelling the flame of a candle or lamp upon any small substance, which the chemist or mineralogist wishes to heat. Stones and ores, are said to be *fusible* when they can be melted in this manner.

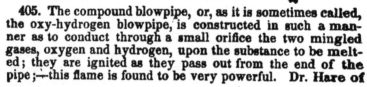

405. The compound blowpipe, or, as it is sometimes called, the oxy-hydrogen blowpipe, is constructed in such a manner as to conduct through a small orifice the two mingled gases, oxygen and hydrogen, upon the substance to be melted; they are ignited as they pass out from the end of the pipe;—this flame is found to be very powerful. Dr. Hare of

401. How extensively does water exist ?
402. How long has water been known as a compound substance ?
403. What are found to be the two most important properties of hydrogen gas, and its most important combination ?
404. Describe the common blowpipe.
405. What is said respecting the compound blowpipe ?

Philadelphia, was the inventor of this important instrument, and the discoverer of the intense heat produced by the united power of the two gases, employed. In no other way, except by means of galvanic agency, can such an intense heat be produced. The compound blowpipe has melted every mineral that has yet been subjected to its operation except the diamond, this is so inflammable that it burns without first melting. All the metals, not excepting platina, gold, and silver, have been melted and burned by this blowpipe. Wire, made of iron or copper, burns in its flame, as a piece of cotton in an ordinary flame; earths burn with great brilliancy; a bit of a China cup under its influence burns with too strong a light to be borne by the naked eye.

CHAPTER XII.

Sulphur. Combination of Sulphur with Oxygen. Selenium.

406. THE new letter in the alphabet of Chemistry, which you are now to learn, is called *Sulphur*, it differs from the elements we have examined, in being found in a solid state, and existing in nature free from any combination. Sulphur was known in very ancient times, and has long been in common use as a medicinal article, while oxygen, nitrogen, and hydrogen, are words familiar only to chemists, because it is only by chemical analysis that they can be obtained.

407. The word sulphur is supposed to be composed of two Greek words, *sal* salt, and *pur* fire, so called from its great combustibility.

408. Pure sulphur has never been decomposed, it is therefore considered as a simple element; but such is its affinity for other substances, that it is seldom found entirely pure. With metals it forms *sulphurets* and *pyrites;* with oxygen it forms *sulphuric acid;* and this acid by its union with lime, soda, &c. forms *sulphates.*

409. Sulphur is abundant in volcanic countries; being combined with metals in the earth, it is separated from them by the heat of volcanoes, and becomes a vapour, which, rising from their craters, falls again upon the surface of the earth,

406. What new element are we now to consider? and why is its name more familiar than oxygen, nitrogen, and hydrogen?
407. From what is the word sulphur derived?
408. What are some of the compounds formed with sulphur?
409. In what situations is sulphur usually found? and in what substances is it contained?

forming a crust, and sometimes beautiful crystals. It exists in some plants, as cabbage and dock, and in some animal substances, especially eggs.

410. Sulphur is known in commerce in two states; the *flowers* or flower of sulphur, and *brimstone;* the latter is in the form of *rolls*, made by pouring melted sulphur into small moulds. The sulphur of commerce is generally obtained by separating sulphur from some of its combinations, as the *sulphuret of iron*, which parts with its sulphur on being sufficiently heated.

Bleaching.

411. The colour and odour of sulphur are familiar to all. When sulphur is thrown upon coals, it rises in vapour, and uniting with the oxygen of the air, forms sulphureous acid gas, which is very useful for bleaching straw and leghorn hats, and other articles.

412. The process of bleaching as practised by milliners, is this; some sulphur is placed in a dish upon the bottom of a barrel, and sticks are laid crosswise for the hats, or articles which are to be bleached, to rest upon. A hot coal is then laid upon the sulphur, and the barrel covered with a thick cloth, to prevent the sulphureous acid gas, which rises, from passing off. Iron moulds and the stains of vegetables may be removed in this way. Articles for bleaching must be wet with water. In the large manufacturing establishments, where cotton cloth, yarn, and other articles in large quantities are to be bleached, they are hung wet upon frames in tight apartments, with floors of sheet lead, on which the sulphur is burned.

Other uses of Sulphur.

413. *Various uses of Sulphur.—*The most important use of sulphur is in the composition of gunpowder, where it is mixed with charcoal and saltpetre. The effects of gunpowder are owing to the sudden change of solids into gases. Sulphur is used in medicine, externally, to cure diseases of the skin, and internally, as a cathartic. It is used to copy medals by being melted, and then poured into hot water; in this soft state the medals are impressed upon it. Small pine sticks, dipped in melted sulphur, form matches used for kindling fires

414. If a bar of hot iron is rubbed with a roll of brimstone the iron will melt and fall to pieces.

---

410. In what two states is sulphur known in commerce?
411. What is the effect of throwing sulphur upon burning coals?
412. Describe the bleaching process.
413. What are some of the uses of sulphur?

The figure shows a gun-barrel, in one end of which, is a piece of sulphur. This end is then closed and the gun-barrel heated to a red heat. The hot sulphureous vapour issuing forth at an orifice near the end of the gun-barrel burns a bunch of iron wire which is held over it, so that it falls in melted globules. These are a *sulphuret of iron*, so called from being a combination of iron and sulphur.

415. Beautiful crystals of sulphur, for ornamental articles, may be made by melting it in a deep vessel. The surface will become solid; this must then be broken, and the liquid below turned off.

416. Sulphur melts or fuses at 218° of heat. At 600° of heat, it *sublimes;* that is, it becomes a vapour, and settles again on the sides of the vessel which is placed over it for that purpose.

417. In order to obtain sulphur purified from the earths, and metallic substances with which it is often combined, it is *sublimed* in a vessel called an *alembic.* The sulphur is put into the lower part, A; this is then placed over a vessel of sand, B, called a *sand-bath*, which is heated by a furnace, C: by means of the sand-bath the sulphur is fused more gradually and equally, than could be done by placing it directly over a fire. When heated sufficiently, the sulphur rises in the form of a thick, white vapour, and settles in the head of the alembic, in clusters resembling *flowers;* from this has been derived the term, *flowers of sulphur.* On account of the minuteness of its particles, it is sometimes called the

414. What is represented by the figure?
415. How may crystals of sulphur be obtained?
416. What degrees of heat are required for melting and subliming sulphur?
417. How is sulphur sublimed?

flour of sulphur.   The product of *sublimation* is a *solid*, that
of *distillation* a *liquid*.

418.   Sulphur possesses the *positive* electricity; it therefore
goes to the negative pole of the galvanic circle.

419. The weight of its atom is 16, hydrogen being unity
or 1.

COMBINATIONS OF SULPHUR AND OXYGEN.

420.   We are now to consider sulphur as united with oxygen; and here we find two important substances, sulphur*ous*
and sulphur*ic* acids.   The ending in *ous* shows a lower proportion of oxygen, the ending in *ic* shows a higher proportion.

Sulphurous Acid.

421.   We have already made some remarks upon the gas
which results from the burning of sulphur in atmospheric air;
you will recollect that this is the *sulphurous acid* gas.   One
atom of sulphur, 16, is here united to two of oxygen, the sum
of which being also 16, makes the *chemical equivalent* of sulphurous acid 32.

422.   Sulphurous acid may be obtained for experiment by
suspending burning sulphur in a glass bottle containing a
little water.   The sulphurous acid gas uniting with the water,
gives it acid properties; this may be ascertained by the taste,
which is disagreeable, and peculiar to this gas.   On mixing
blue vegetable infusions with this liquid, it will be at first
reddened, and then the colour will entirely disappear.

423.   A red rose dipped in water containing a portion of this
gas, loses its colour and becomes white; pieces of calico
which have been dyed with vegetable colours, become white
on being wet with this liquid.   But we have already spoken
of the uses of sulphur in bleaching, or destroying the colours
of different substances; you will however observe, that it is
only when combined with oxygen, in the proportion to form
the gas we are now considering, that it has this effect.

---

418. Why does sulphur go to the negative pole of the galvanic circle?
419. What is the weight of its atom?
420. What two important substances are formed by the union of sulphur
with oxygen?
421. What is the equivalent number of sulphurous acid?
422. How may sulphurous acid be obtained in a liquid state?
423. What change is produced upon vegetable colours by sulphurous
acid?

424. In the *anhydrous* state,* sulphurous acid is a gas without colour, and having a strong smell. It is suffocating to the lungs, and destroys combustion.

Sulphuric Acid.

425. We have, in sulphuric acid, a combination of sulphur with its highest proportion of oxygen; or, 1 atom of sulphur=16, united to 3 atoms of oxygen=24, makes the equivalent of sulphuric acid=40.

426. This acid was formerly called *oil of vitriol;* it has been known since the fifteenth century, and is now a very important article, not only in the laboratory of the chemist, but in the manufacture of other substances. Nitric and muriatic acids are prepared by the assistance of sulphuric acid.

Modes of obtaining Sulphuric Acid.

427. *Exp.*—You have seen that sulphur, burned in atmospheric air, does not unite with a sufficient portion of oxygen to form sulphuric acid; neither if burned in pure oxygen gas will it form any thing more than sulphurous acid. In order to illustrate the formation of sulphuric acid, four parts of sulphur, mixed with one of nitre (saltpetre) may be burned in a glass bottle containing a little water, in the same way as for obtaining sulphurous acid. The water, though slightly sour, will exhibit the properties of weak sulphuric acid, and be very different as to taste from the sulphurous acid.

428. In preparing this acid for commerce, large quantities of sulphur and saltpetre in the proportion of 8 of the former to 1 of the latter, are burned in chambers lined with sheet lead. The mixture being placed in a vessel upon the leaden floor, which has been covered with water, is inflamed; in burning, it absorbs oxygen from the air. New portions of the sulphur and saltpetre are added from time to time, and fresh air admitted into the chamber. The sulphuric acid gas is absorbed by the water upon the floor of the chamber; this is afterwards

* That is, without water.
† = Signifies *equality*, or equal to.

---

424. How does sulphurous acid appear when not combined with water?
425. In what proportions do oxygen and sulphur exist in sulphuric acid
426. Has this acid been long known? and is it a useful substance?
427 How may the formation of sulphuric acid be illustrated?
428. How is sulphuric acid prepared for commerce?

distilled, in order to obtain the acid in a pure and concentrated state.

429. *Explanation.*—Sulphurous acid is first formed by the burning of the sulphur in the air, the nitre furnishes another portion of oxygen, and the *sulphurous*, thus becomes *sulphuric* acid.

430. Some of the properties of sulphuric acid you have already learned—you have seen that many substances have so strong an affinity for it that they leave their old combinations to form new ones with this acid. Thus muriate of soda became sulphate of soda, and muriate of lime, sulphate of lime.* As we proceed, we shall find that it unites with metals, forming substances called *sulphates*, while the sulphurous acid uniting with metals forms *sulphites*.

431. Sulphuric acid is one of the most corroding substances in nature. I could show you a book now lying before me, that seven years ago happened to have one drop of this acid fall upon it; at first it only made a brown stain, but it has continued to eat gradually, until a great many pages have been partly consumed; or, I should rather say, have been *burned*, since the effect is produced by the action of oxygen upon the paper, and indeed its appearance is exactly what it might have been, if burnt slowly by a hot brick.

432. You will, I hope, be very careful in its use, should you attempt to perform experiments with sulphurous acid, and not suffer it to fall upon your clothing, and especially any part of your person. But should such an accident occur you may remember that while water only serves to excite the acid to action, chalk, lime, or any alkaline substance neutralizes it, and of course alleviates its effects. When sulphuric acid is swallowed accidentally, chalk and magnesia are the best remedies. But every person who makes use of this, or any other active substances, should be very careful to have it conspicuously labelled.

433. When sulphuric acid is decomposed by galvanism, the

* See experiments under the head of elective affinity.

429. How is this process explained?
430. Does sulphuric acid combine freely with other substances?
431. What instance is mentioned to prove the corrosive nature of sulphuric acid?
432. What are the most proper applications in case of accidents with sulphuric acid?
433. When sulphuric acid is decomposed by galvanism, to which pole is each element attracted?

(sulphur goes to the negative, and the oxygen to the positive pole.)

Combining Weight.

434. It was mentioned that sulphur was considered as represented by the number 16, it being so much heavier than hydrogen, or 1. Oxygen is 8; therefore the two acids we have been considering, may be thus stated;—*sulphurous acid* composed of one part sulphur, 16, and 2 parts oxygen 16=32. Sulphuric acid composed of 1 part sulphur 16, and 3 parts oxygen 24=40. Therefore 32 is the chemical equivalent for sulphurous acid, and 40 for sulphuric acid.

SELENIUM.

435. We will now introduce an *element* which, being considered as simple, should not be omitted, though little is known of it, or of its combinations. Selenium was discovered in 1817, by the Swedish chemist, Berzelius. It was by him considered as a metal; but as it is found to be a bad conductor of electricity and caloric, which is not the case with the metals, it is not at present ranked as such.

436. Selenium is found in connexion with various metals, as lead, silver, copper, and iron. It was first discovered in iron pyrites, (sulphuret of iron,) which are used in Sweden for the manufacture of sulphuric acid. A reddish substance was observed to remain, after the process for obtaining the sulphur was completed. On burning, a smell like that of horse-radish was given off. Berzelius found this substance resisted all attempts to decompose it, and therefore proposed its admission among the *elements*; and named it Selenium.

437. Its properties, in some respects, resemble sulphur. When powdered, its colour is reddish, but when broken in larger masses, its fracture is metallic. It is soft like wax. Its combinations are not numerous or important, at least as far as is now known respecting it. With oxygen, it forms *selenic*, and *selenious acids*.

---

434. What are the chemical equivalents for sulphurous and sulphuric acids?

435. When and by whom was selenium discovered?

436. What circumstances led to its discovery?

437. What are its properties?

CHAPTER XIII.

*Phosphorus. Impositions practised by means of Phosphorus.
Phosphorus and Oxygen. Phosphorus and Hydrogen.*

438. WE now commence the observation of another element, which, though less commonly known than the one we have last examined, constitutes a portion of our own frame, it being found combined, in large quantities, in animal bones and teeth.   The word Phosphorus is derived from the Greek words *phos* light, and *phero* to bear, and signifies light-bearer.

439. Notwithstanding this substance is as ancient as the creation, it was not discovered until the year 1691, when Brandt, an alchymist of Germany, accidentally obtained it. The reason of its being so long unknown, is, that it is intimately combined with other bodies, and can only be separated from them by a long, and somewhat difficult process.

440. Bones contain phosphorus united to oxygen and lime, forming a compound which is called *phosphate of lime.* The phosphate of lime consists of *phosphoric acid* and lime.   In order to obtain pure phosphorus, the lime, and the oxygen of the phosphoric acid, must be disposed of.   As you are not yet chemists enough to attempt the manufacture of this article, it is not necessary that you should study the operations which this requires; these chiefly depend on that great principle of chemical affinity which we have endeavoured to explain. First, one substance is attracted from the phosphorus by presenting another for which it has a greater affinity, and then the other substance is withdrawn in the same manner.

441. Every lecturer who makes experiments in chemistry does not prepare the phosphorus he uses.   It may be obtained from the shops in the form of yellowish sticks, smaller than a pipe's stem, and a few inches in length. It cannot be put up in papers, and handled like most other solid substances which we purchase.   It is usually kept in vials of water, because, when exposed to the air, it takes fire at the slightest increase of heat.

442. When you see phosphorus, that has for some time been kept in water, you may observe that the sticks are cov-

438. What is the word phosphorus derived from?
439. Has phosphorus been long known?
440. How may pure phosphorus be obtained from the phosphate of lime?
441. In what form is phosphorus usually obtained for chemical experiments?
442. What is the whitish crust that covers the sticks of phosphorus?

ered with a whitish crust, this is an *oxide of phosphorus*. It is formed by the attraction which this substance has for oxygen, which it takes from the water; it is still more combustible than pure phosphorus. If exposed to the sun, it takes fire spontaneously.

443. In former times, wicked and artful people imposed greatly upon the ignorant, by means of the peculiar properties of phosphorus; for instance, words written on a board, with a stick of this substance, will, in the dark, appear like the words of fire. In the dark ages, the monks, who possessed nearly all the knowledge of chemical substances which then existed, are said to have imposed on the credulous novice, by making him believe he saw the devil with flames about his head, and ready to take possession of him, if he refused to pronounce monastic vows. By dissolving phosphorus in oil, and rubbing the face and hair with it, it produces, in the dark, the appearance of a glowing fire, playing over the features and issuing from the head. It does not burn the skin, if the phosphorus is thoroughly mixed with the oil.*

444. It is the great affinity which phosphorus has for oxygen that causes the phenomena we have described; this affinity is so great, that phosphorus unites with the oxygen of the air, and burns at the ordinary temperature of the atmosphere. The burning, or combustion, in this case, is very slow. Inflamed in pure oxygen gas, phosphorus burns with the most vivid brilliancy.

445. You may well suppose that a substance so combustible as phosphorus does not exist in a free state, in nature; it is always obtained by analyzing some of its compounds, usually the *phosphate of lime*. Combined with oxygen, it enters into combination with many minerals; it exists in the nerves and brains of fish, which on this account often have a luminous appearance in the dark.

446. Phosphorus is not an important substance, as respects its application to the arts. It is used in making phosphoric

* A fine young lad, the son of a distinguished chemist, was, a few years since, badly burned in consequence of a failure in this respect, when showing this property of phosphorus before a class of young ladies. Although suffering much from pain, he went through the exhibition with a firmness about as heroic as that of the Spartan youth, who suffered the fox, concealed under his cloak, to gnaw his entrails, without uttering a complaint

443. How has phosphorus been used to impose on the credulous?
444. What causes the phenomena which have been mentioned?
445. Is phosphorus found in nature in a pure state?
446. Is it of important use in the arts and in medicine?

matches, and in testing the purity of the air, by means of an instrument called an *eudiometer*, which shows, by the union of the oxygen with phosphorus, what portion of this gas exists in a given quantity of air. Attempts have been made to use it in medicine, but its effect upon the animal organs is found to be injurious.

Combinations of Phosphorus and Oxygen.

447. There are two acids formed by the union of oxygen and phosphorus; viz. *phosphorous* and *phosphoric* acids.

448. 1. *Phosphorous acid;* this is obtained by the slow combustion of phosphorus in the air; its properties are not remarkable.

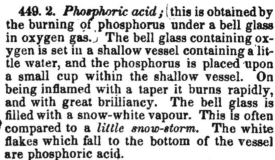

449. 2. *Phosphoric acid;* this is obtained by the burning of phosphorus under a bell glass in oxygen gas. The bell glass containing oxygen is set in a shallow vessel containing a little water, and the phosphorus is placed upon a small cup within the shallow vessel. On being inflamed with a taper it burns rapidly, and with great brilliancy. The bell glass is filled with a snow-white vapour. This is often compared to a *little snow-storm*. The white flakes which fall to the bottom of the vessel are phosphoric acid.

450. The oxygen may be expelled from this acid, and phosphorus again obtained, by heating it with charcoal. The figure shows you a retort *a*, placed over a furnace *b*. The retort, which contains phosphoric acid and charcoal, has its tube immersed in the basin of water *c*. Large quantities of carbonic acid gas, which is composed of oxygen from the phosphoric acid, united to a gas which proceeds from the charcoal, pass over. When the retort is at a red heat, phosphorus, in the form of a reddish wax, appears in the basin of water.

447. What two acids are formed by the union of oxygen with phosphorus?
448. How is phosphorous acid obtained?
449. How is phosphoric acid obtained?
450. How may phosphorus be obtained from phosphoric acid?

451. The weight of an atom of phosphorus is called 12, it being in relation to hydrogen as 12 to 1. The two acids of phosphorus are thus expressed. *Phosphorous acid;* 1 part phosphorus, 12, and 1 part of oxygen, 8, this is represented by the number 20. *Phosphoric acid;* 1 part phosphorus, 12, and 2 parts oxygen, 16, this is represented by the number 28.

Combination of Phosphorus and Hydrogen.

452. In combination with hydrogen, phosphorus forms a substance called *phosphuretted hydrogen.*

453. Here we have two simple *combustible substances* united. You will observe that the termination *uret* or *uretted* is used to denote this union.

454. *Exp.*—Phosphuretted hydrogen may be obtained by heating phosphorus with a solution of potash, and collecting it through a solution of the same kind, instead of water.

455. *Explanation.*—Part of the phosphorus unites with the potash—hydrogen is given off from the solution, and unites with another portion of phosphorus, forming phosphuretted hydrogen gas. This gas passing from the beak of the retort into the solution of potash rises into air, where it inflames spontaneously. Each bubble of gas, after exploding, ascends in the form of a pale wreath of smoke, becoming fainter and larger, as it rises.

451. By what numbers are the acids of phosphorus expressed?
452. What substance is formed by the union of phosphorus with hydrogen?
453. What does the termination *uret* denote?
454. How may phosphuretted hydrogen be obtained?
455. How is this process explained?

456. This gas is produced in nature by the decomposition of animal substances, in which the two elements, phosphorus and hydrogen, exist abundantly; particularly in the brains and nerves. Thus, when a body is buried, as the animal matter putrifies, hydrogen and phosphorus in a gaseous form escape, and uniting, pass up through the earth, and ascend into the atmosphere. Owing to the peculiar nature of this gas, it takes fire at the ordinary temperature : thus it happens that over graveyards, lights are sometimes seen, which the ignorant are ready to believe are indicative of some unearthly visitation.   Children not unfrequently hear about *Jack-o'-lanterns*, or wandering lights, which lead people into bogs and marshes, and then disappear.   It is in damp grounds that the phosphoretted hydrogen is most likely to be formed, and we can therefore see the reason for the Jack-o'-lantern leading its followers through such places. Professor Silliman says, " Travelling once through a deep valley in a dark night, I was surrounded by multitudes of pale, lambent lights; they were every moment changing their position, and some of them were within reach of my whip." But this gentleman, knowing the nature of the lights, did not tremble, nor turn pale, as an ignorant and superstitious person might have done.

457. Knowledge serves to dissipate those superstitious fears which torment the mind when ignorant of the causes of the phenomena of nature.   It was this ignorance which gave rise to a belief in the existence of witches and hobgoblins of various kinds.   By means of knowledge man has subjected the elements of nature to his sway; and although no witches ride through the air on broomsticks, yet people do fly in balloons, ride with almost the rapidity of lightning in rail-road cars, and glide in steamboats with a swiftness which would have been incredible to the people of the last century.   These are some of the effects of knowledge.

---

456. How may the lights be accounted for which often appear in damp grounds, graveyards, &c. ?
457. What are some of the effects of knowledge ?

CHAPTER XIV.

Carbon—Carbonic Acid, and Carbonic Oxide.

458. THE subject of our lesson is *Carbon ;* the word is derived from *carbo,* a coal. This exists in all vegetable and animal matter, being one of the most extensively diffused substances in nature.

459. You are familiar with *charcoal ;* you know it is what remains of wood after it has been exposed to heat. The common charcoal, which is used in household operations, is made by placing sticks of wood in a conical pile, covering them with earth, and kindling a fire in an opening below. The volatile parts of the wood are driven off by heat, and make their way through apertures in the covering, and charcoal remains. This is nearly *pure carbon.*

Diamond.

460. In the diamond you may see pure, crystallized carbon. But diamonds are very rare in our country. There is a great deal of jewelry which is made in imitation of diamonds, but the real diamond possesses a splendour that cannot be imitated. The empress Catherine of Russia, gave 100,000 pounds for a diamond about the size of a pigeon's egg, which was placed in the imperial sceptre.

461. Sir Isaac Newton suggested that the diamond might be made to burn, because its power of reflecting and refracting the rays of light was so great ; and where a body was capable of producing such effects on light, he thought it must be affected by caloric. *It is now proved that the diamond is a combustible substance.*

462. Diamonds may be burned in oxygen gas; the product of this combustion is *carbonic acid gas.* This proves the diamond to be pure *carbon,* for carbonic acid gas is composed of oxygen and carbon.

---

458. What is the word *carbon* derived from ? and where does it exist?
459. What is charcoal? and how is it obtained?
460. What is the real diamond composed of? and what is said of its value?
461. What led Sir Isaac Newton to think that the diamond might be made to burn?
462. What proves the diamond to be pure carbon?

463. You might suppose, since chemists know of what diamonds are composed, and as this material, viz. carbon, is very abundant in nature, that they could *manufacture* diamonds but you must recollect that they are *crystals of carbon*, and no method of crystallizing carbon is known. Scientific men stimulated by the desire of making discoveries, and artists eager for wealth, have sought to learn this; but, like the alchymists of former days, who endeavoured to turn stones into gold,—all have been disappointed in the attempt to make diamonds from charcoal.

464. You must not confound with charcoal the various kinds of coal which are dug out of the earth; the latter are called mineral coal. They contain a large proportion of carbon, but usually mixed with some sulphur and iron. They are heavier than charcoal.

465. Black lead, or *plumbago*, lampblack, and soot, are chiefly composed of carbon.

466. In considering the properties of carbon, we shall confine ourselves to that form of it which is seen in *charcoal.* 1. *It is remarkable for its power of absorbing gases of different kinds, and giving them off again when heated.* The pores of newly made charcoal become filled with the first kind of air or gas which comes in contact with it. In order to purify it from these substances, it must be heated, after which it is again ready to absorb other gases. These gases do not form a chemical combination with charcoal; for when driven off by heat and collected, they are found to be unchanged, and to leave the charcoal so.

467. 2. Charcoal is *one of the most important antiseptics* known. It will purify water that has become putrid, and for this reason is very useful to persons at sea, who cannot obtain fresh water. Tainted meat may be made sweet by being boiled with powdered charcoal, or rubbed thoroughly with it. But the housekeeper who uses it for this purpose should remember that it must be heated to redness, and applied to the

* Antiseptic is derived from the Greek *anti*, against, and *septo*, to putrefy; an antidote to putrefaction. Whatever possesses the power to prevent animal substances from putrefaction, or removes it after it has commenced, is called an antiseptic.

463. Can diamonds be manufactured from carbon?
464. Are all kinds of coal called charcoal?
465. What substances besides coal are chiefly composed of carbon?
466. What is said of the absorbing power of charcoal?
467. What is said of the purifying power of charcoal?

meat before it has absorbed other gas than the putrid odour of the meat. If put into water while hot, it may be thus preserved fit for use. On account of its antiseptic nature, it makes an excellent dentrifice.

468. 3. Charcoal resists decay; for this reason the ends of posts, before being placed in the earth, should be charred, or partly turned to coal. Silliman remarks, that he saw in the British Museum, at London, a pointed stake, which, with many others, was found in the bed of the Thames, in the spot, where, according to the Roman historian, Tacitus, the Britons fixed a vast number of stakes to prevent the passage of Cæsar's army. They were all charred to a considerable depth; they retained their form entirely, and were so firm that knife-handles were manufactured from them, and sold at a great price.

Other uses of Carbon.

469. Charcoal, in the form of lampblack, is used with oil for paints, and for printer's ink; with iron it forms steel; with sulphur and nitre it makes gunpowder. It is in common use for fuel, especially in cooking operations of various kinds. The *diamond* furnishes not only the most elegant ornaments, but is useful in the arts; it is the best substance known for cutting glass.

Combination of Carbon and Oxygen.

470. We here meet with a gas which exists in a vast number of substances, which we throw out of our lungs at every breath, and yet which we cannot inhale in any large quantity without destroying life; this is *carbonic acid gas*, sometimes called *fixed air*, because it exists in a fixed state in lime, and many other minerals.

Modes of obtaining Carbonic acid gas.

471. By burning diamond or charcoal in oxygen gas, pure carbonic gas is obtained. But the burning of diamonds is too expensive an operation to be performed, except for important experiments, and the gas can be obtained still more easily than by burning charcoal in oxygen.

472. There are in nature many *carbonates;* that of lime

---

468. Why are the ends of posts sometimes charred before being put into the ground?
469. What are some of the other uses of charcoal?
470. What is said of carbonic acid gas?
471. How is carbonic acid obtained?
472. What are carbonates?

under various forms, as limestone, marble, and chalk, is the most common. Carbonates are composed of carbonic acid gas, united to some substance called its *base;* thus lime is the base of carbonate of lime.

473. The common method of obtaining carbonic acid gas is, by the decomposition of chalk, or powdered limestone, by means of sulphuric or muriatic acid.

474. In the figure, the bottle *a* is supposed to contain pieces

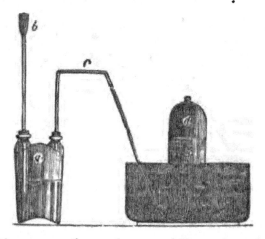

of marble, or any other carbonate of lime; through the tunnel *b*, is poured weak muriatic or sulphuric acid—a violent effervescence takes place, owing to the escape of carbonic acid, which passes through the tube *c* into the bell glass *d;* the receiver is not filled with water, with which carbonic acid gas would unite; but it excludes the common air.

475. Carbonic acid seems held to its bases by a tie which is easily broken, for there are few acids which will not expel it from its combinations: thus vinegar poured upon pearlash, which is a *carbonate of potash*, causes the carbonic acid to pass off; its escape is indicated by the effervescence that takes place. This is owing to *elective* affinity. The acid which exists in vinegar is called *acetic* acid, for this, the potash has a greater affinity than for the carbonic acid, which is expelled.

---

473. What is the common mode of obtaining carbonic acid gas ?
474. What does the figure represent ?
475. Is carbonic acid easily separated from its bases ?

476. Carbonic acid may be driven off from carbonates, merely by the action of heat. Thus quicklime, which is used for whitewashing and plastering, is made from lime- stone, by heating the latter in kilns, and thus expelling the carbonic acid gas.

Properties of Carbonic acid gas.

477. No animal can breathe in an atmosphere of this gas. Thus the entomologist makes use of it to destroy the lives of the insects he wishes to preserve, as there is no method of doing this with more expedition and certainty. It is different in its effects upon the lungs from nitrogen or hydrogen, they *do not support life*, carbonic acid *destroys it.* In the two former, ani- mals *die for want of oxygen*, in the latter, *they are killed.* It is on account of the deadly nature of this gas, that it is so danger- ous to burn in close apartments. The small portable furnaces which are now so much in use for cooking, ironing, and other household operations, should never be used except in the open air, or in a fireplace, and in the latter case, the doors of the room should be opened. Three young women, a year or two ago, were ironing in a close room, with furnaces to heat their irons, and all of them fainted successively. The char- coal, as it burns, gives off carbon, which, uniting with the ox- ygen of the air, forms carbonic acid gas.

478. *Carbonic acid gas does not support combustion:* a lighted taper suspended in it is immediately extinguished. This fact should be known to all. Lives are often destroyed in consequence of people going into wells and vaults where this gas abounds; sometimes when one person faints, others go immediately into the same place, and many lives are thus lost in consequence of ignorance. If people would first test the purity of such places, by suspending into them a lighted candle, they would at once know whether they could live in them;—if the air will not support combustion, it will not support life, or rather, if it destroys the one, it will de- stroy the other.

479. Carbonic acid gas is *heavier* than atmospheric air; this is the reason why it is most abundant in low places. It sinks into them.

---

476. How is quicklime manufactured?
477. What effect has carbonic acid gas upon respiration and life?
478. How can the existence of this gas be ascertained in wells, and other subterranean places?
479. Why is this gas most abundant in low places?

480. *Exp.*—Because it is heavier than the air, it may be poured from one vessel to another like liquids. If you collect this gas in a tumbler it may stand without being covered, for it will not rise and escape like most other gases It is a curious experiment to see a lamp extinguished by holding over it what appears to be an empty tumbler; for carbonic acid gas is without colour and invisible, yet it may be thus poured out upon flame, which it will destroy as if it were so much water.

481. This gas is called carbonic *acid*, because it gives to liquid substances an acid taste of a peculiar kind, which, though not sharp, is lively and refreshing. It is this gas which sparkles and bubbles in good bottled cider and some wines. It causes the effervescence and refreshing taste of soda waters, and the smartness of the Saratoga and some other mineral waters.

480. What does the experiment prove?
481. Why is this gas called carbonic *acid?*

482. Carbonic acid gas unites with water, and imparts to it a peculiar taste. The soda-water which is sold by confectioners is merely carbonated water, prepared as follows. Pieces of pounded chalk or marble, being put into a vessel* and sulphuric acid poured upon them, carbonic acid gas rapidly escapes into a tube B, communicating with the *condenser* or forcing pump A, which on raising the piston forces the gas through the other pipe C, into a vessel containing water. By means of pressure, the water is made to absorb large quantities of gas. When sufficiently impregnated with gas, the water is drawn out by means of a syphon or bent tube D, and flows into the tumbler, where it appears sparkling and foaming. This is improperly called soda-water, since it usually contains no soda.

483. Good yeast contains a large proportion of carbonic acid gas, and to this is owing its peculiar property of *raising* bread. The gas imprisoned in the dough, seeks to expand itself, and the heat of the oven in baking increases its expansive force; thus light bread is spongy, or full of cavities. Pearlash (*carbonate of potash*) is used in making cakes and biscuit, on account of the carbonic acid gas which it contains. Every one who has observed the effect of cake when it is baking, knows that it rises much in the oven; this is owing to the expansion of the carbonic acid gas. When eggs instead of pearlash, for cake, are used, the *air*, which by beating the eggs becomes entangled in their albumen, and causes them to appear light and frothy, makes the cake light by its expansion. It is for this reason that cake made with eggs should not be suffered to stand long before baking, as the imprisoned air would escape, and the cake not rise in the oven.

Existence of Carbonic acid gas in nature.

484. Carbonic acid gas forms nearly half of the marble and limestone which are so abundant in the mineral kingdom, in beds and mountains;—it is thrown from the lungs of animals in breathing;—it is produced by the fermentation of li-

---

* Having shown (at page 127) the manner in which this gas is obtained. it is unnecessary to have the whole apparatus here exhibited. The pipe B, is supposed to communicate with the vessel from which the gas issues. See the figure on the preceding page.

---

482. How is soda water prepared?
483. Why are bread and cakes made light by yeast, pearlash, or eggs?
484. Is carbonic acid gas found extensively in nature?

quors, and the burning of candles, lamps, furnaces, and fireplaces. Oysters, and other shell fish, have a covering of carbonate of lime, which seems to be formed from matter partly
furnished by their own bodies, and partly by the salt water.

485. It would seem as if so deadly a gas, as we find the
carbonic acid to be, in its effects upon animal life, and produced as it is, in such great abundance, from the breathing of
animals, the decomposition of substances, and the burning of
candles and fires, would soon destroy the whole animal creation. Besides, we use oxygen at every inspiration or drawing in of the breath;—does it not seem alarming to think of
the great quantities of the deadly air which is every moment
formed, and the vast portions of the vital air which are at the
same time consumed? Behold here the wisdom of God, who,
when he formed the grass, the herb and tree, and gave them
to man for meat, so made them, that in their growth, they
should absorb and be nourished by this very gas, so fatal to
the life of animals; and, at the same time, throw from their
vegetable lungs, that gas, without which, they would instantly die! Truly, God gave the vegetable world for meat, in
more senses than one; and well might He, in beholding his
work, and its curiously balanced machinery, pronounce it
"good!"

486. The weight of an atom of carbon is reckoned as 6,
that of hydrogen being 1.

487. Carbonic acid being composed of carbon 1 atom= 6
oxygen 2 " 16

The number which represents it is 22
This is called its *chemical equivalent.*

Carbonic oxide gas.

488. There is a combination of carbon with oxygen, called
carbonic oxide; in which the proportion of carbon is much
greater than in the gas we have been studying; indeed, the
term, *oxide,* denotes that the substance contains less oxygen
than is required to form an acid.

489. Carbonic oxide is no less fatal to animal life than car-

485. Why does not the accumulation of carbonic acid, and the constant
waste of oxygen, destroy the whole animal creation?
486. What is the weight of an atom of carbon?
487. What is the chemical equivalent of carbonic acid?
488. What combination is there of carbon and oxygen besides the one
we have just been examining?
489. What is the effect of carbonic oxide when taken into the lungs?

bonic acid. The great chemist, Sir Humphrey Davy, of England, who often exposed his life, in his zeal for making discoveries, once attempted to inhale it, with one fourth part of common air, but the attempt had nearly proved fatal. Another person, attempting to breathe it, appeared to fall into an apoplexy, from which he was restored by inhaling oxygen gas. Though some may foolishly expose their lives from an idle curiosity, or mere love of novelty, it is often necessary for the man of science to expose himself to dangers in his investigations. Thus Franklin dared to bring down lightning from heaven, in order to prove its identity with electricity, and chemists, inhale deadly gases, that they may test their properties by experience. In some cases, they have fallen victims to this desire of enlightening the world.

490. You will recollect that 22 is the representative number of carbonic acid. Carbonic oxide being composed of one atom of carbon, 6, united to one atom of oxygen, 8, 14 is the representative number of this gas;—one additional atom of oxygen, being 8, would change it into carbonic acid gas.

491. *Carbonic oxide will not support combustion;* but it is inflammable, and will, itself, burn in oxygen or in common air. But the product of its combustion is not water, as in the case of hydrogen; it is carbonic acid. You may here see an inverted jar, placed over a vessel of carbonic oxide which is burning in a jet, as it issues from the tube, at the mouth. The inverted jar will soon be filled with carbonic acid gas. The air furnishes another atom of oxygen, (8,) which, uniting with the carbonic oxide, (14,) makes the chemical equivalent of carbonic acid 22.

CHAPTER XV.

Boron. Iodine. Fluorine. Bromine.

492. THERE is a substance known in commerce by the name of *borax;* it is found abundantly in various parts of Asia, es-

---

490. What is the representative number of carbonic oxide?
491. When carbonic oxide gas burns in air, what is the product of this combustion?
492. Where is borax found?

pecially in the East Indies, from whence it is exported to
Europe in large quantities, under the name of *tincal.* It is
found in crystalline masses, resembling alum, a little below
the surface of the earth. It is sometimes obtained by evaporating the waters of certain lakes, or found in a solid form a
the bottom of salt lakes, which is the case in Peru.

493. But borax is a *compound* substance, consisting of an
acid called *boracic** acid, united to soda as its base. Borax
is a *borate of soda,* and is classed among the salts.

494. In 1702, a chemist in Paris discovered in borax the
boracic acid. This acid is obtained by means of decomposing, with sulphuric acid, borax, or the borate of soda.

495. *Exp.*—A small piece of borax being put into a vessel,
hot water and sulphuric acid are poured upon it. The mixture is then placed over burning coals for a few minutes.
The borax decomposes, and a solution of sulphate of soda is
formed; when this solution cools, solid scales of a white and
shining appearance may be collected; these are *boracic acid.*

Explanation.—You will at once perceive here the agency
of elective affinity; the soda having a greater affinity for sulphuric, than for boracic acid, unites with it and expels the
latter.

496. But *boracic acid, itself, is a compound;* its base was
discovered about one hundred years after the acid itself, by
Sir Humphrey Davy. He found by heating the acid with a
metal called potassium, that oxygen was liberated, and a dark,
olive-coloured mass remained. This he named *boron,* and as
no succeeding chemist has been able to decompose it, it is
ranked among the *elements,* or simple substances.

497. The weight of its atom is 8, the same as oxygen. In
boracic acid, 1 part of boron, 8, is united to two parts of oxygen, 16; this makes the chemical equivalent of this acid 24.

498. Boron is a combustible substance, resembling carbon
in some respects—the product of its combustion when burnt
in the common air, or in oxygen gas, is boracic acid.

* Pronounced *borasic.*

---

493. Is borax a simple substance?
494. What acid is obtained from borax?
495. By what process is boracic acid separated from borax?
496. How did Sir Humphrey Davy discover boron?
497. What is the weight of an atom of boron? and what is the chemical
equivalent of boracic acid?
498. What is the product when boron is burned in oxygen, or common
air?

. Boracic acid, dissolved in alcohol, burns with a pecu-
lame, the edges and top being of a beautiful green
ir.)

Uses of Borax.

0. Borax is used in the arts, to assist in the melting of
ls and other substances, with some of which, it forms
pus coloured glass.   It is used in medicine, as a remedy
ore mouths, especially for young children.)

SUPPORTERS OF COMBUSTION.

✕ Iodine.

loron, we found to be a *combustible* substance. *Iodine,*
ich we shall now consider, is ranked among the *supporters*
combustion; that is, though it does not burn, it is supposed
promote the burning of other substances.   All combustible
bstances possess the *positive* electricity, while the support-
s of combustion possess the *negative* electricity.   Hitherto
we have examined but one supporter of combustion, viz.
oxygen, and this, for a long time, was considered the only
one.

502. Iodine has been known only since the year 1812.   It
was discovered in Paris, by a manufacturer of soda, as he was
burning seaweeds to obtain soda.

503. Iodine exists in the form of a solid, of a gray colour,
it is remarkable for passing from a solid state to that of a vapour, by a small increase of temperature.   Almost every solid
passes through the liquid state before becoming a vapour; but
this springs into vapour at once, or if it exist at all as a liquid,
the change is so sudden to a gaseous state, that it is not
perceptible.

504. The name *iodine,* is from the Greek *iodes,* signifying
violet-coloured. This is the colour of its vapour, which
appears very beautiful when seen through a clear, transparent
glass vessel.

---

499. What is the appearance of boracic acid, dissolved in alcohol, when
burning?
500. What are some of the uses of borax ?
501. In what important particular does iodine differ from boron ?
502. When and by whom was iodine discovered?
503. In what form does iodine exist ? and for what is it remarkable?
504. What does the word iodine signify ?

505. A small piece of iodine (which may be obtained at a druggist's shop) put into a vial, will be sufficient to show many interesting properties or this substance. On holding it near the flame of a lamp, the solid will disappear and the vial be filled with a purple vapour. As soon as the vial is removed from the lamp, the iodine is again seen in the form of a solid lump, of a gray colour and without appearing to have undergone any change in its nature.

Properties of Iodine.

506. Its odour is very disagreeable—its taste acrid. It is very corrosive, eating quickly through a cork, if a bottle containing it, is stopped by one—for this reason, glass stoppers are used. Its vapour is heavier than that of any other vapour: it being about nine times heavier than the air. The weight of its atom is 124. It destroys vegetable colours. With starch it produces a blue colour, a circumstance which always shows its presence.

Combinations of Iodine.

507. Iodine unites with oxygen, forming *iodic* and *iodous* acids. With hydrogen, it forms *hydriodic* acid, and with metals, *iodides*. With soda, lime, and other alkalies, it forms *iodates*.

Method of obtaining Iodine.

508. The figure shows a flask *a*, which contains crystals formed by evaporating the ley of seaweed ashes. Sulphuric acid is poured into the flask, and on the application of a gentle heat, the violet-coloured vapour of iodine rises in the head *b*, and passes through the tube into

505. What experiment may be made with iodine?
506. What are some of the properties of iodine?
507. What combinations does iodine form with other substances?
508. Describe the mode of obtaining iodine?

the receiver *c*, where they are condensed into the solid sub stance, iodine.

Fluorine.

509. You will perhaps smile when you learn, that chemists have placed among the elements, a substance which does not exist, or, at least, which has never yet been obtained. But such is the case, and the name which they have given to this imaginary element is *fluorine.*

510. There is a beautiful mineral found in England, called, from the place where it is most common, Derbyshire spar. It is sometimes called *fluor-spar ; fluor*, because it melts easily, and *spar*, on account of its appearance being similar to that of minerals which are called *spars*, or *sparry*. Fluor-spar is found to consist of lime united to an acid, which is named *fluoric acid ;* therefore the chemical name for fluor-spar is *fluate of lime.*

511. But you undoubtedly would like to know why chemists *imagine* the existence of a substance, called fluorine. You remember that *boracic acid* has been found to consist of a base, called *boron*, united to *oxygen ;* and that *carbonic acid* is composed of a base, *carbon*, united to *oxygen*, and so on with respect to all the acids we have noticed ; they all consist of a *base* united to an *acidifying* substance. Reasoning therefore from *analogy*,* chemists have thought that fluoric acid must also be a compound, consisting of a base united to oxygen, or to some other acidifyer ; this imaginary base has received the name of fluorine, because it is thought in some respects to resemble iodine, and some other substances ending in *ine*, which we shall soon examine. We shall not attempt to say any thing about this fluorine, which, like the hero of a novel, has but an imaginary existence. Fluoric acid has hitherto resisted all attempts to decompose it, so that, if fluorine does exist, it is so well satisfied with the companion to which it is united, that no temptations can induce it to separate.

---

* If the young pupil does not fully understand what is meant by *reasoning from analogy*, he will do well to refer to a dictionary, or what is better, to some work on logic.

---

509. What imaginary substance do chemists class among the elements?
510. What is fluor-spar?
511. Why is fluorine supposed to have an existence?

Method of obtaining Fluoric Acid.

512. *Exp.*—Fluoric acid is obtained in the gaseous state from fluor-spar, by means of elective affinity. For this purpose, sulphuric acid is poured upon pulverized fluor-spar. Heat is applied, and the fluoric acid gas immediately begins to ascend. The apparatus for collecting this gas must be of silver, as glass would not answer, for reasons we shall soon mention. The fluor-spar and sulphuric acid are put into the flask *a*, the gas passes through the tube *b* into the receiver *c*.

Explanation.—Fluor-spar, or the fluate of lime, consists of lime and fluoric acid. Lime has a strong affinity for sulphuric acid and unites with it, while the fluoric acid, being set free, escapes. The substance remaining in the flask is now *sulphate* of lime, while that in the receiver is *fluoric acid* in a gaseous state.

Properties of Fluoric Acid.

513. One of the most important properties of fluoric acid is its great affinity for a mineral called *silex*, which constitutes the gritty part of stones, and forms a considerable portion of glass. This acid dissolves or corrodes glass, by uniting with the silex; and this is the reason that glass vessels cannot be used for obtaining fluoric acid.

514. *Exp.*—In the figure is a representation of an *etching* box, placed over a furnace of coals; some fluor-spar being pounded, is put into the box, and sulphuric acid added. As soon as the gas begins to rise, a piece of glass, having been previously coated over on one side, with beeswax, and written upon, or sketched through the wax with a pin, is placed over the box, with the waxed side down.

512. How is fluoric acid obtained?
513. What are some of the most important properties of fluoric acid?
514. Describe the process of etching, or engraving on glass.

To prevent the wax from melting by the heat, a sponge, wet in cold water, is applied to the upper side of the glass. In a few seconds after the gas has begun to act, the glass may be removed. On scraping off the wax, the words written, or the picture sketched, will be found engraven upon the glass. Were it not for the wax, the glass would in every part be equally acted on by the acid.

515. Fluoric acid gas produces this effect on glass by act ing upon a portion of the silex of which glass is composed, united to silex, fluoric acid forms a new compound, called *silicated fluoric gas.*

516. The vapours of fluoric acid are very dangerous when brought to act upon any part of the body, and especially when inhaled in breathing. One writer on Chemistry mentions that his assistant suffered severely, for several weeks, in consequence of the vapour of this acid acting upon his finger, and that six drops of the acid falling upon the back of a dog, produced great agony, and death in a few hours.

Bromine.

517. Bromine is a newly discovered element; the name is from the Greek *bromos*, signifying an unpleasant odour, a circumstance which marks this substance. It was discovered by a French chemist in making some experiments with the ley obtained from the ashes of seaweed and other marine plants. It exists in seawater in the state of a *hydro bromic** acid united to magnesia. The process of collecting bromine separate from its combinations, is long and difficult.

518. It is a *liquid* of a deep red or brown colour, much heavier than water; its chemical equivalent is 75. It is very *volatile,* that is, it has a tendency to pass into the state of a vapour; a drop or two will fill a quart vessel with red vapours. It is very poisonous; its vapour supports combustion feebly, but before a candle is extinguished in it, the flame presents a singular appearance, being green at the bottom, and red at the top. Bromine does not change vegetable blue col-

* *Hydro* signifies, in *a moist state,* or combined with hydrogen, to form water.

---

515. Why does fluoric acid produce the effect on glass which takes place in the process just described?

516. What is the effect of fluoric acid upon the animal system?

517. What does the name bromine signify? and when and how was the substance which is so called discovered?

518. What are its properties?

lours red, therefore it is not an acid; but it bleaches them, and even destroys the colour of indigo.

519. The chemical affinities of bromine are numerous; it forms *acids* with hydrogen and oxygen; it forms *salts* with alkalies; these salts are called *bromates;* and it combines with metals, forming *bromides.*

520. You will perceive that bromine in some respects resembles iodine, in connexion with which, it is usually found. Like iodine it is attracted to the *positive* pole of the galvanic battery, and is therefore classed among the *electro-negative* substances, oxygen, iodine, fluorine, and one which we have not yet examined, called *chlorine.*

521. Bromine is very rare and dear in this country. Professor Silliman, a few years ago, in his "Elements of Chemistry," said, "I have just obtained from Paris, two vials, containing each, not more than a thimble full; the price was eight dollars."

CHAPTER XVI.

Muriatic Acid. Chlorine.

522. WE have deferred the study of *chlorine,* not because it is an unimportant substance, but because there is some dispute among chemists as to its being *an element,* and we did not wish to perplex you with arguments about this, while you were ignorant of the nature of substances which are more easily understood.

523. You have often been told in the progress of your study, about *muriatic acid;* now according to the present opinion of most chemists, respecting the nature of chlorine, and according to the rules by which acids are named, muriatic acid ought to be called *hydro-chloric* acid, it being considered as a compound consisting of *hydrogen* and *chlorine;* but the name having been long established, it is not easy to alter it, although, for the sake of greater uniformity and clearness, many scientific men would be glad to do it.

519. Does bromine readily unite with other substances?
520. In what respects does bromine resemble iodine?
521. Is it a common substance?
522. Why has the study of chlorine been so long deferred?
523. What does muriatic acid consist of? and what is a more proper name for it?

Muriatic Acid.

524. Before proceeding to treat of chlorine directly, we will consider the substance from which it is obtained : this is (muriatic acid) or, as before remarked, more scientifically (though not so commonly) called *hydro-chloric acid.*

525. Muriatic acid is so called from *muria,* the Latin name for sea salt, from which it is usually obtained.

526. Liquid muriatic acid has long been known, but the discovery of its gas was not made till (the latter part of the last century.)

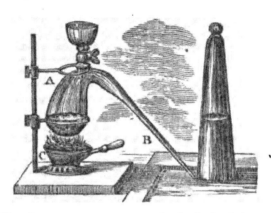

527. The figure represents a method of obtaining muriatic acid gas—at *A* is a retort containing common salt ; some sulphuric acid is poured through the glass tunnel, and the stop-cock turned to prevent any gas escaping in that direction. *B* shows the tube of the retort passing under a receiver filled with mercury and inverted over a trough of mercury. At *C* is the chaffing dish of hot coals to hasten the process that is going on in the retort.

528. *Explanation.*—Common salt is a *muriate of soda ;* that is, it is composed of muriatic acid united to soda ; the latter having a greater affinity for sulphuric acid, unites with

---

524. From what substance is chlorine obtained?
525. Why is muriatic acid so named ?
526. When was muriatic gas discovered ?
527. Describe the process for obtaining muriatic acid gas.
528. How do you explain this process ?

it, forming *sulphate of soda*, and excludes the muriatic acid; this rises in the retort, and is conducted through the tube into the receiver filled with mercury; as fast as the gas rises, the mercury sinks into the trough below; as the receiver now appears, it is a little more than half filled with gas. You will recollect that such is the affinity of muriatic acid gas for water, that it cannot be collected through it like many of the other gases, as it unites with the water and assumes the liquid state.

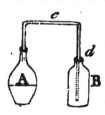

529. *Exp.*—Muriatic acid gas is heavier than common air;—this is shown by collecting it, by the following experiment. The bottle *A* being filled with the substances which produce the gas,* communicates with an empty receiver *B* by the tube *c*. As the gas passes over, it settles at the bottom of the vessel, and the air consequently rises, until the whole space being filled with the gas, it begins to issue forth from the mouth at *d*. Muriatic acid gas may be known by its peculiar smell, and the white cloud which it forms by uniting with aqueous particles in the air.

Explanation.—The muriatic acid gas *sinks to the bottom* of the receiver *B*, because it is heavier than the air with which it was at first filled.

Properties of Muriatic Acid gas.

530. It is colourless, of a sharp odour, and extinguishes combustion. Its affinity for water is such, that it attracts it from the atmosphere, and forms white vapours. It turns vegetable blue colours red. It melts ice with great rapidity, and is strongly absorbed by water. It is fatal to animal life.

Liquid Muriatic Acid.

531. Every chemical laboratory ought to be furnished with liquid muriatic acid, as it is necessary in many experiments. It is obtained by saturating water with muriatic acid gas by means of Woulfe's apparatus, so called from the name of the

* That is, common salt and sulphuric acid.

---

529. What experiment proves muriatic acid gas to be heavier than common air?
530. What are the properties of this gas?
531. How is liquid muriatic acid obtained?

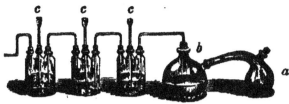

inventor.* The retort *a* contains common salt and sulphuric acid; the muriatic acid gas passes into the glass globe *b*, where it is washed from some sulphuric acid which is generally carried along with it—the gas then passes through the tube to the bottle next the globe, where it is received into water; when this water is saturated, the gas passes on through another tube to the next bottle, and thus the process is continued.—The number of bottles may be increased or diminished. The straight tubes *c, c, c,* are called safety tubes; being open at top, they admit atmospheric air into each bottle when the gas ceases to come over from the retort, thus preventing a vacuum, which might draw in the impure acid from the globe or first bottle.

532. Silliman observes, " *the sulphuric, the nitric, and the muriatic, are the three cardinal acids of Chemistry and the arts. We could effect very little in practical Chemistry without them.* Of the three, the sulphuric is the most useful, because, besides its own numerous and important applications, it is the principal instrument in making the other two."

Uses of Muriatic Acid.

533. Besides its many applications in assisting the chemist in his analysis of other substances, muriatic acid is of important use in medicine, and in the arts. It is very useful in a sick room, by destroying disagreeable odours, and preventing contagion. A little common salt in an earthen vessel, placed over coals, requires only the addition of a small quantity of sulphuric acid, in order to obtain muriatic acid gas, the fumes of which are powerful to destroy the effect of other gases; and all contagion is conveyed by means of bad air, or unwholesome gases. An instance of the power of muriatic acid

* For a further description of Woulfe's Apparatus, see Dictionary of Chemistry, articles " Absorption," and " Apparatus."

532. What does Silliman observe of the importance of three of the acids?

533. What are some of the uses of muriatic acid?

gas as a disinfecting agent, is thus related by professor Silliman. "At Dijon, in France, there is a cathedral which in 1773, was, from the corpses interred beneath it, so infected with putrid miasmata* that it had been deserted, after a number of unsuccessful attempts to remove them and purify the air by explosions, aromatics, &c. Application being made to Professor Morveau† for a remedy, he took a glass vessel, supported by one of cast iron, and placed it on a few live coals in the middle of the church. He then put into it six pounds of common salt, and two pounds of sulphuric acid, and hastily withdrew, closing the doors after him. The muriatic acid gas soon filled the vast space, and could be perceived even at the doors. At the end of twelve hours, the church was thrown open and ventilated." Thus by means of chemical science, that vast and ancient church which otherwise must have been destroyed or given up to owls and bats, and lizards and noxious reptiles, was purified and rendered a meet temple for the worship of God.

534. Muriatic acid forms many combinations with other substances. With nitric acid it forms a compound called nitro-*muriatic acid.* It was at first called *aqua regia*, a Latin name signifying kingly or powerful water. This name was given by the first chemists, who were called *alchymists*, and whose great object was to change all metals into gold. *Nitro-muriatic acid*, or aqua regia, is the only liquid known which has power to dissolve gold.

535. With alkalies, muriatic acid forms salts, called *muriates*, as common salt, which is usually called the muriate of soda, &c.; but which, according to late discoveries, is a *chloride* of sodium.

Muriatic acid is composed of 1 part chlorine, whose atom is called 36, united to 1 part of hydrogen. The number, therefore, which represents this acid, is 37; this is its *chemical equivalent.* You will remember that hydrogen is the unit or 1, to which all other elements are compared, and one atom

* *Miasma* is a Greek word, signifying noxious matter, or small particles which float in the air, and produce diseases, or bad smells. *Miasmata* is the plural of miasma.
† A distinguished French chemist; see Dictionary of Chemistry, page 21.

534. What is nitro-muriatic acid? and by what name was it known to the alchymists?
535. What other combinations are formed with muriatic acid?—What is its chemical equivalent?

of chlorine weighs 36, while one atom of hydrogen weighs only 1.

Chlorine, or Oxmuriatic Acid.

536. We have now to consider the nature of chlorine, an element, which is obtained by the decomposition of muriatic acid. It was in the year 1774, that Scheele, a Swedish chemist, being engaged in some experiments with the oxide of manganese, added to it some liquid muriatic acid, when a gas, of a yellowish green colour, and a very strong and disagreeable smell, was observed to issue forth from the combination. Since that period, this gas and its compounds have been considered as among the most interesting subjects of study in the whole range of chemical science.

537. It was at first thought, as the oxide of manganese contains a large portion of oxygen, that some of this oxygen by uniting to the muriatic acid gas, produced the newly discovered gas; on this supposition, it was named *oxmuriatic* acid.

538. As chemists attempted to decompose it, they found it resisted all the agents which they could employ for this purpose; they, therefore, began to believe it was a simple substance, and gave it the new and independent name Chlorine, from the Greek *kloros*, green, on account of its peculiar colour.

Method of obtaining Chlorine Gas.

539. Chlorine may be obtained with muriatic acid and the

oxide of manganese, as has already been mentioned, or by the use of some other substances. The following process is described by Silliman. Into a pot of sheet lead are put some *common salt, oxide of manganese, and sulphuric acid.* To the cork is fitted a leaden tube. The pot is then placed in a tin vessel containing hot water, and standing over a furnace. The gas must be collected in vessels filled with warm water, as the water, if cold, will absorb the gas.

---

536. When and by whom was chlorine discovered?
537. Why was chlorine at first called oxmuriatic acid?
538. Why was its name afterwards changed to chlorine?
539. How may chlorine be obtained?

510. *Explanation.*—How is chlorine obtained from the substances which were put together in the leaden vessel? This question those will ask who desire to understand the causes of things; we will therefore tell you what most Chemists now believe to be the *rationale** of this process.

They think that *chlorine*, combined with *hydrogen*, exists in muriatic acid, forming *hydro-chloric acid*, which you will recollect we mentioned, as being, now, the scientific name for muriatic acid. Now, in order to obtain the chlorine, it is only necessary that the hydrogen shall be separated from the muriatic acid which the salt furnishes; this is supposed to be done by means of the oxygen which comes from the oxide of manganese, and which is pressed out by the union of the manganese with the *sulphuric acid*, forming a *sulphate of manganese.* The oxygen furnished by the oxide of manganese, uniting to the hydrogen of the muriatic acid, forms water. One portion of the sulphuric acid unites with the soda of the common salt, (muriate of soda,) forming the sulphate of soda, while the muriatic acid being set free, gives its hydrogen to the oxyen of the manganese, and chlorine gas appears. In short, it is supposed that if muriatic acid be divested of its hydrogen it becomes chlorine.

541. Liquid chlorine may be obtained by putting pounded red lead, (oxide of lead,) and common salt into a bottle containing water, and adding sulphuric acid; after agitating the contents of the bottle, and plunging it into cold water to promote the absorption of the gas by the water in the bottle, the liquid will assume the yellowish green colour peculiar to chlorine. Any piece of calico, or other coloured substance, if introduced into a bottle of liquid chlorine, will soon appear colourless.

Properties of Chlorine gas.

542. The colour is greenish yellow; the smell suffocating and offensive: it is very dangerous to the lungs, its effects

---

* Pronounced ra-shun-a-le, signifying the reasons for any process. This is a term so common in Chemistry, that the author would not think of defining it, if this were not a work for "*Beginners.*"

---

540. Can you explain the rationale of the process by which chlorine is liberated from salt with the help of the oxide of manganese and sulphuric acid?
541. How may liquid chlorine be obtained?
542. What are the most important properties of chlorine gas?

sometimes appearing long after the gas has been inhaled.[*] One of its most remarkable properties is that of (destroying all animal and vegetable colours ;) on this account it is of great use in manufactories, where it is used in a combination with lime, called *chloride of lime*. *Chlorine is a supporter of combustion*, though far inferior to oxygen in this respect; a burning candle, held by a wire in a vial of this gas, burns a short time, though dimly, and with a reddish flame. Phosphorus, and many other substances, are inflamed spontaneously in

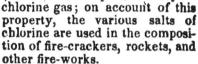

chlorine gas; on account of this property, the various salts of chlorine are used in the composition of fire-crackers, rockets, and other fire-works.

543. *Exp.*—(The figure represents a tubulated bottle of chlorine gas into which some phosphorus being introduced, it burns spontaneously, and throws off brilliant jets of fire. A bladder is fastened at the *tubulure* to give room for the expansion of the chlorine gas by heat.) The product of this combustion of phosphorus in chlorine, is called *chloride of phosphorus*.

---

[*] I cannot refrain from giving here a little notice of two young men, who have fallen victims to their zeal and boldness in the cause of science, especially Chemistry; I allude to two sons of Professor Amos Eaton, one of whom, Hezekiah, died recently at Lexington, Ky., filling with distinguished honour the station of assistant professor of Chemistry in Transylvania University. His brother Dwight died at Troy, N. Y., several years before, too young to have made himself extensively known abroad. But those who witnessed the enthusiasm and courage of these young men, for making the boldest experiments, the intuitive readiness with which they seized upon facts, and the clearness of their judgment in making deductions from these facts, can never cease to lament that they should so often have exposed themselves to the deleterious influence of deadly gases, which, operating like a slow poison, undermined their constitutions, and laid them in an early grave. To their father, science is indebted for the costly sacrifice of these two sons, the glory and pride of his declining years; while his own impaired health shows that neither has he withheld the sacrifice of himself.

---

543. How is the chloride of phosphorus formed?

CHAPTER XVII.

Compounds. Ammonia. Coal Gas. Oil Gas. Carburetted Hydrogen. Safety Lamp.

544. WE have now completed our view of the *ponderable elements* which are *not metallic.* You will recollect, that we first noticed the imponderables, caloric, light, electricity, and magnetism, and then proceeded to the consideration of those elements which have definite weight, and are therefore called ponderable. The ponderable elements consist of two classes *supporters of combustion* and *combustibles.*

545. The supporters of combustion are Oxygen, Chlorine Iodine, Fluorine, and Bromine; oxygen, by way of distinction, is called " *the great supporter of combustion.*"

546. The *combustibles not metallic*, are, Hydrogen, Nitrogen,* Sulphur, Phosphorus, Selenium, Carbon, and Boron.

547. We did not follow the arrangement above given, of combustible and non-combustible substances, in our view of these substances, because we wished first to examine oxygen and nitrogen, that we might show the constituents of the atmosphere; and then we examined hydrogen, in order to illustrate the composition of water. Chlorine was considered last, because the doctrines respecting it are not so simple, or so fully established, as those which relate to the other elements. With those elements, or that part of the alphabet of Chemistry which we have examined, are formed, either amongst themselves or with other substances, all of the most important combinations in nature. We shall now consider some of these combinations of non-metallic substances with each other, which we have hitherto omitted, that your attention might be chiefly given to the elements themselves.

* Nitrogen is combustible in the sense in which chemists consider combustion, viz. the union of a substance with oxygen; but nitrogen does not take fire on being brought in contact with a burning substance, and is not therefore combustible in the common understanding of the term.

544. Of what two classes do the ponderable elements consist?
545. Which are *supporters of combustion?*
546. Which are *non-metallic combustibles?*
547. What reasons are assigned for the order in which subjects have considered?

AMMONIA.

A compound of Nitrogen and Hydrogen.

548. Ammonia* consists of one atom of nitrogen, which is represented by 14, and of three parts hydrogen, which are called 3 ; therefore, as 14 and 3 are 17, the latter number represents ammonia, or is its *chemical equivalent.*

549. Hartshorn (sometimes called *volatile* salts, and *volatile* spirits) is an article in very common use. In powder it is used in *smelling-bottles*, and in a liquid state it is used for medicine. Hartshorn is so called because it is obtained by burning the horns of harts or deer. Hartshorn is a *carbonate of ammonia.*

550. By applying heat to liquid ammonia, a gas of a very powerful nature is disengaged, this is called *ammoniacal* gas. *a*, is a vessel containing liquid ammonia; *b*, a lamp ; *c*, a receiver, and *d*, a tube which connects the receiver to the flask. Ammoniacal gas being lighter than the air, rises, and takes its place in the upper vessel.

551. The annexed figure represents the receiver filled with mercury, and inverted over a mercurial trough. The retort contains powdered *muriate of ammonia*, and slaked quicklime.† The muriatic acid leaves the ammonia to unite with the lime, and the ammonia is set free. This experiment shows the power of elective affinity operating upon two solids, and causing the decomposition of one of them.

* The name ammonia is, by some, supposed to be derived from *ammos*, sand, because it was first procured from the sandy country Lybia, by others it is thought to be named from the temple of Jupiter Ammon, in the vicinity of which it was found.

Quicklime is pure lime; it is usually obtained from the carbonate of lime by burning it in kilns, the carbonic acid being expelled by heat. Slaked lime is a combination of lime and water, called, in Chemistry, *hydrate* of lime.

548. What does ammonia consist of? and what is its chemical equivalent?
549. What is said of hartshorn ?
550. How may ammoniacal gas be obtained from liquid ammonia ?
551. How may it be obtained from muriate of ammonia and lime ?

552. *Muriate of ammonia* is known in the shops of druggists as *sal-ammoniac,* which means, salt of ammonia.

553. Ammonia cannot be produced by *synthesis,* or mixing hydrogen and nitrogen gases; but it seems necessary that they should be brought in contact, at the instant they pass from other combinations, in order to unite in the proportions necessary to form ammonia.

554. During the decomposition of animal substances, both hydrogen and nitrogen are given off; these unite, and form ammonia; thus, from putrid and offensive matter, arises a gas of a refreshing odour, and which is a preventive to putrefaction.

555. The figure shows a method of obtaining liquid ammonia. The retort contains the muriate of ammonia and lime; the tube conducts the gas into a bottle containing cold water, which absorbs it rapidly.

556. Ammonia is an alkali;—that is, it changes vegetable red colours blue; it changes blue colours green, and yellow colours brown: it is *caustic* to the taste; it combines with acids to form salts, and with oils to form soaps.

557. The *volatile liniment,* used for burns and sore throats, is c mposed of ammonia and sweet oil.

COMPOUNDS OF CARBON AND HYDROGEN.

558. Combinations of carbon with simple bodies are called *carburets ;*—the most important of these is *carburetted hydrogen,* one kind of which forms the gas which is used for lighting the streets of cities.

559. Those of you who have walked out of an evening in

552. What is the common name of muriate of ammonia?
553. Can ammonia be produced by a mixture of the gases which compose it?
554. What gas is produced during the decomposition of animal substances?
555. How is liquid ammonia produced?
556. Why is ammonia considered as an alkali?
557. What is volatile liniment?
558. What are carburets?

the principal streets of New York, or some other large city, must have noticed the beautiful and brilliant lights which illuminate the streets, shops, and public places, sometimes issuing forth in many small jets of flame from elegant chandeliers of curious construction, and at others, appearing in one large effulgent blaze. *These lights burn without any wick; they are caused by the combustion of gas.* You will recollect that carbon and hydrogen are both highly combustible substances; we should naturally infer that when united, they would burn with force and brilliancy.

560. There are several varieties of carburetted hydrogen; that which is used for gas-lights is obtained either from coal or oil. Coal, we have found, is chiefly composed of carbon; that which is used for gas-lights, is a damp kind, called *pit coal;* it is dug from mines. Water in the coal furnishes the hydrogen. Oil is composed principally of carbon and hydrogen; the gas obtained from it is much purer than *coal gas.*

Coal Gas.

561. An apparatus for furnishing *coal gas-lights* consists of a large iron vessel which contains the coal; this vessel is placed over a furnace, and the gas which rises is made to pass through a tube into a vessel of cold water, called a *condenser,* which cleanses it of many impurities; it is then conducted through a mixture of quicklime and water, called the *purifier,* which absorbs the *carbonic acid* and *sulphuretted hydrogen;* the gas is then transmitted into a *gasometer,* or vessel prepared for its reception. In some large gas manufactories, the gasometers are twenty feet high and thirty in diameter. They are made of sheet iron—from these great fountains of gas, tubes placed under ground proceed to the different streets and buildings where it is used, in the same manner as water is conducted from one place to another through pipes placed under ground.

Oil Gas.

562. *Oil gas* is obtained chiefly by the distillation of whale oil, which is made to drop slowly into a vessel containing pieces of red hot bricks or coal; the apparatus in other respects resembles that for obtaining coal gas. Oil gas is most pure, and brilliant; it is the cheapest, except in places where coal is very abundant.

559. How are cities chiefly lighted at night?
560. From what substances is the carburetted hydrogen, used for gas lights, commonly obtained?
561. How is coal gas manufactured, and conveyed to different places?
562. What is said of oil gas, and the mode of obtaining it?

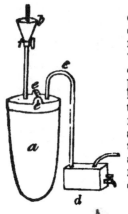

a represents a cast iron vessel with a copper tube and funnel *b*, into which the oil is poured, *c* is a bent iron tube communicating with a copper condenser *d*; when this apparatus is used, the vessel *a* is placed over a furnace; and the pieces of brick within the vessel being heated to redness, oil is poured in at *b*, the stop-cock at *f* being turned, the oil falls drop by drop upon the hot bricks, and becomes gas, which, issuing through the tube *c* passes into the condenser *d*, and may be conveyed to a gas-holder by means of a leaden pipe at the top of the condenser.

563. Spirits of turpentine and common resin may be used in the manufacture of gas-lights. If you have ever noticed the brilliant light made by the burning of a pine knot, you can readily believe that turpentine, which is the substance that causes it to burn so brightly, might afford a very luminous gas.

564. The figure shows a *portable gas-light*, or a copper vessel, which being filled with gas can be conveyed from one place to another. The flexible pipe serves the purpose of conveying the gas into the receiver, after it has been exhausted of air; the stop-cock near the insertion of the pipe is then turned to prevent the escape of the gas. The stop-cock below the perpendicular tube being turned, the gas issues forth at the orifice, where, after being inflamed, it continues to burn till the whole is consumed.

---

563. What other substances, besides coal and oil, may be used for gas-lights?

564. Describe a portable gas-light apparatus?

Bi-Carburetted Hydrogen, or Olefiant gas.

565. The gas, chiefly used for light, is *bi**-*carburetted hydrogen;* that is, 2 atoms of carbon united to 2 atoms of hydrogen—carbon being represented by 6, we have 12 of carbon to 2 of hydrogen, (an atom of hydrogen being 1,) so that 14 is the *chemical equivalent* of this gas.

566. Bi-carburetted hydrogen is called *olefiant* gas, because with chlorine it forms an oily substance; it is also called *heavy carburetted hydrogen,* on account of its specific gravity being greater than that of the other combinations of carbon and hydrogen.

567. The bi-carburetted hydrogen or olefiant gas gives the most luminous flame of all gases—hydrogen burns with a pale light; simple carburetted hydrogen, which contains but one atom of carbon, burns more vividly; but the additional atom of carbon which exists in the olefiant gas renders it still more brilliant.

568. This gas is obtained for experiments by heating, in a retort, alcohol and sulphuric acid. Alcohol is supposed to consist of one proportion of olefiant gas and one of water. The sulphuric acid having a great attraction for water, unites with it, and the olefiant gas is set free. If a small quantity of pounded coal be put into the bowl of a tobacco pipe, covered over the top with clay and then placed in burning coals, a stream of olefiant gas will issue forth, which may be known by applying to it a lighted taper, when it will be inflamed.

Light Carburetted Hydrogen.

569. We have here but 1 atom of carbon to 2 of hydrogen; therefore, as 6 the atom of the one, to 2 the two atoms of the other, make 8, this number is the representative of carburetted hydrogen—the difference between this gas and the bi-carburetted hydrogen, consists then, in the different proportion of carbon which exists in them.

570. The specific gravity of this gas is less than that of the *bi-carburet,* on account of its containing less carbon.

* From the Greek *bis,* two, meaning *twice* carburetted hydrogen.

---

565. What are the proportions of carbon and hydrogen in bi-carburetted hydrogen?
566. Why is bi-carburetted hydrogen called olefiant gas?
567. Why is olefiant gas the most luminous of the gases?
568. How may olefiant gas be obtained for experiments?
569. What are the proportions of hydrogen and carbon in light carburetted hydrogen?
570. Why is its specific gravity less than that of the bi-carburet?

Carburetted Hydrogen.

571. It is called *inflammable air*, and sometimes the *inflammable air of marshes*, because it is formed in low, damp grounds, during the decomposition of animal substances. It may be collected over stagnant waters, by stirring the mud at the bottom; the gas rises in bubbles, and may be collected in a receiver, through water.

572. Coal mines, which furnish in abundance the elements of carburetted hydrogen, are often scenes of fatal accidents to the workmen engaged in them. Ascending from the coal beds, the gas remains floating in the air, and the instant it comes in contact with a flame, takes fire, and explodes with great violence.

573. In England there are many coal mines; whole villages of people attend to the mining business as their only way of getting a support; some families live wholly in the mines; and people are often born in them, who live to old age without ever leaving them. It was a dreadful thing to these poor people to feel in constant dread of the *wild-fire damp*, as they called this gas, for they cannot work without a light, and their lamp must have exposed them every moment to this destruction.

574. Many dreadful accidents having occurred, in some instances destroying nearly a hundred workmen at a time. Sir

571. Why is it sometimes called the inflammable air of marshes?
572. In what way does this gas cause accidents in coal mines?
573. Why did this gas become a terror to the miners of England?
574. What is said of the application made to Sir Humphrey Davy?

Humphrey Davy, who was known as a man of much science, was applied to, with the hope that he might discover some means by which the miner could pursue his employment, and thus furnish the country with fuel, without being in constant danger of such a catastrophe. Sir Humphrey listened to the application with deep interest, and immediately took a journey to the coal region: he went into the mines, conversed with the miners, and obtained from them all the information they could give respecting the nature of this *fire-damp.* He then collected the gas, and examined its properties by various experiments.

575. He discovered one fact with regard to this substance, which suggested to him a way of preventing its explosion. He found that even red hot iron, in contact with the gas, did not set it on fire, while the smallest point of flame would cause an immediate explosion; this brought to his mind the fact, that another chemist, Dr. Wollaston, had discovered, viz.: "that an explosive mixture cannot be kindled in a glass tube so narrow as one seventh of an inch in diameter." This fact

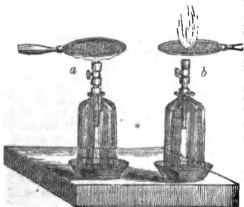

he proved by the experiment represented in the figure. He procured two vessels of the light carburetted hydrogen gas, or fire-damp, each fitted with a tube and stop-cock, and as the gas issued forth at each orifice he set fire to it; when it was burning he held over one orifice *a*, a piece of fine wire gauze, or net-work; but, as you see in the figure, the blaze, instead of passing through it, was turned away. He set fire to the gas of the other orifice *b*, *above* the wire gauze, and although it burnt freely, the flame had no effect upon the gas below. The net-work of wire is made of a vast number of very small *tubes* connected together. Sir Humphrey Davy having proved that such a net-work would secure the flame from the external air, then went to work and constructed a lamp, which is known throughout the civilized world as *Davy's Safety Lamp.*

575. What suggested to him the idea of his safety lamp?

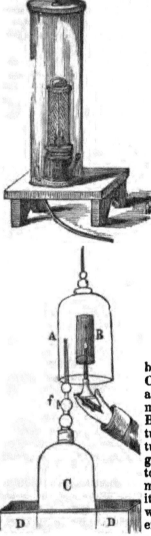

As the miner now goes forth to his daily toil with his safety lamp, which secures him against danger from the fire-damp, how ought he to bless the benefactor to whom he is indebted for this security! But it is probable that very few of this class of persons ever heard his name, for they are obliged to labour very hard, and have no means of gaining knowledge like the young persons who are now studying this book.

576. This is the safety lamp. The oil and wick are in the lower part, which is fed with oil from the spout on the side. The flame is surrounded by a cylinder, or cage of wire gauze, so fine that in every square inch there are at least 625 apertures. At the top, where the greatest heat exists, the wire gauze is double. There are conveniences for raising the wick, and replenishing the oil, without opening the lamp, and thus exposing the flame to the external air.

577. This figure represents a large bell glass A, suspended over a jar C, filled with carburetted hydrogen, and standing over water of the pneumatic cistern D D. A safety lamp B is held under the bell glass. On turning a stop-cock, fitted to the tube of the jar C which contains the gas, the *inflammable air* is allowed to pass up into the bell glass A, and mingle with the common air which it contains; a certain portion of which renders the fire-damp more explosive than when unmixed. The

576. Describe the safety lamp?

577. What experiment proves that the safety lamp is secure even when burning in an atmosphere of inflammable air?

flame of the lamp will now change its appearance, and exhibit a green, or delicate blue colour, and finally be extinguished; but it will not set fire to the external gas, which would be the case, should the smallest portion of flame come in contact with it.

578. From the little sketch we have given of the method pursued by Sir Humphrey Davy in his invention of the safety lamp, the young may see that knowledge does not come into the mind without labour. When a person begins to search into the nature of things, then it is that new ideas seem to arise in the mind—one experiment suggests another, and so on until the investigator often ends in the discovery of some new principle, or some new application of principles before known. In this way oxygen gas, and all the other gases, so important in chemical science, were discovered; and to such a process of inquiry we owe, not only the invention of the safety lamp, which gives security to thousands of labourers, as they go forth to their daily toil, but that of the steam engine, the printing press, and a vast number of improvements which tend to the comfort of life, and promote the good of society.

---

† CHAPTER XVIII.

Compounds.   Sulphuretted Hydrogen.   Cyanogen.   Prussic Acid.

SULPHURETTED HYDROGEN.

Compound of Sulphur and Hydrogen.

579. By a union of one atom of sulphur, represented by the number 16, and one atom of hydrogen, represented by 1, a gas is produced called *Sulphuretted Hydrogen*, of which the chemical equivalent is 17; that is, this is the sum of the two elements when added together.

580. The termination *uret* is applied to combinations of combustible, non-metallic substances with each other, and with metals, alkalies, and earths; thus we have *sulphuret of*

---

578. In what way have most important discoveries among men been made?

579. What is sulphuretted hydrogen?

580. How are the terminations *uret* and *uretted* applied?

phosphorus, sulphuret of iron, phosphoret of lime, &c. But when the compound is gaseous, this is signified by the termination *uretted*, as we have in the combinations of carbon and hydrogen, called carburetted hydrogen.

Modes of obtaining Sulphuretted Hydrogen.

581. Sulphuretted hydrogen is obtained by heating sulphur with hydrogen gas, as represented in the figure; the sulphur or brimstone is contained in the lower vessel, and the upper one is filled with hydrogen gas, which, from its specific levity, keeps its place; as heat is applied, the sulphur becomes a vapour, rises and unites with the hydrogen, forming *sulphuretted hydrogen*.

582. The same gas may also be obtained by heating sulphuric acid and the *sulphuret of iron*, (a combination of sulphur and iron.) This is an instance of *double elective affinity*; the oxygen of the water in the liquid sulphuric acid, unites to the iron of the sulphuret, and sets the sulphur free; while the hydrogen of the water, being at liberty, unites with the sulphur, and forms sulphuretted hydrogen.

583. This is one of the most offensive of all the gases; it is not only highly disagreeable in its odour, which resembles that of bad eggs, but is very destructive to animal life. Sulphuretted hydrogen, when pure, kills almost instantly; and it is very noxious, even when mingled with a large proportion of common air.

584. This gas is formed in nature in various places, particularly about wharves, and in sinks where filth is suffered to accumulate. It exists in the atmosphere around sulphurous springs.

585. One property of this gas renders it of much importance to the world, viz., its power as a test to show the existence of poisonous substances; many of the most active poisons have a metallic basis—sulphuretted hydrogen has such

---

581. How is sulphuretted hydrogen obtained ?
582. By what process is sulphuretted hydrogen obtained from sulphuric acid and the sulphuret of iron ?
583. What are some of its properties ?
594. Does it exist in nature ?
585. What important property does this gas possess ?

an affinity for metals that it unites with them, and, by a change of colour, indicates their existence, where it otherwise might not be suspected.   Thus arsenic, one of the most deadly poisons, may be detected by a yellow precipitate, and mercury by a black precipitate, with sulphuretted hydrogen.

586. White lead (*carbonate of lead*) becomes black when exposed to sulphuretted hydrogen gas; and bismuth, another metal, becomes dark brown—both these substances are used as the basis of the paints or cosmetics, which are used by silly females, under the mistaken idea of improving their complexions.   Bismuth is manufactured into a brilliant, white powder, sold under the name of *pearl-powder;* now it would be a very unpleasant circumstance to a beautiful, painted lady, walking near a sulphur spring, or other place where the atmosphere contained a portion of sulphuretted hydrogen, to have her colour suddenly changed to that of a tawny mulatto; but this is a risk that must always be incurred by those who use cosmetics prepared from mineral substances.   .

Suppose a sketch to be made with the *acetate of lead,* which is colourless, and this sketch in a moist state exposed to the action of a stream of sulphuretted hydrogen gas, the lines will become black as if made with a lead pencil.   The lead, combining with the sulphur of the gas, has formed sulphuret of lead. -

587. You have probably observed that a silver spoon, after

586. To what accident are persons exposed who use such cosmetics as pearl-powder, white paint, &c. ?
587. Why does a silver spoon become blackened in boiled eggs?

being put into a boiled egg, becomes blackened; (this is the effect of sulphuretted hydrogen—the yolk of eggs contains sulphur, the watery part contains hydrogen; when heated, the two elements unite.

588. There is a combination called *bi-sulphuretted* hydrogen, in which 2 atoms of sulphur unite to 1 of hydrogen.)

CYANOGEN.

Compound of Nitrogen and Carbon.

589. The word cyanogen is derived from the Greek, *kuanos* blue, and *gennao* to produce, signifying the producer of blue.) This substance gives its colour to the paint called *prussian blue.*

590. Prussian blue was discovered at Berlin, in Prussia, in the year 1704, and was then supposed to consist of an acid called *prussic* acid, united to iron;—by chemists prussian blue was for more than a hundred years considered as a *prussiate of iron.* • The discovery of cyanogen, by one of the French chemists, a few years since, has wholly altered the names of the substances with which it combines.

591. It is obtained from a substance now called the *cyanuret* or *cyanide* of mercury, (formerly prussiate of mercury,) which on being heated, in a small glass retort, gives off the cyanogen gas.

592. This is found to consist of 2 parts of carbon 12, and 1 part of nitrogen 14—thus the representative number of cyanogen is 26. Cyanogen, therefore, is not a simple element, though it forms combinations with other substances, much in the same manner as our chemical alphabet, oxygen, nitrogen, &c. It combines with oxygen to form *cyanic* and *cyanous* acids, and another acid called *fulminic.**

Prussic acid—hydro-cyanic acid.

593. The acid which was obtained from prussian blue was at first called *prussic acid;*—as it is now known to be a com-

* From *fulminate,* to thunder; this acid forms explosive mixtures when combined with some of the metals.

---

588. What is bi-sulphuretted hydrogen?
589. Why is cyanogen thus named?
590. What was Prussian blue, when first discovered, supposed to consist of?
591. How is cyanogen obtained?
592. Is cyanogen a simple substance?
593. What is the scientific name for prussic acid?

bination of hydrogen and cyanogen, its scientific name is *hydro-cyanic acid.*)

594. (This is an extremely poisonous substance; it kills small animals instantly—a single drop of it falling upon the arm of a German chemist, is said to have destroyed his life. Silliman relates that a medicinal preparation of this acid, which he had received from Paris, happening to get spilled upon the floor, although it was immediately covered and removed, produced alarming effects upon those present, such as fainting, loss of pulse, &c. which continued for several days.

595. Prussic acid exists in some vegetables, as the leaves and blossoms of the peach, and the kernels of the fruit of the laurel and almond.

596. It is used in medicine, but much diluted. So powerful an agent as this, should never be used at all but by a person of science and experience.

597. Prussic acid, combined with iron, forms prussian blue, which is scientifically called *hydro-ferro cyanate of iron.**

598. Prussic acid is remarkable for its tendency to decomposition, as its elements seem so feebly united that they separate spontaneously. These elements, you will recollect, are three, nitrogen, carbon, and hydrogen.

599. No oxygen exists in this acid. It has neither an acid taste, nor does it turn blue vegetables red; but it is called an acid, because it combines with alkalies to form salts; these salts are termed *hydro-cyanates* or *prussiates.*

600. Cyanogen, you will recollect, is represented by the number 26,—one part of hydrogen being added, gives 27 as the representative number of hydro-cyanic or prussic acid.

601. Cyanogen is a substance about which much might be said, but in a Chemistry for Beginners it is not to be expected that the different subjects named will be thoroughly investi-

* *Hydro* from hydrogen, *ferro* from the Latin *ferrum*, iron. For a particular account of the discovery of prussian blue, and the manner of obtaining it, see Dictionary of Chemistry, p. 122.

594. What are the properties of this acid?
595. Does it exist in nature?
596. What is said of its use in medicine?
597. What is the scientific name of prussian blue?
598. What are the elements which form prussic acid?—Are they easily separated?
599. Why is this substance called an acid?
600. What is the representative number of prussic acid?
601. What do we find in pursuing our chemical researches, with respect to the creations of God?

gated. It is the object of this book to give young persons a taste for the science, so that they can understand more extensive works, and especially to direct their attention towards the Great Volume of Nature, of which God is the Author. We find, in pursuing our researches in Chemistry, how He has distributed around us the most deadly elements, as if to show that while He holds in his hand powers that would instantly destroy us, He has been pleased so to arrange and temper them, as to render them harmless or conducive to our service and comfort.

602. We have, in the progress of our work, concluded our examination of the *imponderable* elements, of all the *non-metallic*, ponderable elements; we shall, in our next chapter, commence with a new class of simple substances.

CHAPTER XIX.

Metalloids. Alkaline Metals.

ALKALINE METALS,—*Potassium, Sodium, Calcium, &c.*

603. WE shall now examine a class of elements called *metalloids ;*—the termination *oids* is from the Greek, and signifies like, or similar to. (The word *metalloids* means *similar to metals.*)

604. The metalliods are usually classed among the metals, but they differ from them in their greater *affinity for oxygen ;* this circumstance renders it difficult either to obtain or preserve them in a state of purity; they differ greatly from the metals in their *specific gravity.* It is but recently that they have been known to exist; the substances from which they are obtained, were considered simple, until late discoveries proved them to be compound.

605. Potash, soda, and lime were formerly considered as pure alkalies, but they are now known to be *oxides of metals.*

POTASH.
Combination of Potassium and Oxygen.

606. The potash of commerce is obtained by evaporating the ley of wood ashes, and that of other vegetables. It was

602. What subjects have now been considered?
603. What is understood by the term metalloids?
604. How do the metalloids differ from the proper metals?
605. What are potash, soda, and lime?

formerly called *vegetable alkali*. The name potash was given because the ley was boiled down in pots.

607. Potash was known to the ancients. The Romans in the days of Julius Cæsar, are said to have used soap made of ashes and tallow; and at Pompeii, which was buried by the eruption of Mount Vesuvius, 79 years after Christ, a soap-boiler's shop has been discovered, which contained soap that appeared to be of the same nature as our common soap, and which, although it must have been made more than seventeen hundred years, was in a state of perfect preservation.

608. The ley that is obtained from the common wood ashes, and used in families for making soap, is a very impure solution of potash; as it usually contains more or less *carbonic acid*, *quicklime* is thrown into it, to which the acid unites, forming a *carbonate of lime*, and leaving the potash to act upon the grease.

609. Potash, in its purest state, is not an *element*, but an *oxide* of a metal called *potassium*.

610. Sir Humphrey Davy, in 1807, discovered the compound nature of potash. He subjected this alkali to the action of a powerful galvanic battery; it melted, *oxygen appeared at the positive pole, and some metallic globules at the negative pole.*

The figure represents a galvanic battery; A is the wooden trough with partitions, the spaces between which, are filled with weak brine, or with a weak solution of sulphuric, or some other acid. The plates B, which are alternately of zinc and copper, being shut down into the cells of the trough A, galvanic action commences, or, in other words, opposite electricities are disengaged. Z being connected with a zinc plate, represents the zinc, or *positive pole*, and C being connected with a copper plate, repre-

606. How is potash obtained? and why is it so called?
607. Has it been long known and used?
608. Why is lime used in making soap?
609. Is potash an element, or a compound?
610. How did Sir Humphrey Davy discover the compound nature of potash?
14*

sents the copper, or negative pole. The substance to be acted upon is placed in contact with the two poles;—if it is a
compound body, its elements will go to the different poles.
As in the *oxide* of a metal, the *oxygen* will always go to the
positive pole, and the *metal* to the *negative*. We will now
suppose Sir Humphrey Davy attempting to learn the nature
of potash—he brings a piece of dry, solid potash, places it
upon a plate of platina within the galvanic circle (P)—the
potash begins to melt, and soon vanishes, while oxygen appears at the positive pole Z, and little metallic drops at the
negative pole C. When he saw this, the philosopher knew
that he had made a grand discovery, which would greatly
change the science of Chemistry, and be followed by many
other discoveries.

611. This indeed was the case, for as soon as other chemists knew of Davy's discovery, they began to make new experiments; and it was but a short time before several alkalies
hitherto considered as elements, were proved to be compounds, among these were soda and lime.

612. Potassium has such an affinity for oxygen, that in the
air or in water, it combines with it; for this reason, it is
preserved by chemists, in an oily substance, called *naptha*.
It is on account of this affinity for oxygen, that potassium is
found highly useful in decomposing other substances, by
combining with their oxygen.

613. The union of potassium with oxygen, forms potash;
thus the compound nature of this substance is proved by synthesis as well as analysis.

614. Potash is an *oxide* of potassium. Pearlash is a *carbonate of potash*. Saltpetre is a *nitrate of potash.*

615. Pure potash dissolved in water is a *hydrate of potash.*

616. Potassium does not exist in nature, except in a state
of combination; this you will at once perceive must be the
case, as it takes oxygen from both air and water, and becomes
potash.

617. Potash is a powerful alkali, and therefore has a strong
tendency to unite with acids; the effect of this union is a
neutral salt, which exhibits neither acid nor alkaline proper-

611. What effect had Davy's discovery upon the science?
612. Why cannot potassium be preserved in water, or in the open air?
613. What substance is formed by the union of potassium with oxygen?
614. What are the chemical terms for potash, pearlash, and saltpetre?
615. What is a hydrate of potash?
616. Does potassium exist pure in nature?
617. What is the effect of the union of potash with acids? and how may
a knowledge of this effect be turned to an economical purpose?

ties. If the colour of a carpet or a garment is changed by an acid, a solution of potash, by neutralizing the acid, would remove the stain. Pearlash is better for this purpose, as pure potash is very caustic, and has such an affinity for animal substances as to destroy them. Woollen cloths are made of an animal substance.

618. Besides its use in making soap, potash is employed in the manufacture of glass, by melting it with sand; under the form of pearlash, it is much used by the housekeeper to make gingerbread and other cakes light; it is often called *sal-aratus*.

619. Potassium is soft like wax, and has a beautiful metallic lustre, but it is immediately covered with a coat of potash, if exposed to the air; if thrown upon water, it floats and burns on its surface, so rapidly does it unite with oxyen.

620. The specific gravity of potash is 1.700, that of potassium 0.805, or less than water.

621. The weight of potassium compared with hydrogen is 40; potash consists of 1 atom of potassium, and 1 of oxygen, 8; ts *chemical equivalent* is 48.

SODA.

(*Compound of Sodium and Oxygen.*)

622. You will readily comprehend, from what has been said respecting the nature of potash, that *soda*, another powerful alkali, is also a *compound substance*. It is the *oxide of sodium*.

623. The soda in common use is not, however, the pure oxide of sodium, but a *carbonate of soda.* It was formerly called *barilla*.

624. By an Arabian chemist of the ninth century, soda was described, but considered the same substance as potash. The difference between them is, in many respects, great. (Soda is obtained by the burning of *salt water plants ;* the ashes are leached, and the ley is then evaporated. The *attraction of soda for acids is less than* that of potash; the salts of soda are decomposed by potash, which attracts from them their

---

618. What are some of the uses to which potash is applied ?
619. What are some of the other properties of potassium ?
620. What is the specific gravity of potash and potassium ?
621. What is the weight of an atom of potassium, and the representative number of potash ?
622. What is soda?
623. What is the soda in common use?
624. How do soda and potash differ ? and in what respects are they similar?

acids. Soda forms with oil hard soap; potash forms soft soap.
Soda is used in the manufacture of glass, and is for this purpose preferred to potash. Both the carbonate of soda and that
of potash are used in weak solutions, to correct acidity of the
stomach. Potash is found in the mineral kingdom; as in felspar, one of the constituents of some of the primitive rocks,
it composes 10 parts in 100. Soda is the basis of common
salt, and therefore extensively diffused throughout the mineral kingdom in beds, and even mountains of salt, and in the
waters of the ocean, and salt lakes and springs.)

625. Common salt was long known among chemists as *muriate of soda;* but late discoveries of the existence of chlorine
and of the metallic bases of the alkalies, have changed its
name to *chloride of sodium,* it being considered as a compound
of *chlorine* and *sodium.* *Sulphuric acid* united to *soda* forms
sulphate of soda, commonly called Glauber's salts.)

626. *Sodium,* the *element* which forms the base of soda, is
obtained by means of galvanic decomposition; it may also be
obtained by heating in a gunbarrel with iron filings, which
take up the oxygen, and the melted sodium flows down in a
liquid state. Potassium may also be obtained by this latter
mode, which was first practised by two distinguished French
chemists, Gay-Lussac and Thenard. In many of its properties, sodium resembles potassium.)

627. The weight of sodium compared with hydrogen is 24;
combined with 1 atom of oxygen, 8, it forms the *oxide of sodium or soda,* whose chemical equivalent is 32.

LIME.

Combination of Calcium and Oxygen.

628. Lime was known to the ancients, though, probably, not
so early as the attempt to build the tower of Babel, for it is
said in Scripture, that they had "bricks for stone, and *slime*
for mortar." This slime was a substance dug from pits in
the earth; it contained an oily, adhesive substance, called bit-
umen, the same with which Noah coated the ark, and the
mother of Moses lined the little basket in which the child was
exposed on the banks of the Nile.

629. Lime was formerly called *calcareous* earth. Its Latin
name, *calx,* is derived from the Arabian word *kalah,* to burn,

625. What is said of common salt, and Glauber's salts?
626. How is sodium obtained? and what metal does it resemble?
627. What is the chemical equivalent of soda?
628. Was lime known to the ancients?
629. What was lime formerly called?

from this comes *calcine*, which signifies to burn; thus, any mineral which has been subjected to a high degree of heat is said to be *calcined*.

630. Lime is not a simple substance, but the *oxide* of a metal called *calcium*.

631. Lime is never found in nature free from combination, but always united with an acid, most frequently the carbonic. The limestone so common in marble quarries, limestone rocks, and chalk hills (as in England,) is all *carbonate of lime*.

632. Chemists who wish to prepare pure lime for experiments, put some pieces of white marble into a retort, and then heat it to a red heat; a gas is driven out, which, when collected, is found to be carbonic acid—when the gas ceases to issue from the retort, the marble, if examined, will be found greatly changed—before, acids poured upon it would cause an effervescence; now, acids have no effect upon it. Its taste is very bitter and caustic. This substance is called *quicklime*, and sometimes *alkaline earth*.

633. For commerce, quicklime is obtained by heating limestone in large kilns. The lime, thus manufactured, is used for whitewashing, for mortar, and various other purposes.

634. It is probable that most who study this book, have observed the process which is called slaking lime. (When whitewashing is to be done, the quicklime is put into a tub or pail, and water gradually poured upon it.) It absorbs a great deal of water; about 700 times its own weight. The lime will not, at first, appear moistened by the water, because it absorbs it so rapidly; a hissing noise is heard, and soon the lime begins to fall to pieces. So great is the quantity of heat given off in this process, that tinder may be set on fire.) This heat is caused by the loss of caloric, which passes off in consequence of *a liquid*, viz. water, becoming a solid. (See section 226.) On continuing to add water to the lime, it forms a thick, liquid mixture, suitable for laying on walls with a brush.

635. Lime united to water is called a *hydrate*; so great is its affinity for water, that if it stands for a short time exposed to the atmosphere, it attracts moisture from it and slakes itself, or becomes a *hydrate of lime*.

636. Lime is not easily fused or melted; but it greatly pro-

---

630. Is lime a simple substance?
631. Is it found pure in nature?
632. How is pure lime prepared?
633. How is the lime of commerce obtained?
634. Describe the process of slaking lime?
635. What is a hydrate of lime?

motes the melting of other substances, and on this account is
called a *flux*. Clay which contains lime cannot be used for
pottery, because the vessels made of clay must be baked, and
the lime would cause them to melt while they were exposed
to the necessary heat.

637. The *carbonate* of lime is marble, The *sulphate* of
lime is plaster of Paris, or gypsum. The *phosphate* of lime
exists in animal bones. The uses of lime in its various combinations, and in a pure state, are many and important in building, statuary, manufactures, agriculture, and medicine.

638. *Calcium*, the metallic base of lime, was discovered by
Berzelius of Sweden, in 1808, the year after the discovery of
the bases of potash and soda by Davy. The weight of calcium is stated as 20, this being united to one atom of oxygen,
8, forms lime, or the *oxide of calcium*, the *chemical equivalent*
of which is 28.

639. We have now considered three of the most important
alkaline metals, viz. *potassium*, *sodium*, and *calcium*; the
others are *lithium*, *barium*, and *strontium*.

Lithium, (from lithos, a stone.)

640. Lithium is the newly discovered metallic base of *lithia*,
an alkali found in a mineral called *petalite*, also in the *tourmaline mica*, and some other minerals. Lithium is a metal of
a white colour, resembling sodium in its properties, especially
in being the base of an alkali. Lithia is the *oxide* of *lithium*; it
is composed of 1 atom of the latter, which is called 10, to 1 of
oxygen, which equals 8; its chemical equivalent is therefore
18. There are various salts of lithia, as the *nitrate*, sulphate,
phosphate, &c.

Barium.

641. Barium is the metal of a mineral called *barytes* or *ba-
ryta*, (from the Greek, *barus*, heavy;) it is found in many
places in the United States. As barytes combines with acids
to form salts, is very caustic to the taste, and gives the alkaline
test with different colours, it is very properly classed among
the alkalies. Barium is very little known. It is much heavier

636. Is lime easily fused?
637. What are some of the combinations of lime? and what are their common names?
638. What can you say of calcium?
639. Which are the most important alkaline metals? and what others remain to be considered?
640. What is said of lithium?
641. Describe barium.

than the other' alkaline metals, is of a dark gray colour, with little lustre. It readily attracts oxygen from the air, thus forming a white powder, which is barytes, or *oxide of barium.* The specific gravity of barytes is 4, that is, it is four times heavier than its own bulk of water. It has a strong affinity for water, and slakes in this liquid in the same manner as quicklime, but with a more intense heat. The result of this process is a *hydrate* of *barytes.* One atom of barium, 70, united to one of oxygen, 8, makes the chemical equivalent of the oxide of barium (or barytes) 78.

642. The *sulphate of barytes* is called *Heavy Spar.* It is common in the mines of England, in the lead mines of the United States, and in various situations. The chemical equivalent for the sulphate of barytes is 118—for it contains one portion of sulphuric acid, whose equivalent is 40, united to one equivalent of barytes, which is 78; and 40+to 78=118.

Strontium.

643. Strontium is the metallic base which forms, by its union with oxygen, an alkaline mineral, called *strontia;* this received its name from Strontian, in Scotland, where it was first discovered in a lead mine. Strontia gives a blood-red colour to burning alcohol; for this purpose it is sometimes used to give a peculiar effect to fire in theatrical representations. This mineral exists on Strontian island in lake Erie, in the state of a *sulphate.* The base of strontia or strontium, was discovered in the same manner as that of the other alka--line metals, and about the same time.

CHAPTER XX.

Metalloids, or Earthy Metals.

644. We have, in the last chapter, considered certain substances which, before the late discoveries of Davy and some other chemists, were called simple *alkalies;* but are now known to be compound, consisting of a metallic base united to oxygen; these bases are called *alkaline* metals.

645. There is another class of minerals which were called

---

642. What is said of the sulphate of barytes?
643. Describe strontium.
644. What is said of the substances considered in the last chapter?
645. What is said of the minerals called *earths?*

earths, and considered as *elementary substances ; these are now regarded as compounds*, consisting of *oxygen* united to metals called *earthy metals.* Their oxides are white, and of an earthy appearance, and do not generally exhibit strong alkaline properties.

MAGNESIA.

Compound of Magnesium and Oxygen.

646. The common magnesia, which is used for medicine, is an *oxide of magnesium ;* it is a white, soft powder, without odour or taste. This substance is very common in nature. It usually exists as a carbonate of magnesia, and is obtained pure for medicine by heating it, until the carbonic acid is driven off; it is then called *calcined magnesia*, and is sold in the form of a loose powder—the carbonate of magnesia is sold in little square cakes.

The atom of magnesia is reckoned as - - 12
That of oxygen being - - - - 8
———
The equivalent of the oxide of magnesium is - 20

Magnesia forms a part of the clay used for porcelain; it is one of the constituents of rocks, especially soapstone, or, as they are called in geology, *talcose rocks.* Soapstone, which is known in mineralogy as *steatite*, is remarkable for its property of resisting fire; this is owing to the magnesia it contains, a substance, which, of all others, the chemist finds it most difficult to fuse. Magnesia is generally obtained from the *sulphate of magnesia.*

SILEX.

Compound of Silicon and Oxygen.

647. Silex exists in almost all stones and earth; it is the gritty part of them: it is abundant in quartz and flint.

648. Silex has been known from the earliest times. By the Arabians it was called *Selag;* from this was derived the name *silex.* The ancient chemists called it *vitrifiable earth,* because it was melted to make glass. Afterwards it was named silex, but is now known as the *oxide of silicon ;* it being a compound of *oxygen* and *silicon.*

649. Mixed with potash, or some other alkali, sand (which

646. What is said of magnesia?
647. What is said of silex?
648. What was silex formerly called? and what is its name in Chemistry?
649. What is said of glass-making?

is mostly silex) is melted to form glass;—the dark-coloured glass, such as you see in common junk bottles, is made from impure sand, mixed with some oxide of iron; the finest and clearest glass is made with pure, white sand. The ancients understood the process of making glass. Glass beads were found upon the mummies in the catacombs of Egypt, supposed to have been placed there 1600 years before Christil. But glass, as an article of common use, was not known until the thirteenth century; about this time some of the nobles of Europe began to have glass windows in their houses. The articles which are sold by jewellers as an imitation of precious stones, and called *paste*, are composed of very fine glass, coloured by the *oxides of metals*—thus we have green, in imitation of the emerald; violet, of the amethyst; red, of the ruby; and limpid, of the diamond; the latter, however, is colourless.

650. Silicon, though classed among the metals, is thought by some chemists to be improperly placed here. Berzelius of Sweden, who has made many experiments upon it, asserts, that it bears no resemblance to any of the metals, but is, in some respects, like carbon and other of the combustible non-metallic substances.

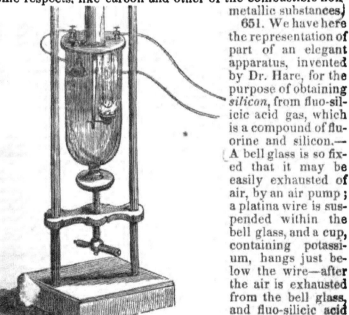

651. We have here the representation of part of an elegant apparatus, invented by Dr. Hare, for the purpose of obtaining *silicon*, from fluo-silicic acid gas, which is a compound of fluorine and silicon.— A bell glass is so fixed that it may be easily exhausted of air, by an air pump; a platina wire is suspended within the bell glass, and a cup, containing potassium, hangs just below the wire—after the air is exhausted from the bell glass, and fluo-silicic acid

650. What does Berzelius assert respecting silicon?

gas admitted, the platina wire is ignited by an electric spark communicated to a part of the wire extending without the bell glass, this inflames the potassium, which burns and decomposes the fluo-silicic acid, giving rise to a peculiar, deep red flame, and chocolate-coloured fumes, which condense into flakes, resembling (except in colour) a miniature snowstorm. On washing the substance which is collected after this combustion, pure *silicon*, which is insoluble, is obtained, the residue is chiefly *fluoride of potassium*.

ALUMINE.

Compound of Aluminum and Oxygen.

652. The name *alumine*, is from *alum,* which has this earth for its base. (Alumine is very abundant in nature, existing in clay, and giving it that peculiar quality necessary for the manufacture of porcelain.) In all manufactures of bricks and pottery, whether of the coarser kind, as the gardener's flowerpots, or of the most beautiful porcelain vases, alumine and silex are essential constituents. The rudest nations know something of the art of making vessels of wet sand and clay, hardened by baking. Felspar, one of the minerals which is of important use in making fine porcelain ware, consists, in 100 parts, of silex 65, alumine 25, and potash 10. All these constituents are important in the manufacture of porcelain ware.

653. Alumine is obtained by chemists for experiments, by the decomposition of alum, (*sulphate of alumine.*) To a solution of alum, carbonate of potash is added; a carbonate of alumine is precipitated. The carbonic acid is driven off by heat, and pure alumine obtained.

654. *Aluminum,* (the metal of alumine, burns readily in the air; the produce of this combustion is the *oxide of aluminum,* or alumine. The metal is obtained by the analysis of the earth, *alumine.* The combining weight of

$$aluminum \text{ being} \quad 10$$
$$oxygen \quad 8$$

The chemical equivalent of *oxide of alumine* is $= 18+$

651. Describe Dr. Hare's method of obtaining silicon from fluo-silicic acid.
652. Of what is alumine the base? Is it abundant? and for what is the clay which contains it useful?
653. How is it obtained?
654. What is said of aluminum? and what is the weight of its oxide?

YTTRIUM, GLUCINUM, ZIRCONIUM, AND THORIUM.

655. Besides the earthy metals magnesium and aluminum, there are four others, *yttrium,* the base of an earth called yttria, *glucinum,* the base of an earth called glucina, *zirconium,* the base of the earth zirconia, and *thorium* the base of the earth thorina; but as these metals are little known, and the earths in which they exist unimportant, we shall not dwell upon them. We name them because they are to be found in the alphabet of Chemistry, and are therefore objects of interest. Their discovery has severally been registered by men of science, and the names of their discoverers are now connected with the history of science.

656. There may be among the young persons who are gaining from this book the first elements of Chemistry, some who are destined to make discoveries even greater than any preceding chemist has yet done. There was a time when the terms used in Chemistry sounded as new and strange to the ears of the most celebrated chemists as they now do to yours. These men became learned and eminent only by long and persevering study. Following what, at first, was a feeble light, they gradually attained clearer views, until they became themselves lights of their age; and are there not among the youth of our country, those, who, inspired by the example of our own scientific men, and those of foreign countries, will bestir themselves, that they may become worthy to succeed those whose places will ere long be vacant, that they may attain strength to gird themselves with their armour, when they shall lay it aside it for ever?

Hopes like these encourage the author who labours to prepare works of instruction for the young. This is not a field for honour and fame; but as the parent toils cheerfully to elevate his children beyond his own sphere, so we labour, cheered with the thought that our humble efforts may be the means of raising up among the children of our country those who are, hereafter, to add to her glory and prosperity.

---

655. What is said of some other substances which belong to the class we have been considering?

656. What remarks close this chapter?

CHAPTER XXI.

Metals. Metalloids. Proper Metals.

657. Even young children know something of the character of metals. They can tell their silver sixpence from a copper cent; and they understand that silver is more valuable than copper, and that gold is more valuable than silver: they know that the pot is made of iron, the andirons of brass, and the shovel and tongs of steel. There are, probably, few who study this book that could not readily answer, if asked, which is the most useful metal. They know that *iron* is used for almost every kind of machinery, for stoves, cooking vessels, and other domestic utensils, as the plough, the hoe, and spade.

658. Metals are not usually found pure in nature, but in the state of *ores*, that is, connected with minerals of various kinds, from which they are separated by different means, chiefly by a process called *roasting*—the metal being more easily melted than the earths or stones to which it is united, runs down in a liquid state, and is thus separated from them. In some cases, as in the *sulphurets* of metals, the sulphur is driven off, or *sublimed* by heat, and the metal remains. The art of refining metals is of great importance, and requires much care and experience as well as science; it is called *metallurgy*.

659. The knowledge of metals is of great antiquity. Tubal Cain, the grandson of Methuselah, was an artificer in brass and iron.

660. 1. The metals possess a peculiar brilliancy called *metallic lustre.*

2. They are *opaque*, that is, the rays of light do not pass through them.

3. They *fuse*, or melt at different temperatures. Mercury is liquid at the ordinary temperature, and even below zero. The metal called platinum can be melted only when exposed to a stream of oxygen gas, directed upon burning charcoal. Mercury is therefore the most fusible of the metals, and platinum the least so.

4. The metals are good *conducters of heat and electricity.*

657. What is said of the general knowledge which all have of metals?
658. What is said of refining metals?
659. Were metals known to the ancients?
660. Mention some of the most important properties of metals.

5. Metals, when combined with other substances, always go to *the negative pole* of the galvanic battery.

6. They *reflect light* powerfully; this causes their metallic lustre.

7. The metals were all formerly considered as *heavier* than water; but potassium and sodium, were not then known—these metals are lighter than water. Platinum, one of the heaviest metals, is 23 times heavier than water.

8. Metals *burn* brilliantly, and with different coloured flames, when subjected to the action of galvanism.—Lime (*oxide of calcium*) can be volatilized, and become vapour by a very intense heat.

9. The *tenacity* of metals depends on their cohesive attraction; it is the power they possess of bearing weights. An iron wire, one tenth of an inch in diameter, will hold a weight of two pounds. Iron has more tenacity than any other metal.

10. Metals are said to be *ductile* when they can be drawn out into wire. Gold and platinum are most remarkable for this property.

11. *Malleable* refers to the property which metals have of being hammered or rolled into thin plates. Gold possesses this property in the highest degree.

12. The *colour* of metals is various, but they generally appear white, gray, red, or yellow.

661. The first rude attempts made in Chemistry, were in the fourth century, by a set of men called alchymists, who laboured with great patience and perseverance in making experiments to change the baser metals into gold.

662. Metals have a *strong affinity for oxygen*, though in very different degrees. Iron attracts it from the air; therefore it rusts easily, for the rust of a metal is caused by its union with oxygen,—rust is, therefore, an *oxide*. Gold and silver do not attract oxygen from the air or water; therefore they do not rust easily. Gold, for this reason, is used for filling cavities in the teeth—even the acid substances which are taken into the mouth with food, in various ways, do not oxidate gold. Silver oxidates more easily, and therefore when used in the same way, soon becomes discoloured and tarnished.

663. The oxides of metals *unite with acids and form salts*, thus the *sulphate of soda* is a salt, formed by the union of *sulphuric acid* with *soda*, which is the *oxide of sodium*.

661. By whom were the first rude attempts in Chemistry made?
662. What is said of the affinity of metals for oxygen?
663. What substances are formed by the union of the oxides of metals with acids?

664. (Metals *unite with each other*,) and form a class of bodies called *alloys*. These furnish some of the most important materials for the use of mankind. Brass is a compound of copper and zinc; pewter of tin and lead; and bell metal of copper and tin.

665. (Mercury combines with other metals) and forms *amalgams*.*

666. The ancients were acquainted with but *seven* metals, viz : gold, silver, copper, mercury, iron, tin, and lead. These are still the most important to mankind, notwithstanding many others have been since discovered.

CLASSIFICATION.

Metallic substances may be divided into two great classes, *Metalloids* and *Metals*.

CLASS I.—METALLOIDS.

667. Metalloids have properties in common with the true metals, but they differ from them in being much lighter, and in having so great an affinity for oxygen that they absorb it from the atmosphere in a dry state.

This class we divide into two orders.

ORDER 1.—*Alkaline metals*, or metalloids, whose oxides are *alkalies*.

Potassium,	Lithium,
Sodium,	Barium,
Calcium,	Strontium.

* With silver, mercury readily unites, to form an amalgam. Two little girls, wishing to do some meritorious act in the absence of their mother, attempted to brighten her silver spoons by rubbing them over with quicksilver, (mercury.) At first they were delighted with their success, but they found, that on coming in contact with other substances, the spoons tarnished, and looked dark-coloured like old pewter—the little girls were then greatly troubled, believing they had spoiled the spoons. When their mother returned, they very sorrowfully informed her of the accident; she told them that the mercury had formed an amalgam with the silver, but that by heating the spoons it would be driven off, and the silver restored; she advised them, however, not to attempt making experiments upon articles of so valuable a nature, until they had more experience.

---

664. What are alloys?
665. What are amalgams?
666. What metals were known to the ancients?
667. Describe the first class of metallic substances, and the orders it contains.

ORDER 2.—*Earthy* metals, or metalloids, whose oxides are *earths:*

Magnesium,	Glucinum,
Silicon,	Zirconium,
Aluminum,	Thorium.
Yttrium,	

CLASS II.—THE PROPER METALS.

668. This class we divide into two orders.

ORDER 1.--*Metals* which are of important use to man, either in *agriculture,* for *domestic purposes,* or in the *arts.*

Platinum,	Zinc,
Gold,	Bismuth,
Silver,	Antimony,
Mercury,	Cobalt,
Copper,	Arsenic,
Iron,	Manganese,
Lead,	Chromium.
Tin,	

ORDER 2.—*Metals* which are of little use in the arts.

Palladium,	Uranium,
Rhodium,	Tellurium,
Iridium,	Titanium,
Osmium,	Molybdenum,
Nickel,	Columbium,
Cadmium,	Cerium,
Tungsten,	Vanadium.

669. Of the Metalloids, we have already treated; these we found to be of little importance, except as exhibiting the compound nature of substances until lately considered simple—we therefore paid more attention to the *oxides* of these metals, than to the metals themselves. Potash, soda, and lime are known to almost every one, while potassium, sodium, and calcium, their metallic bases, are scarcely known beyond the chemist's laboratory. Potassium is indeed of great use to the chemist, in enabling him to decompose other substances, a fact which has been already mentioned. The metals of the second class we shall now briefly notice.

---

668. How are the proper metals divided?
669. What general remarks are made respecting the metalloids?

ORDER 1.

670. *Platinum,* (was so called by the Spaniards, from *plata,* which, in their language, signifies silver.) The largest mass of silver which has been found does not exceed a pigeon's egg, in size. This metal is found in the vicinity of the Rio de la Plata, in South America, and with it are found the four new metals, *palladium, iridium, osmium,* and *rhodium.* Pure platina is the heaviest of all known substances. Its specific gravity is 22. On account of its hardness, infusibility, and difficulty of being acted on by most substances, it is of great value for making vessels to be used in chemical experiments.

671. *Gold* was called by the ancients the "king of metals." Its *specific gravity* is 19; it is the heaviest of all known substances except platina. No substance is capable of such *extension* as gold. One ounce of gold is sufficient to cover a wire that may be extended more than 1300 miles. The thin sheets of gold, called goldleaf, are the lightest of all solid substances. Gold melts at 1300° of Fahrenheit's thermometer, which is above red heat. It does not *oxidize* by exposure to the air, heat, or moisture, and may therefore be preserved for ages without change. When exposed to the action of the galvanic battery, goldleaf burns brilliantly with a red light, and an *oxide of gold* is the product of the combustion. Goldleaf introduced into chlorine gas unites and burns, forming *chloride of gold.* There is but one acid which can dissolve gold; this is the *nitro-muriatic,* or a mixture of nitric and muriatic acids. The gold coin of the United States is alloyed with about one part in twelve, of a mixture of copper and silver. The chemical equivalent of gold is 200.

672. *Silver.* (The alchymists called silver *Luna,* or the moon, and they also called gold *Sol,* or the sun. Silver and gold were called by the ancients *precious metals,* and also *noble metals.* It is unnecessary to tell those who study this book what the colour of silver is, and whether it exists in the state of a liquid or a solid. Our silver dollars, half-dollars, and the smaller pieces of silver coin, are known to all—silver spoons, which were formerly only used by the rich, are now very common. They seem indeed to be almost an article of necessity, since silver is little acted upon by acids, or other substances which corrode iron and blacken pewter. From the fact that silver is little affected by acids, you will perceive that

670. What is said of platinum?
671. What is said of gold?   672 What is said of silver?

it has not much affinity for oxygen. It resembles gold in many of its properties. Nitric acid dissolves silver, forming *nitrate* of silver, commonly called *lunar caustic; lunar* from the ancient name of silver, and *caustic* from its power to act upon and decompose animal substances. The silver of the nitrate of silver is separated from its combination with nitric acid by many other metals—if a piece of bright copper is immersed in a solution of nitrate of silver, it will be instantly covered with beautiful white crystals of silver. The chemical equivalent of silver is 110.

673. *Mercury* is commonly called *quicksilver;* the alchymists gave it this name because they supposed it to be silver in a fluid state, quickened by some substance which they hoped to expel, that they might obtain from it solid silver. The name is from the planet Mercury, which the alchymists supposed had a peculiar influence upon the metal. This is the only metal which is fluid at the common temperature. You can see it in thermometers and barometers, and on the backs of looking-glasses, where it is laid over tin-foil, making with it an amalgam. At 40° below zero, a cold which is produced by mixing nitric acid and snow, mercury becomes solid, and may be cut with a knife, and flattened by a hammer. At 656° of heat mercury can be made to boil, and is converted into a vapour. If a lump of mercury be dropped into a cup of warm water, the solid metal will immediately become fluid, while the fluid water will become solid. At the poles it is probable that mercury would always be solid. With oxygen, mercury forms compounds, which are of great importance in medicine. An article in great use by physicians, called the *blue pill,* is an oxide of mercury; another medicinal article called *red precipitate,* is an oxide with a higher portion of oxygen. Chlorine forms with mercury some important combinations which will be mentioned under the head of *chlorides.* The fine scarlet colour, called vermilion, is the *red sulphuret of mercury.* Mercury is found in a pure, or native state, and as an ore, in various parts of Europe and South America. This is one of the most useful metals; its importance in science is very great, as without the thermometer no precise principles could be established with respect to heat and its effect on substances; and without the barometer no certain observations could be made of the pressure of the atmosphere. Medicine owes to mercury some of its most powerful and effective agents.

674. *Copper* was first known in the island of Cyprus, from

673. Give some account of mercury. 674. What is said of copper?

whence came the Latin name *cuprum*, and the English name copper. The brass of the ancients is, by some, supposed to have been an alloy of copper and tin, but they seemed to have used the words copper and brass as synonymous. The colour, and other external properties of copper, it is unnecessary to enumerate, since in the form of coin, as cents, and in various articles in common use, it is known to all. Copper is not, affected by the dry atmosphere, but when in contact with damp air, its surface becomes covered with the *oxide of copper*. It is *combustible*, and burns under the compound blowpipe with great brilliancy, throwing off a green-coloured flame. Copper alloyed with zinc forms *brass ;* with a different proportion of zinc it forms *pinchbeck*. Copper forms various alloys with tin, as *bell-metal, cannon-metal*, bronze, and a coating for the inside of copper vessels. Copper is found in a pure state, in the state of an *oxide, a sulphuret, a sulphate, and a carbonate.* It should be known by all housekeepers that the compounds of copper are highly poisonous. Clean and bright copper vessels may be used with safety for scalding vinegar for pickles, for making sweetmeats, and in other culinary operations; but these substances should not be allowed to stand in them. For instance, vinegar contains *acetic acid ;* if this stands, for any length of time, in a copper vessel, it corrodes it, forming an *acetate of copper*, a very poisonous substance, commonly called *verdigris.**

675. *Iron.* The affinity of this metal for oxygen is very great. You will recollect that iron filings decompose water by uniting with its oxygen, and that hydrogen gas being set free, is obtained in this manner. So great is the affinity of iron for oxygen, that even at the common temperature it decomposes water; thus if you leave water to stand a few days in an iron vessel, it will appear rusted ; iron rust is an *oxide of iron.* Even if left to stand dry for any length of time, iron will oxidate by attracting oxygen from the air. Iron is the most useful of metals, for which reason the Creator and Benefactor of man has caused it to exist in great profusion in every country. Our own country is very rich in iron ores.

* Ammonia affords a test to detect the presence of copper. A slight portion of ammonia will give a *blue* colour to a liquid holding copper in solution. The green sugar ornaments for cake are sometimes covered with salts of copper; when this is the case, by cutting through them with a clean knife blade, the copper *will adhere to the metal,* and show itself by a streak upon the knife.

New villages, in consequence of the discovery of iron ore, have recently sprung up in the wilderness, and the busy hum of industry is now heard, where silence and desolation lately reigned. Most mineral substances contain some iron. It is found in the state of an *oxide, a sulphate, sulphuret, carbonate,* &c.; but the *oxides* are the ores from which the metal is usually obtained. Iron combined with carbon forms *steel,* which is a *carburet* of iron; with a greater proportion of carbon, it forms *black lead, or plumbago.*

Iron, as you have already seen, burns brilliantly in oxygen gas. Even in the common air, as may be seen in the blacksmith's shop, a bar of iron heated to a white heat throws out brilliant sparks when withdrawn from the fire. Iron is a good conductor of heat and electricity; it is the basis of ink-powder.

676. *Lead* was by the ancients called Saturn: this deity, according to the fables of mythology, devoured his children; thus lead *absorbs,* or devours all the metals, except gold and silver. Lead is a soft metal of a bluish white colour; it is not very *ductile,* but very *malleable,* as it can be beaten into thin leaves. It melts easily. When black lead pencils, and sheets of ruled lines were less common than at present, plummets of lead were used for ruling paper. These were made by melting lead, and pouring it into moulds. Nitric acid easily dissolves lead, but sulphuric and muriatic acids have little effect upon it. It combines with oxygen in three proportions, forming a *protoxide, deutoxide,* and *peroxide.** Lead is sometimes found pure, but generally in combination with sulphur, forming a *sulphuret of lead,* called, in mineralogy, *galena.* This is very common, and when once known, is easily recognised by its fine metallic lustre.

677. A beautiful experiment may be made by suspending from the stopper of a decanter a small *piece of zinc* in a solution of the *acetate of lead;* if suffered to stand undisturbed a few days, a beautiful figure will be formed resembling a tree; this is called

* For an explanation of these terms, see *oxides.*

the *lead tree,* and forms a handsome and scientific ornament for a mantelpiece. The *zinc* attracts the *acetic acid* from the solution of acetate of lead, and the *lead* being precipitated from this combination, collects upon the zinc, branching forth in various directions. The salts of lead are mostly very poisonous.

678. *Tin.* On account of its shining appearance, tin was called Jupiter by the alchymists. Believing there was some intimate connexion between the planets and the metals, and that the number of each was equal, they thought each planet had its metal, and each metal its planet. We smile at what we conceive to be the ridiculous notions of men of former ages, but those who come after us may be as much amused with the folly of many of our opinions, as we are with those of our predecessors. Tin is very flexible; it dilates much by heat, and is among its best conductors. It attracts oxygen from the air less freely than some of the metals, of course it does not rust so easily. Tin burns brilliantly in the focus of the compound blowpipe, with a lively white flame; the result of the combustion is a white *oxide of tin.* Tin combines with but two simple combustibles, sulphur and phosphorus. An alloy of tin with zinc, and sometimes with other substances, forms pewter. Tin is not found in this country; the most important tin mines known are in Cornwall, England.

679. *Zinc.* This metal has a bluish white colour, and a strong metallic lustre; it is obtained from two ores, the *carbonate of zinc,* called *calamine,* and the *sulphuret of zinc,* called *zinc-blende.* All the zinc of commerce was formerly brought from China, as the secret of obtaining it from its ores was not known to Europeans. It is now manufactured in Europe in great quantities, and exists in many places in the United States. Zinc has a strong affinity for oxygen, and is, therefore, often used for obtaining hydrogen, by the decomposition of water; it is for the same reason used for the positive side of the galvanic battery. It is to this side that oxygen always goes. Zinc is very *combustible;* if a small quantity is put into a crucible, it may soon be heated by a common furnace, and made to boil; a little more heat causes it to burn; a light, white substance rises and floats about the room—this was formerly called *white nothing,* and *philosopher's wool.* It is the *oxide of zinc.*

680. *Bismuth* is a metal of a reddish white colour; it is very brittle and fusible. A preparation of bismuth forms the

678. Describe tin. 679. What is said of zinc? 680. Of bismuth?

pearl powder, which is used as a cosmetic, and becomes dark coloured by the vapour of sulphur, hydrogen, or phosphorus. A solution of the nitrate of bismuth forms a *sympathetic ink ;* letters written with it, although at first invisible, when exposed to sulphuretted hydrogen gas, become distinct and legible. Bismuth is not found abundantly ; one locality only is known in the United States, this is in Connecticut, where it is found in connexion with silver, galena, zinc-blende, and some other minerals.

681. *Antimony.* The name of this metal is said to be derived from *anti*, against, and *monakos*, a monk, it having been first applied to medicine by Basil Valentine, a Benedictine monk, who, using it injudiciously among the brethren of his order, killed many of them. It is of a greenish white colour, and very brittle; it is seldom found pure in nature. The *sulphuret* is the most abundant of its ores. It is a constituent of the metal of which printers' types are made. With tartaric acid (an acid obtained from the fermentation of grapes) and potash, antimony forms an important medicinal substance called *tartar emetic.*

682. *Cobalt* is found in connexion with ores of iron, copper, and arsenic, and is separated from them by subjecting the ores to a high heat. These ores were used in Europe, as early as the fifteenth century, for the purpose of colouring glass blue; but it was not until the last century that they were known to contain a peculiar metal. Solutions of cobalt form *sympathetic ink.* The nitrate of cobalt, when pure, is of a beautiful blue colour, or if iron is present, of a pea green; when much diluted, it is a pale rose or pink. Writing, with this solution, appears invisible on white paper when cold, but when held to the fire, it takes a blue or green tinge, and may be

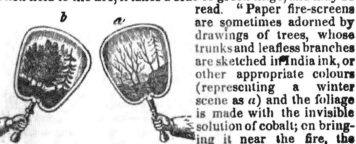

read. "Paper fire-screens are sometimes adorned by drawings of trees, whose trunks and leafless branches are sketched in India ink, or other appropriate colours (representing a winter scene as *a*) and the foliage is made with the invisible solution of cobalt; on bringing it near the fire, the

green leaves at once appear, (and spring returns," as *b*.*)
It is supposed that this effect is caused by the agency of oxygen, in some manner not well understood. Most of the cobalt
of commerce is obtained from a combination with arsenic,
called *arsenical cobalt*. In Saxony, this manufacture is very
extensive, and carried on by criminals who are condemned to
this labour for crimes, that by law deserve death. The fumes
of the arsenic, which is a deadly poison, render this business
destructive to the health of the miserable beings who are thus
cruelly punished. The children of luxury, when partaking
of their rich beverage from porcelain cups painted with the
beautiful blue of cobalt, think not of the dreadful sufferings
their fellow creatures have endured, in order to procure this
costly embellishment. An oxide of cobalt mixed with silex
forms a substance called *zaffre;* this, heated with sand and
potash, forms a beautiful blue glass, called *smalt;* this latter,
powdered very fine, is called *powder-blue*. This is said to be
more delicate than indigo for bluing muslins and laces. "The
name, cobalt, is said to be derived from *cobalus*, the supposed
demon of mines, who opposes the operations of the miners,
and this metal appearing at first mysterious and untractable,
was nick-named cobalt." It is found in Chatham in Connecticut, and Franconia in New Hampshire.

683. *Arsenic*. This metal is supposed to have derived its
name from an Arabic word, *arsanek*, signifying strong and
deadly qualities. Arsenic is found in connexion with cobalt,
from which it is separated by roasting. The arsenic being
volatile, vapourizes and condenses in receivers prepared for
that purpose. Arsenic may be detected by a strong smell of
onions or garlic, when thrown upon burning coals; in burning, it unites with oxygen and forms the *oxide of arsenic*, or
as some consider it, *arsenious* acid. With the alkalies, this
acid forms salts called *arsenites*. The *deutoxide of arsenic*
has a greater portion of oxygen; by some, it is considered as
arsenic acid; combined with alkalies, as potash and soda, it
forms salts called *arseniates*. The equivalent number of the
arsenic is 38. King's yellow, which is considerably used in
painting, both in water-colours and oil, is made of a *sulphuret
of arsenic*, called *orpiment*. People who make use of these
colours, ought to be very careful never to put paint brushes
into the mouth, as most of the colours are based upon poisonous substances.

* Silliman's Elements of Chemistry.

683. What is said of arsenic?

684. *Manganese.* The affinity of this metal for oxygen is such that it is never found in a pure metallic state, but always as an oxide. It is found in connexion with iron ore, which it resembles in colour, and other external properties. You will recollect that the *peroxide* of this metal, (that is, the oxide with the most oxygen,) gives off oxygen when heated to a red heat. (The equivalent of manganese is 28.) It is not of much use, except in decomposing other substances which furnish oxygen and chlorine gases. The rationale of the process by which chlorine is obtained through the agency of manganese is still disputed. We will state this process, and give that explanation of it which we think most reasonable. The *peroxide of manganese,* and *muriatic acid* (hydrochloric) are put into a vessel and exposed to heat; chlorine gas is then given off. It is supposed that the muriatic acid decomposes; that its hydrogen unites with the peroxide of manganese, and one part of the liberated chlorine combines with the manganese, while the other portion is disengaged; there is then in the process a formation of *water,* of the *chloride of manganese,* and a disengagement of *chlorine.** On account of the utility of manganese in disengaging chlorine from muriatic acid and common salt, it is indispensable in the bleaching processes of manufactories.

685. *Chromium.* The name of this metal is from the Greek *kroma,* colour, because it is remarkable for giving colour to its combinations. The metal is of no use in its pure state; it is generally found combined with oxygen. There are two *oxides* of chromium, the *protoxide,* which is green, and the *deutoxide,* which is brown; the *chromic acid,* which has a higher portion of oxygen, is scarlet. The compounds of this acid with bases are called *chromates;* these salts are all coloured.

The metal, chromium, was first obtained by the celebrated French chemist, Vauquelin, from the chromate of lead, a brilliant yellow substance, used as a paint under the name of *chrome yellow.* Chromium is the colouring matter of many minerals; the emerald is coloured green by its oxide, the ruby red by its acid. Chromate of iron is found in marble and serpentine, and in connexion with the oxide of iron is thought to produce the green and most other colours with which they are variegated.

---

* See Dictionary of Chemistry, page 159.

ORDER 2.

We shall do little more than name the metals of the 2d order of the class of proper metals, because they are of less importance than those of the first order.

The four following metals have been found in connexion with the ore of platinum.

686. 1. *Palladium* was discovered in 1803 by Dr. Wollaston. It is a very rare metal. It was named after the late discovered planet, Pallas. 2. *Rhodium* was discovered by Dr. Wollaston about the same time that he found palladium, and in the same metal. It has been combined with several of the metals, but it is too rare to be applied to any use. Its name is from the Greek, *rodon*, a rose, on account of the colour of its salts. 3. *Iridium*, a metal found in connexion with another called *osmium*, in the ore of platinum. The name (from Iris, the rainbow) is given in allusion to the changeable colour of some of its solutions. According to Berzelius, "solutions may, without the aid of foreign matter, be obtained with all the colours of the rainbow." 4. *Osmium*, from the Greek, *osme*, odour, is named in allusion to the peculiar smell of its oxide, which somewhat resembles chlorine. It is found only in platinum ore, either combined with other metals, or with iridium. The four metals we have just described, viz. palladium, rhodium, iridium, and osmium are called *platiniferous* minerals from the ore with which they are usually combined. The method of obtaining them from this combination is very complicated, and shows the great accuracy and delicacy of chemical analysis.

687. *Nickel* is found in connexion with the ore of cobalt; it also exists with iron in what are called *meteoric stones*,[*] (substances which occasionally fall to the earth from the surrounding atmosphere, and whose origin is unknown.) Nickel is a white metal, somewhat like silver in appearance. It is thought to possess magnetical attraction, a property which belongs to no other metals except iron and cobalt. It forms a green *oxide of nickel*, when heated in the air, or with oxy-

---

* Silliman observes that "large masses of meteoric iron, in Siberia, Peru, Louisiana, &c., have lain in the open air apparently from age to age without rusting, or only superficially." It is supposed that the nickel they contain prevents their rusting.

---

686. What four metals have been found in connexion with platinum ore, and what is said of these metals?
687. Describe nickel.

gen. Pure nickel is never found in nature; it is obtained from its ores by a complicated process. Although a highly valuable metal, it is too rare and costly to be applied to use in the arts.

688. *Cadmium* was first discovered in 1817, in an oxide of zinc. It is a white, brilliant metal resembling tin; it receives a high polish.) Though an interesting metal, it is not yet obtained in sufficient quantities to cause it to rank among the useful ones. It has not been found in this country, though it is thought that it may exist with zinc in the Missouri lead-mines.

689. *Tungsten.* The name of this metal signifies, in the Swedish language, *heavy stone.* It was first discovered in a Swedish mineral, called in mineralogy, *wolfram*, but known in Chemistry as the *tungstate of iron and manganese.* There is a combination of oxygen and tungsten, forming *tungstic acid;* this acid, with bases, forms *tungstates;* of these, there are some with alkaline, and some with metallic bases. The metal tungsten is said by Silliman to exist in Connecticut.

690. *Uranium,* was discovered in 1789, and named from the Greek, *ouranos,* the heavens. It was found in a mineral called *pechblend,* which is the *oxide of uranium.* It is obtained by calcining the ore or expelling the oxygen with heat. Combined with carbonic acid it forms *chalcolite,* or green mica.

691. *Tellurium* was named in 1789, by Klaproth, the discoverer of uranium, from *tellus,* the earth; thus following the example of the ancients, who named minerals from the planets. Tellurium is a brilliant metal; it burns with splendour in oxygen gas. Silliman thinks it exists in Connecticut in connexion with the ore of tungsten.

692. *Titanium* resembles bright copper in its colour and lustre; its crystals were at first mistaken for iron pyrites in England and Scotland. It is found in primitive rocks, and exists in many places in the United States.

693. *Molybdenum,* is so called from a Greek word signifying lead; this was long supposed to be the same substance as black lead, or plumbago. It does not exist pure in nature, but is found either as a *sulphuret of molybdenum* or a *molybdate of lead;* the latter substance is composed of *molybdic acid* and lead.

694. *Columbium* was first sent by Governor Winthrop of

---

688. What is said of cadmium? 689. Of tungsten? 690. Of uranium?
691. Of tellurium? 692. Of titanium? 693. Of molybdenum?

the Massachusetts colony, to Sir Hans Sloane, the founder of the British Museum. The name was given in honour of the discoverer of America. The metal is of a dark gray colour. It was formerly called *tantalium.*

695. *Cerium* was discovered in 1804, and afterwards investigated by Vauquelin. It is found in a mineral called *cerite,* which is the *oxide of cerium.* In some respects, the metal is said to resemble iron, though it is harder and whiter.

696. *Vanadium.* This is the most recently discovered metal. It was found in 1830, in connexion with iron ore, by a director of the school of Mines of Fahlun, in Sweden. This metal is said to resemble chromium, and therefore easily mistaken for it. Since its discovery, it has been found in the lead ore of Mexico. In this same ore, a number of years since, a professor of Chemistry asserted that he had found a new metal; but another chemist, to whom he submitted some specimens, said it was impure chromium. Combined with oxygen vanadium forms *vanadic acid,* and this, with bases, forms salts called *vanadiates.*

697. The division of metals into such *as are useful in the arts,* and *such as are little known and used,* seemed very proper, as there is, at present, a broad and plain distinction between them in this respect;—though it is very probable, that in the progress of science, means will be found for obtaining in plenty some of those rare metals which are now scarcely known but in name, and that these may, hereafter, become as common for useful and ornamental purposes as any which are now in use.

698. The attentive pupil has now learned the *Alphabet of Chemistry,** with some of the combinations of the elements to form compound substances. Thus as *b a* make the word *ba,* so do the elements oxygen and nitrogen form *air ;* oxygen and hydrogen, *water ;* oxygen and sulphur, *sulphuric acid,* &c. In some cases, three or more elements unite to form a compound, and again, compounds themselves, combine to form more complex compounds. From these elements are formed every thing, on, and around the earth, that we have any knowledge of; the rocky foundations of th earth, the air; the water, the vegetable creation, and the ani

* For the Alphabet of Chemistry, see section 303.

---

694. What is said of columbium ?   695. Of cerium ?   696. Of vanadium ?
697. What division of the metals seems very proper ?
698. What is the concluding remark ?

mal frame—every product of land or sea, of heaven and earth, so far as science has discovered, may be resolved into a few of these elements.

CHAPTER XXII.

Oxides. Chlorides. Salts.

BINARY COMPOUNDS,

Consisting of two elements.

699. WHEN any *two* elements are united, they form what is called a *binary compound,* (from the Greek *bis,* two.) They are of (three kinds:) 1. *acids ; oxides;* and 3. those which are *neither acids nor oxides.*

Acids.

700. Acids were long supposed to be produced by oxygen only, as its name signifies the producer of acids ; but chlorine and the other supporters of combustion, together with hydrogen, have been found to form acids.*

701. *Nitric acid* is composed of *nitrogen* and *oxygen.*
    Sulphuric acid   "   *sulphur* and *oxygen.*
    Carbonic acid   "   *carbon* and *oxygen.*
Muriatic acid, which is composed of *hydrogen* and *chlorine,* is among the most powerful of the acids, though it contains no oxygen. *Prussic acid†* (hydro-cyanic) is a compound of *cyanogen* and *hydrogen,* and is also a very powerful acid.

Oxides.

702. Oxides are formed by the union of oxygen with various elements ; the metallic oxides were formerly called *metallic*

---

* The same elements also form atmospheric air, but the proportion of oxygen in nitric acid is much greater than in air.
† Prussic acid is not, however, a *binary* compound, since its base, cyanogen, is composed of two elements. This is a *ternary* compound, or one that consists of three elements.

---

699. What is a binary compound ? and how many kinds of binary compounds are there ?
700. Is oxygen the only acidifying element ?
701. Of what are some of the principal acids composed ?
702. What are oxides ?

ashes and *burnt metals.* You have seen that the non-metallic substances, nitrogen, phosphorus, &c. form acids by their union with oxygen; but that a lower proportion of oxygen produces with them compounds which do not affect vegetable colours, nor give other acid tests; the latter are, therefore, called *oxides,* as *nitric oxide,* &c.; water is the *deutoxide of hydrogen.*

703. The *metallic oxides* are formed by the union of oxygen with a metal; thus when iron wire is burned in oxygen, we have an *oxide of iron,* or when copper is burned in oxygen, we have an *oxide of copper.*

The most important metallic oxides are those which we have already noticed under the head of *alkaline* metals, as the *oxide of potassium,* the *oxide of sodium,* &c.; which are the chemical names for potash, soda, &c.

704. Some metals unite with oxygen in more than one, and some, in more than two proportions; thus we have *protoxide* for the *first degree of oxidation, deutoxide* for the *second,* and *tritoxide* for the *third; peroxide* signifies the *highest state of oxidation* of which a substance is capable.

Chlorides.

705. Another important class of *binary* compounds are the *chlorides;* these consist of substances formed by the union of *chlorine* with *metals.* They were formerly ranked among *salts;*—but salts are formed by the union of *oxides,* and are therefore composed of *four* elements; while chlorides consist of but *two* elements. When common salt was named *muriate of soda,* it was supposed that muriatic acid was composed of a base, *muriatium,* united to oxygen, and that this acid combined with soda to form the salt: but since muriatic acid is found to consist of hydrogen and chlorine, and soda is found to have a metallic base, *dry* salt is called *chloride of sodium.* A *solution* of salt, is now considered the true *muriate of soda;* the *hydrogen* of the water goes to the *chlorine,* forming *hydro-chloric* or *muriatic acid,* and the *oxygen* of the water goes to the *sodium,* forming the *oxide of sodium* or soda, and thus is formed a proper salt, consisting of four elements, *chlorine* and *hydrogen, oxygen* and *sodium.* But common salt, in a dry state, is a binary compound, consisting only of *chlorine* and *sodium,* it is not, therefore, according to the chemical definition, a salt, but a *chloride.*

703. What are metallic oxides?
704. What terms denote the different degrees of oxidation?
705. What is the difference between *salts* and *chlorides?*

706. *Chloride of sodium*, or common table-salt, consists of one proportion of sodium whose

combining number is	24
one of chlorine "	36
	—
Chemical equivalent is	60

Of the important uses of this substance in preserving meat and preparing food, it is unnecessary to remark. It is of great use in bleaching manufactories, by furnishing chlorine. It is highly esteemed as a preventive of contagious diseases, and was used very extensively and with great success, in the form of chloride of soda, during the late alarming prevalence of the cholera in the United States.

707. Chloride of *calcium* is composed of *chlorine* and *calcium*, the metallic base of lime. Slaked lime, which is called a *hydrate* of lime, unites with chlorine gas and forms a hydrated *chloride of lime*, this is called bleaching powder; it is useful for many of the purposes to which the chloride of soda is applied, and is less expensive.

708. *Proto-chloride of mercury* forms a very important medicine called *calomel*. The *deuto-chloride* of mercury is commonly called *corrosive sublimate;* it is a deadly poison, and is used for destroying insects and bugs.

709. There are chlorides of silver, of gold, and of other metals, which furnish interesting subjects for the observation of the chemist, but our limits will not permit us to examine them.

710. *Fluorine, iodine,* and *bromine,* the three supporters of combustion in the class with oxygen and chlorine, form, with metallic bases *fluorides, iodides,* and *bromides.*

711. Among the binary compounds are *carburets, sulphurets, phosphurets, &c.* the termination *uret,* being applied to combinations of the non-metallic substances among themselves.

QUARTERNARY COMPOUNDS.
Consisting of four elements.

712. The properties of acids have been mentioned: *alkalies*

---

706. Give some account of the chloride of sodium ?
707. What is observed respecting chloride of calcium ?
708. What are the chlorides of mercury commonly called ?
709. Are there any other chlorides besides those already described ?
710. What compounds are formed by fluorine, iodine, and bromine, with metallic bases ?
711. What other binary compounds are there besides those which have just been named ?

(or the oxides of *alkaline* metals) possess properties essentially different—acids are compounds consisting of *oxygen*, or some *other acidifiable* element united to a base; thus *nitric acid* is composed of *oxygen* and *nitrogen*.   Alkalies are composed of *metals* united to *oxygen*, as *potash*, which consists of *oxygen* and the metal *potassium*.   Acids turn vegetable blue colours red; alkalies turn them green.   Acids (with very few exceptions) taste sour; alkalies have a pungent taste of a very different kind.   *Acids are attracted to* the *positive pole* of the galvanic circle, *alkalies to the negative.*

713. By the union of acids and alkalies, *salts* are formed which, in most cases, bear no resemblance to the substances of which they are composed.   These are called *neutral* salts. *But there are some cases when the salt appears to partake of the character of the acid, and others, in which the alkali seems to predominate.*

714. *Action of water upon salts.*   Some of the salts can be dissolved in water, as the *sulphate of soda*, (Glauber's salts,) others are insoluble, as *carbonate of lime*, (marble.)   Salts are soluble in proportion to their affinity for water, and the feebleness of their cohesive attraction.   They are more soluble in warm than cold weather.

715. *Action of ice.*   When pounded ice is mixed with a soluble salt, the one melts rapidly, and the other is quickly dissolved; cold is produced in consequence of the absorption of heat from surrounding bodies in causing solids to pass to a liquid state.   Thus, in making ice-cream, common salt and ice are placed around the vessel containing the cream to be congealed.

716. *Action of air.*   Some salts absorb moisture from the air and become damp; this is called *deliquescence.*   Housekeepers know that pearlash, (carbonate of potash,) if left exposed to the air, soon becomes wet, and at length wholly dissolves.   Some salts fall to powder on exposure to the air; this is called *efflorescence.*

717. *Action of fire.*   When submitted to the action of fire, some salts lose their water of crystallization, and break in pieces with a crackling noise; this is called *decrepitation;* you can observe an instance of this, by throwing a piece of common salt upon burning coals.

---

712. How do alkalies and acids differ?   713. How are salts formed?
714. What is said of the action of water upon salts?
715. Of the action of ice upon salts?
716. Of the action of air upon salts?
717. What is said of the action of fire upon salts?

718. Action of galvanism. When submitted to galvanic action, the *acid* of the salt goes to the *positive*, and the *oxide* to the *negative* pole. When the galvanic action is powerful, the acid is decomposed, and its oxygen then goes to the positive, and its metal to the negative pole.

719. Action of metals upon solutions of the salts. Metals have a powerful action upon the solutions of some of the salts. When a piece of zinc is introduced into a solution of the acetate of lead, the acetic acid having a greater affinity for the zinc, leaves the lead, which being precipitated or thrown out of the solution, attaches itself to the zinc, forming what is called the *lead* tree, (see section 677.) There is something very curious in this process; as soon as the zinc unites with the lead, a new principle begins to operate; viz. that of galvanism.. The two metals form the poles of the galvanic pile, of which the zinc is positive; the *precipitating metal being always positive,* and *the precipitated negative.* From hence arises the decomposition of the *water,* of the *salt* which was dissolved in it, and of the *oxide* of the metal. This tendency of metals to act on solutions of salt was found very destructive to ships with copper bottoms, as the plates of copper, in consequence of decomposing the salts held in solution by the water, became corroded by the action of the acid thus set at liberty. Sir Humphrey Davy was again consulted, and by studying and experimenting, he ascertained that a double lining of zinc and copper, would change the electrical state of the copper, and prevent its being injured by the decomposition of seawater. But though Davy discovered this mode of protecting the copper, he was not wholly successful in the result of his plan, because it was found, that though this change of the electrical state of copper prevented its injury from corroding and oxidizing agencies, it now attracted a new set of enemies, viz. all *electro-positive* bodies, among which are the EARTHY SUBSTANCES contained in seawater, as lime, magnesia, and some of their compounds; when a vessel had been some time at sea, these were found to have fastened themselves upon the copper bottom. To the crust thus formed, weeds and sea-shells would soon adhere, and thus the sailing of the vessel become impeded.

720. Action of the oxides upon the salts. Some oxides, when brought in contact with salts in a state of solution, take the place of the oxides which formed the bases of the salts.

---

718. What is said of galvanic action upon salts ?
719. Of the action of metals upon salts ?
720. Of the action of oxides upon salts ?

Sometimes the new oxide displaces a part of the base and combines with the salt, thus forming a *double salt*, as *alum*, which is a *sulphate of alumine and potash.*

Nomenclature of the Salts.

721 *Names given to the salts.* The acids which contain most oxygen, terminate in *ic*, those with a lower portion of oxygen terminate in *ous ;* thus, we have sulphur*ic* and sulphur*ous* acids. The acid whose name ends in *ic*, forms a salt whose name terminates in *ate ;* while the acid whose name ends in *ous*, forms a salt whose name terminates in *ite.* Thus, sulphuric acid forms, with bases, salts called *sulphates*, and sulphurous acid, forms *sulphites.*

722. The chemical name of the salts, shows of what they are composed; and are therefore preferable to names which were merely fanciful or arbitrary ; thus Plaster of Paris (or gypsum) is now *sulphate of lime*, Epsom salts is *sulphate of magnesia*, Saltpetre is *nitrate of potash, &c.*

723. The salts are divided into *genera* and *species ;* a genus contains such *species* as are formed by *one* acid with different bases. We will consider some of the most important genera with some of their species.

Genera of Salts.

724. *Borates.* Combinations of *boracic acid* with different *bases.* This genus is divided into sections :—*Neutral* borates are such salts as exhibit neither acid nor alkaline properties. *Sub*-borates* are deficient in acid, or show an excess of the base, exhibiting *alkaline* properties,—they are by some called *basic* salts. The *sub-borate of soda* is the most important of them. This is called *borax*, and by its decomposition affords boracic acid. Borax is useful in promoting the melting of other oxides, and forms with them glass of various colours.

725. *Carbonates.* Combinations of *carbonic acid* with different *bases.* Most of the salts of this genus are decomposed by heat, which expels the carbonic acid. Many of the acids decompose the carbonates, by uniting with their bases, and thus disengaging carbonic acid : minerals containing carbonic

---

* *Sub* is a Latin prefix, signifying under ; *sub*-salts are those which do not contain sufficient acid in their composition to neutralize the alkaline qualities of the base.

---

721. By what rule are the salts named ?
722. Why are chemical names the best to distinguish salts ?
723. What do you understand by a *genus* of salts ?
724. Describe the borates. 725. What are carbonates ?

acid will effervesce with other acids. The effervescence is caused by the escape of carbonic acid, which is expelled by the new union formed between the base and the new acid.

The most important *species* found in the genus carbonates, are,—

726. 1. *Carbonate of Lime.* This is one of the most abundant of all mineral substances. It is known under various names, as limestone, chalk, marble, &c. It exists, in some waters, in a state of solution. Pure, or quicklime, is obtained by calcining, or heating the carbonate, and thus expelling the acid. This salt is composed of

1 proportion of carbonic acid gas = 22
1   "   lime   28
                                                               ——
Chemical equivalent   50

Thus we learn from Chemistry that nearly half the matter of the solid limestone rocks is a gas.

727. 2. *Carbonate of potash* is made from the ashes of vegetables; the strong ley obtained from them is evaporated, and a dry substance of a dark red colour remains. This is potash, or the *oxide of potassium*; it is very caustic at first, but loses this property on being exposed to the air, from which it attracts carbonic acid, and becomes a carbonate of potash. *Pearlash* is a more pure carbonate of potash; it is now generally sold at the shops under the name of *sal-eratus.* The *bi**-carbonate of potash is formed by passing carbonic acid into a solution of the carbonate, which thus receives a second portion of the acid. This is recommended as a valuable medicine for removing acidity in the stomach.

728. 3. *Carbonate of soda* is prepared like potash, except that the ashes of seaweed, or vegetables growing near salt-water, are used. It is commonly known by the name of *soda.*

729. 4. *Carbonate of magnesia* is sold by apothecaries in cakes or lumps. It is used in medicine, but is less valuable than *calcined magnesia*, or that from which the carbonic acid has been expelled.

730. 5. *Carbonate of copper* is found native in a mineral called *malachite*, of a beautiful green colour; it also collects

* From the Greek *bis*, two.

728. What is said of carbonate of lime?
727. Describe carbonate of potash.
728. What is said of carbonate of soda?
729. What is said of carbonate of magnesia?
730. What is said of carbonate of copper?

17

194   CHEMISTRY FOR BEGINNERS.   [Ch. XXII.

like a green rust upon copper vessels exposed to the air. The blue paint *verditer* is an impure carbonate of copper.

731. 6. *Carbonate of lead* is the *white lead* used by painters; it is prepared by exposing sheet lead to the vapour of vinegar; the fumes of the acid first form the acetate of lead, and this gradually attracts carbonic acid from the atmosphere, and becomes a carbonate.*

732. 7. *Carbonate of barytes* was discovered by Dr. Withering in the lead mines of England, and is called in mineralogy, in honour of its discoverer, *Witherite*.

733. 8. *Carbonate of ammonia* is a white powder used in smelling-bottles, under the name of *salts of hartshorn*. It is the product of animal substances, by the action of heat.

734. II. GENUS CHLORATES. The salts of this genus are composed of *chloric acid* and *bases;* they are not found in nature, but are always the product of art. They were formerly called *oxymuriates*. The difference between them and chlorides may be thus stated ;—a *chloride* is a *binary* compound, consisting of *chlorine* and a *simple element; chlorates are quarternary compounds,* formed of *two* binary substances, one of which is *chloric acid,* (chlorine and oxygen,) and the other an *oxide.* It might be said, here are but three elements, oxygen and chlorine, and the base of the oxide, as the oxygen of the oxide cannot be called a fourth element, when it has been already counted—but you must observe that in the salts, the four elements are not all mingled together, but two binary compounds, viz. the acid and oxide, must unite to form them, and thus we consider the oxygen of the acid, and that of the oxide, as performing distinct offices. From what has been observed, you will perceive that chlorides differ much in their composition from chlorates; the former are sometimes improperly classed among salts, but do not belong to them more than acids, oxides, or any other binary compound.

735. We shall mention but one species under this genus.

Chlorate of potash, when thrown upon burning coals, parts with the oxygen of its acid and of its oxide, and becomes

* Although carbonic acid is not a constituent portion of the atmosphere, yet some portion always exists in it.

731. What is said of carbonate of lead?
732. Of the carbonate of barytes?
733. Of the carbonate of ammonia?
734. What is said respecting the general characteristics of the genus chlorates?
735 What are the properties of chlorate of potash?

chloride of potassium ; on account of parting with so much oxygen, this substance has a powerful effect on combustion. When mixed with sulphur, or any resinous body, it will inflame and burn spontaneously. Allumetts, or matches, are made of little sticks of pine, the ends of which are coated with a kind of paste, formed of chlorate of potash and resin; on being lightly plunged into a little vial of sulphuric acid, fire bursts forth. Chlorate of potash enters into the composition of most *fulminating* powders, so called on account of the noise produced in their explosion. Carbon, sulphur, and phosphorus are also used in these compositions. Attempts have been made to introduce chlorate of potash as an ingredient in gunpowder, but it is found to be so sudden in its operation as to render it a very dangerous instrument to the operator.

736. Chlorate of potash is obtained by *saturating a solution of sulphate of potash, with chlorine gas.* The figure represents part of the apparatus used for this purpose. A is the

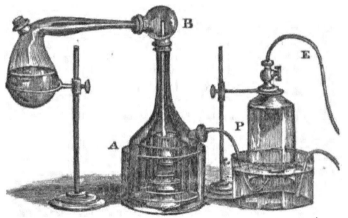

outer one of three jars filled with a solution of *sulphate of potash.* The retort contains the *oxide of manganese,* upon which *muriatic acid* being poured, chlorine gas is disengaged, and passes through the neck of the retort to the ball B, and from the trumpet-shaped tube into the liquid of the inner jar; after saturating the liquid in all the jars, the gas which is not absorbed escapes through the pipe P. The pipe E conducts off any superfluous gas into vessels prepared to receive it.

736. How is the chlorate of potash obtained?

737. The saturated solution of chlorate of potash must be crystallized, in order to obtain the salt in its purest state. The figure represents the manner of doing this. The solution requires to be filtered or strained, and this must be done while it is hot. For this purpose Dr. Hare contrived a large vessel of sheet tin containing an aperture for a funnel, and another to serve the purpose of a chimney by conducting off the smoke of the lamp below. This lamp keeps the water hot with which the tin vessel is filled; the hot water surrounding the solution prevents its cooling. A coarse fibrous paper is laid into the funnel for the solution to filter through; it is received in the decanting jar beneath, and there crystallizes in beautiful, silvery white plates.

738. *Hydro-chlorates* differ from chlorates in being formed with *hydro-chloric* acid, (muriatic acid,) instead of chloric acid. These substances were called *muriates* before the discovery of chlorine.

739. The *hydro-chlorate of ammonia,* (or muriate of ammonia,) is the salt usually called *sal-ammoniac;* it may be formed by mingling in equal volumes, in a dry glass vessel,

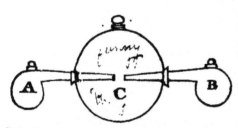

the two gases, ammonia and muriatic acid. Thus A represents a retort containing the one gas, and B a retort containing the other; C is a glass vessel, in which the two gases uniting, form a solid

737. How are crystals of chlorate of potash obtained?

738. How do hydro-chlorates differ from chlorates, and what were they formerly called?

739. How is the hydro-chlorate, or muriate of ammonia, obtained?

hydro-chlorate (or muriate) of ammonia, which is precipitated in snow-white vapours.

740. The *hydro-chlorate of soda* (or muriate of soda) is common salt in solution; the manner in which it differs from the chloride of sodium has been already explained in treating of that substance.

741. III. GENUS NITRATES. There are only four nitrates found in nature, those of *potash, lime, soda,* and *magnesia.* They are found in solution, in water, in the earth of old cellars, and under the floors of stables. The most important species of this genus are—

742. 1. *Nitrate of potash,* or *saltpetre;* this has been already noticed under the head of potash. The nitrates resemble chlorates in many of their properties, particularly in easily parting with oxygen, which renders them important agents in *fulminating* or detonating powders. The nitrate of potash is an important constituent of gunpowder. It is of general use in putting up meat for salting, through the fibres of which it penetrates, giving it a fine, red colour, and aiding in its preservation.

743. 2. *Nitrate of bismuth* is used in the manufacture of *pearl powder.*

744. 3. *Nitrate of soda* is found in beds of a mile or two in length, in South America, and in smaller quantities in other parts of the world, generally in connexion with nitre, or, as it is more commonly called, saltpetre.

745. 4. *Nitrate of silver* is known by the more common name *lunar caustic.* It is very powerful in its effects in disorganizing animal substances; for this reason it is used to remove warts and other excreseences; it does this by a slow burning. oxygen leaving its old combination unites with the animal fibre, and thus decomposes it. The nitrate of silver is used in a weak solution for dyeing the hair black; it is also used for indelible ink. *Nitric acid* forms *nitrates* with most of the alkalies and the metals, but those which we have mentioned are the most important.

746. IV. GENUS PHOSPHATES; these are salts arising from the combination of phosphoric acid with different bases. Its

---

740. What is the hydro-chlorate of soda?
741. How many nitrates are there? and how do they exist in nature?
742. What is said of the nitrate of potash?
743. Of the nitrate of bismuth?   744. Of the nitrate of soda?
745. Of the nitrate of silver?
716. What is said of the genus phosphates? and which are its most important species?

most important *species* are, 1. *phosphate of lime,* which forms an important part of the bones of animals, and is used in the manufacture of phosphorus: 2. Phosphate of cobalt, by calcining with alum, forms a beautiful colour, called, after its discoverer, Thenard's blue.

747. V. GENUS SULPHATES; none of the acids has a stronger tendency to unite with other substances than the sulphuric; for this reason, the genus sulphates contains many species.

748. 1. *Sulphate of lime,* (*plaster of Paris,* or *gypsum,*) was at first used in the vicinity of Paris; it is common in various parts of the earth, sometimes in crystals, when it is called *selenite,* sometimes in large, rough masses, called *plaster-stone.* The many busts and mantel ornaments, resembling marble, which are now so common, are made of a pure and white plaster. Gypsum is used under the name of *stucco,* to give to the outsides of buildings the appearance of marble, and is very useful as a manure, to promote the growth of vegetation. It is said, that after Dr. Franklin's residence in France, where he had witnessed the effects of plaster in promoting vegetation, he wished to introduce its use into his own country. But the farmers believing that they knew better how to raise crops than he did, refused to follow his advice. Dr. Franklin was not accustomed to give way to discouragements, when he had a good object in view, and accordingly he caused a field to be prepared in the common way; but in the middle of the field he wrote with plaster these words—*Effects of Plaster,* and then sowed the whole with grass seed. The grass soon appeared, but that which had been sown upon the plaster, far exceeded the rest in vigour and height. The Doctor then invited the farmers to go into his meadow; astonished with this indisputable evidence of its utility, they all hastened to enrich their fields with plaster manure.

749. 2. *Sulphate of magnesia* exists in solution in the waters of Epsom and Seidlitz springs in Europe; from whence it is commonly called *Epsom salts.*

750. 3. *Sulphate of Soda* was first introduced into medicine by a physician of the name of *Glauber;* from this circumstance it is called *Glauber's salts.*

751. 4. *Sulphate of potash* is used in medicine; it was formerly called *vitriolated tartar,* and its composition considered an important secret.

747. What is said respecting the genus sulphates?
748. Of sulphate of lime?   749. Of sulphate of magnesia?
750. Of sulphate of soda?   751. Of sulphate of potash?

752. 5. *Sulphate of copper* is commonly called *blue vitriol*; it is found in a state of solution in copper mines.)

753. 6. *Sulphate of iron* is called copperas, and sometimes green vitriol; this is important in the arts, especially in dyeing. Ink powder is made with the sulphate of iron and a vegetable substance called nut-galls.

754. 7. Douole *sulphate of alumine and potash.* This, though not strictly belonging to the genus sulphates, we shall here mention; it is the well known substance, *alum.*
It is composed of 3 parts of the sulphate of alumine,   174
added to 1 part of the sulphate of potash,   88

                                                                        ———
making the equivalent number of alum,   262
The peculiar taste of alum is well known. It may be dissolved in boiling water. Large and beautiful crystals for baskets and other ornamental work, may be obtained by evaporating its solutions. It is of great importance to the dyer in fixing those colours that are soluble in water.

755. VI. GENUS CHROMATES are composed of chromic acid with alkaline and metallic bases. The chromates are of various colours, and many of them are valuable in the arts of dyeing and painting.

756. Species 1. *Chromate of lead* is a brilliant yellow, sometimes called *chrome yellow.*

2. *Chromate of silver* is of a deep purple colour.

3. *Chromate of potash* is of a lemon yellow colour, when melted it becomes green. It is used in calico printing, in painting, and in the preparation of chromic acid.

757. We have now given an outline of the principal salts known in Chemistry, with the exception of some important ones which are formed in part, or entirely of vegetable compounds. But we could only notice, comparatively, few of the whole number now known to chemists, exceeding, it is said, more than a thousand. You have seen something of the wonderful manner in which a few elements are made to unite, and form an almost infinite variety of substances. Thus when we examine the works of God, we are ever struck with a union of simplicity and grandeur!

---

752. What is said of sulphate of copper? 753. Of sulphate of iron?
754. What is alum? 755. What is said of chromates?
756. What is said of the chromates?
757. What remark closes this chapter?

CHAPTER XXIII.

ORGANIC CHEMISTRY,

VEGETABLE CHEMISTRY.

Vegetable Acids.   Vegetable Alkalies.   Oils, &c.

758. WE have completed our view of Chemistry so far as relates to the mineral kingdom, under which we include water and air, as well as stones, earths, and metals. The term *inorganic*, is applied to every thing in nature which is not animal or vegetable.

759. Chemistry may be divided into *organic*, and *inorganic*. Vegetables and animals are called *organic*, because they are composed of parts or organs which are connected, and mutually dependent on each other; the remaining objects in nature are called *inorganic*, because they do not consist of such parts, but every portion is a perfect specimen of its kind; and (except in the case of crystals, which have a regular figure) inorganic substances are shapeless masses of inert matter.

760. We have found, in the progress of our study, of what elements these inorganic substances are composed; the chemist, availing himself of this knowledge, is able to recompose many of them, or put them together after he has destroyed their composition by analysis.

761. The chemist is able to separate from their combination the elements which compose animals and plants. He can tell us of what they are made, but he cannot put them together again, to make an animal or a plant; not even a weed, or the meanest worm that crawls, can be imitated by man in one respect, and that the one of all others which makes it what it is, a *living* thing.

762. The *living principle* both in plants and animals is concealed from the search of man; although he has been prying into the mystery ever since Satan tempted our first parents to disobey God, saying, "thou shalt not surely die." Their limbs were then active, the warm current flowed in their veins,

---

758. What substances are included under the mineral kingdom?
759. What two divisions may be made in Chemistry?
760. Can the chemist recompose inorganic compounds?
761. Why cannot the chemist recompose organic compounds?
762. What constitutes the living principle in organic beings?

and they doubtless thought that these were properties of their bodies which could not be taken from them. But God commands, and plants and animals flourish in vigour and beauty; ne says, let life depart, and they die and return to the dust from whence they came.

763. All that can be done in organic Chemistry is to examine, by means of chemical analysis, the elements of which bodies are composed, and to learn the various combinations which exist in animal and vegetable substances. Of these substances new compounds have been formed, which have proved of great importance in the arts, and especially in medicine.

764. Organic Chemistry is divided into Vegetable and Animal Chemistry.

Ultimate Elements of Vegetables.

765. Organic substances, when analyzed, are found to contain carbon, oxygen, hydrogen, sulphur, silex, the oxide of iron, soda, magnesia, and chalk. Iodine and bromine are obtained from seaweeds. Nitrogen is found in few plants though it was formerly thought peculiar to animal and mineral substances.

766. The *ultimate elements* of organic substances, such as carbon, oxygen, &c., are obtained by what is called *destructive distillation*; that is, submitting the vegetable matter to the action of heat in close vessels, and collecting all the products. Oxygen, carbon, and hydrogen form the most important ultimate elements of plants, although other substances are often found at their last, or *ultimate* analysis. We shall not attempt to explain to the beginner the complicated process of analyzing organic substances, which is so delicate, that little progress has hitherto been made in this department, in comparison to what might have been expected from the discoveries in organic Chemistry.

767. *Proximate principles* are produced by plants and animals in their living state; these are gums, resins, honey, sugar, &c., besides various animal products.

768. The ultimate elements of organic bodies are the same

763. What can be effected in organic Chemistry?
764. How is organic Chemistry divided?
765. What are organic substances composed of?
766. How are their ultimate elements obtained? and which are the most important?
767. What are proximate principles?
768. Do the ultimate elements of organic bodies differ from those of inorganic bodies?

as those we have already examined under inorganic Chemistry.) Plants are nourished by inorganic bodies, as the air, earth, and water. Animals feed on plants, and upon other animals which have gained their subsistence from plants.

769. It is wonderful that of so few elements, such a variety of combinations are produced; in organic bodies, but few of the elementary substances which exist in nature are employed. A slight difference in the *proportions* of the elements, or *in the manner in which they are put together or combined*, seems to produce all this variety.

770. Organized bodies are distinguished from inorganic by the following characters.

1. They are composed of the same elements, but in different proportions.

2. They are decomposed, in general, by a lower degree of heat.

3. They cannot be produced by art.)

VEGETABLE CHEMISTRY.

Proximate Principles of Plants.

771. The *proximate principles of plants* are distinguished into two classes.

CLASS I. contains such principles as carbon, oxygen, and hydrogen, without any nitrogen. This class is divided into three orders.

772. 1. Where oxygen is in excess; these are *acids.*

2. Where hydrogen is in excess; these are *resins, oils, alcohol, &c.*

3. Where oxygen and hydrogen exist in the same proportions, as in water; these are *gums, sugar, &c.*)

773. CLASS II. contains such principles as are composed of the elements of the first class, with the addition of nitrogen;) this class includes vegetable alkalies. We can do little more than name a few of these proximate principles.

774. CLASS I.—*Order* 1. Vegetable acids.

Acetic acid exists in the sap of some plants and is the acid-

---

769. What produces the variety which exists in organic substances, when so few elements are employed?
770. In what particulars are organic substances different from inorganic?
771. What elements compose the first class of proximate principles?
772. What are the orders of this class?
773. What element does the second class contain that does not exist in the first class?
774. What is said of acetic acid?

ifying principle of vinegar. With various bases it forms *acetates.* Acetate *of lead* is the *sugar of lead; acetate of copper is verdigris.*

775. *Oxalic acid* is usually obtained from wood-sorrel, known in botany as belonging to the genus *oxalis;* it exists in several other plants. It is a powerful acid, and a fatal poison.

776. *Tartaric acid* is obtained from the tamarind, the grape, and several other acid fruits; combined with potash, it forms *cream of tartar,* which is a *tartrate of potash.* Rochelle salt is a tartrate of potash and soda.

777. *Citric acid,* is so called from the genus *Citrus,* the lemon or orange, from which it is obtained. This often constitutes one of the powders sold under the name of soda powders, which consist of one paper of an acid, and another of an alkali, usually carbonate of soda. The effervescence is caused by the escape of the carbonic acid, as the alkali unites to the new acid. Citric acid removes iron stains, though not as readily as oxalic acid.

778. *Malic acid,* from *malus,* the genus of the apple; it is found in many other fruits, as currants, strawberries, &c. The flavour of fruits is chiefly owing to the citric, tartaric, and malic acids which they contain.

779. *Gallic acid* is obtained from *nut galls,* an excrescence upon the limbs and leaves of the oak caused by the puncture of an insect that deposites its eggs in the spot, and is usually found in the centre of the nut. Gallic acid exists in white oak bark, with a principle called *tannin.* Gallic acid turns iron black; it is contained in tea. If you drop strong tea upon a knife, you will see a black spot upon the place. Gallic acid, with tannin and sulphate of iron, forms ink and black dyes. The tannin unites with the sulphuric acid of the sulphate, and the iron is precipitated by the gallic acid in the form of a *gallate* of iron.

780. *Benzoic acid* is obtained from a gum called *benzoin,* the product of a plant whose botanical name is *styrax benzoin;* it is supposed to exist in the sweet-scented vernal grass. (*anthoxanthum odoratum.*) It is used in the preparation of the paregoric elixir, and gives it a peculiar aromatic taste and smell.

781. *Kinic or quinic acid* exists in peruvian bark, known in medicine as the *cinchona bark.* It is said to be formed of two equivalents of carbon, 12; four of hydrogen, 4; and three of oxygen, 24; this would make 40 its representative number, *Indigotic* acid is obtained from indigo.

775. What is said of oxalic acid? 776. Of tartaric acid? 777. Of citric acid? 778. Of malic acid? 779. Of gallic acid? 780. Of benzoic acid? 781. Of kinic acid?

782. *Prussic* acid is obtained from peach meats and blossoms, bitter almonds, laurel, &c. It is now generally known in Chemistry as *hydro-cyanic* acid.

783. *Order* 2, *of proximate principles*, contain such as have *hydrogen in excess*, as oils, resins, &c.

784. *Oils* are known by a greasy touch, by being easily inflamed, and by not uniting with water, unless through the medium of an alkaline substance.

785. Oils are of two classes, *fixed* and *volatile*; the former make grease spots on paper, as olive or sweet oil; the latter fly off and leave no stain, as the oil of peppermint, of cloves, &c.

786. *Fixed oils* are usually obtained from the seeds of plants. Olive oil is pressed from the pulp of the olive berry, which is of the size of a small plum. The oil of *flaxseed*, called *linseed** oil, dries without losing its transparency; this renders it valuable to painters, being used not only in house painting, but in the nicer colouring of the limner. Oils, which, like linseed, dry rapidly in the air, are called *drying oils*. They combine with oxygen while drying, and much latent caloric is brought into a free state;—if light combustibles, such as cotton or flax, are wet with these oils, there is danger of spontaneous combustion—this is one cause of the frequent burning of cotton and other manufactories. The kernels of walnuts and butternuts, on being heated and pressed, afford oil; beech nuts and sunflower seeds are rich in this product. Palm and castor oil are used in medicine.

787. *Volatile oils* give to plants their odour; they are found in blossoms, fruit leaves, barks, and roots, and are obtained by distilling these with water. The common still (see section 400) is used for this purpose. The water and oil flow together into a *recipient*, like the vessel represented in the figure; the water having reached the level *a*, *b*, runs off by the spout *c*; and the oil being lighter, floats upon its surface in the space *d*. Volatile oils are reduced, by

* The botanical name of flax is *linum*, from *lin*, a thread; from this comes *linseed*.

782. What is said of prussic acid?
783. What principles does the second order of the first class contain?
784. What are some of the properties of oils?
785. What two classes of oils are there?
786. What are fixed oils? and which are the most important of them?
787. What is said of volatile oils? and which are some of the most important?

alcohol, they are then called *essences*. (The oil of turpentine) is the most important of these substances; it is used in varnishing and in medicine. The oil of cloves is recommended as a cure for the toothache; the oil of aniseseed, of peppermint, of nutmeg, cinnamon, &c., are used in medicine, and by the housekeeper as a substitute for the spices from which some of them are made. The oils are so powerful that one or two drops contain more of the real aroma of the plant, than twenty or thirty drops of the essences.

788. Camphor is classed among volatile oils; it is mostly obtained from Borneo and Sumatra, where it is extracted from the leaves of a large tree.) In Japan it is found in the roots, branches, and leaves of the *Laurus Camphora*. Camphor cannot be dissolved in water. Alcohol, or spirits containing it, are the best solvents for camphor.

789. *Resins* are (the dried juices of plants) they are of various kinds.—*Gum resins;* among these is the yellow substance used in painting and medicine called gamboge; it is the juice of the gamboge tree, called in botany the *Stalagmitis gambogoides*, from the Greek *stalagmos*, a dropping or distillation, because the gum escapes in this manner. It grows in Gambaja in the East Indies. (*Aloes, myrrh*, and *Indian rubber* belong to the gum resins. Indian rubber, called also *caoutchouc** or gum elastic, is the resinous product of a tree found in hot countries. On exposure to the air, it becomes brown like leather; it cannot be dissolved by water or alcohol. *Wax* is obtained by bees from the pollen of flowers. The bay-berry plant,[†] which grows in sandy plains in the United States, near the sea-shore, furnishes a wax of a beautiful green colour, called by housekeepers bay-berry-tallow, and used with common tallow for candles. The vegetable wax makes them hard, and gives them a pale green tint.

790. *Alcohol* is not a product of nature, but is formed by the fermentation[‡] of certain vegetable juices. It is the intoxicating principle of liquors. If a mixture of one part of

* Pronounced ka-ot-chok.
† Called in botany *myrica cerifera;* the specific name *cerifera* means wax-bearing.
‡ For information respecting the various kinds of fermentation, see Dictionary of Chemistry, pages 214, 215, and 216.

788. What can you say of camphor?
789. What are resins? and which are some of the most important gum-resins?
790. What is said of alcohol?

18

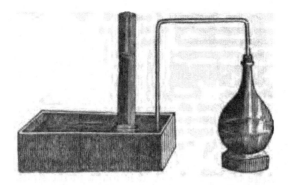

sugar, four of water, and a little yeast; be subjected to a suitable degree of warmth, the fermenting process begins, and carbonic acid gas may be collected; the figure shows the flask containing the fermenting materials, and the receiver inverted over water into which the gas passes. In this process, carbon and oxygen, forming the carbonic acid, are given off. Spirituous liquor is obtained by the distillation of fermented liquors. Spirits of wine, or pure alcohol, differs from wine, brandy, or rum, only in being more thoroughly distilled. It is highly inflammable—many instances are recorded of the bodies of persons accustomed to the free use of spirituous liquors burning, taking fire internally. Though cases of sudden spontaneous combustion are rare, yet every one, who for a length of time indulges freely in the use of alcohol, experiences a slow combustion of the vitals, and what is still more dreadful, a destruction of the mental powers. It is a sad sight to behold a human being thus madly seizing the poisonous cup, which must prostrate in ruin both soul and body. And yet, so pleasant seems the entrance to dissipation, that many a heedless youth, who would shudder at the name, has become a *drunkard*, before he has even thought himself in danger. The peculiar effect of indulgence in drinking ardent spirits is to blind the mental sight and confuse the judgment, so that, at length, the votaries of intemperance can scarcely be considered as moral agents. Alcohol, like opium, and even arsenic, has its valuable applications. It is useful in medicine, and is the only liquid which will dissolve many substances. Wine, cider, and ale, contain alcohol combined with other vegetable principles, and are therefore less intoxicating

* The literal meaning of *ardent* is *burning*, a term which seems most appropriately applied to alcoholic liquors.

than brandy in proportion to the alcohol which each contains; in the latter, the alcohol is combined with water only, and thus acts directly upon the system.

791. *Ether* is a term derived from the Greek *æther*, and signifies spirit. (It is a liquor obtained by distilling alcohol with a strong acid; its properties must, of course, be very active.) It is a powerful agent in medicine, and in Chemistry affords many striking experiments. On account of its volatile nature, when exposed to the air it flies off in a gaseous form, and takes caloric from surrounding bodies.) *Sulphuric ether*, which is obtained by distilling sulphuric acid with alcohol, is most common.

792. *Order 3, contains (such principles as have oxygen and hydrogen in the same proportions as they exist in water.)*

793. Sugar is contained in ripe fruits, and in the sap of many trees and other plants, but is made in the United States, chiefly from the sap of the maple. It has been made from beets, from the juice of cornstalks and grapes. Most of the sugar of commerce is made from the sugar-cane, a plant which flourishes only in warm countries. Sugar is made by boiling and evaporating the juice of the sugar-cane or other substance; when properly made it is obtained in imperfect crystals. *Molasses* is the thick juice which runs off when sugar is drained; it is called *treacle*. When exposed to the action of heat, sugar swells and diffuses a peculiar smell; a large quantity of carbon remains after its combustion. Sugar-candy is crystallized sugar.

794. *Starch* is a very abundant vegetable product; it exists in the seeds, roots, and stems of plants. For domestic uses it is obtained from wheat, potatoes, or Indian corn.) Among farmers in the country, it is very common for each family to manufacture their own starch. The green ears of Indian corn or potatoes are grated into large tubs of water; the starch settles at the bottom; the water is then poured off, a fresh quantity of pure water added, and the starch broken up and again mixed with the water; it is then allowed to settle again. The process is repeated until the starch is perfectly clean and white; it is then laid on large platters and dried in the sun. There are now many starch manufactories; near Utica is a village where the business is extensively carried on. Under the name of Poland starch, much that is made in

791. What is ether, how obtained, and what are some of its properties ?
792. What principles does the third order contain ?
793. What substances afford sugar ?
794. How is starch obtained, and what are some of its properties ?

the United States is sold. ' Starch is insoluble in cold water, boiling water converts it into a jelly.) Iodine gives with starch a blue colour, and its presence in any substance may always be known by this circumstance. *Arrow root, sago, and cassava* resemble starch in most of their properties.

795. *Gum* is a proximate principle; it is found upon many of our trees, as the cherry and plum tree.) *Gum Arabic* is obtained from the species of a plant called *mimosa,* found in various parts of Africa and Arabia. These gums differ, in their constituent principles, from the gum-resins, already named, the latter contain oil.

Vegetable Alkalies.

796. CLASS II. contains such vegetable principles, as, in addition to carbon, hydrogen, and oxygen, contain some *nitrogen.* These are *vegetable alkalies,* or *salifiable* bases ; that is, they unite with acids to form salts; they turn blue vegetable colours green, and exhibit some other properties of mineral alkalies. Most of them are poisonous. They are of modern discovery, and are now ranked among the most important articles in medicine.

797. *Morphia* was first described in a manner to gain the notice of chemists in 1816, although it had been discovered by a German engaged in the preparation of medicine some time before this. It is obtained from opium, which is the dried juice of the poppy. Morphia is supposed to be that principle in opium which causes sleep) Another principle in opium, called *narcotine,* is supposed to cause its sickening effects ; as these effects are counteracted by acids, citric and acetic acid are combined with opium, forming a new and popular preparation, called the "black drop."

798. *Quinine* and Cinchonia are alkaline substances, obtained by the analysis of the Cinchonia, or Peruvian bark. The *sulphate of quinine* is much used in medicine.

799. *Strychnine* is the poisonous principle of the Bohon Upas tree of the island of Java, which is said to infect the air around it. This principle is found in some other plants.

800. *Emetine* is extracted from a plant called *ipecacuanha,* which grows in Brazil and Peru, and is well known as affording, from its root, an emetic powder, sometimes called *ipecac.* Emetine is very powerful, as it contains the concentrated energy of the emetic principle.

---

795. What is said of gum ?   796. What principles does class 2 contain ?
797. What can you say of morphia?   798. Of quinine ?
799. Of strychnine?   800. Of emetine ?

801. These peculiar principles seem to be almost as extensive as the vegetable kingdom itself, and discoveries in this part of the field of science are continually made.   The peculiar properties of the blood root (*sanguinaria*) are found in its extract *sanguinarine;* of tobacco (*nicotiana*) in *nicotine;* of pepper, in *piperine;* and *polenin* is obtained from the pollen of plants; this is very combustible.

802. *Vegetable principles not included under any particular class.* There are some vegetable principles that have not been analyzed with sufficient accuracy to enable chemists to class them in relation to their elements, as *colouring matter, tannin, gluten, yeast,* &c.

803. *Colouring matter.*   The vegetable kingdom is rich in colouring matter; every young girl knows that saffron makes a fine yellow, and the leaves of one species of balm a beautiful red; and most housekeepers in the country know that butternut bark affords a brown colour, and that maple bark with copperas (sulphate of iron) furnishes a good black.

804. *Dyeing depends on a chemical affinity* between the colouring matter and the fibres of the fabric to be coloured. Wool receives colour the most readily of any substance, and next to this, silk.

805. Most colours require the agency of something to fix them firmly, or they will be destroyed by washing.   These intermediate agents are called *mordants,* from *mordeo,* to bite, as it was imagined that they corroded, or eat into the fibres of the coloured fabrics; they are also called *bases.*   Among the mordants used in dyeing are alum, copperas, and the oxides of tin and iron. These not only fix the colours, but often give them a brighter hue, and a different shade.

806. The most important colours for dyeing are blue, red, yellow, and black.

807. Blue is chiefly obtained from a plant called *indigo;* it is cultivated in India, from whence it was first imported into Europe; it is also cultivated in South America, and in the southern United States.   The botanical name of the plant is *indigofera;* of this genus there are several species.

---

801. Do these peculiar vegetable principles seem to be extensive in nature ?
802. Have the elements of all the vegetable principles been analyzed ?
803. Are there many vegetable dyes ?
804. On what principle does dyeing depend, and what substances receive colour most readily ?
805. What are mordants, and which among them are most useful ?
806. Which are the most important colours ?
807. What is blue chiefly obtained from ?

18*

808. Red dyes are *logwood,* which grows in South America; *madder,* the root of a plant, (rubia tinctorum;) *safflower,* the flower of a plant (carthamus tinctorius) which grows near the Mediterranean, and from which *rouge** is made; *litmus,* a lichen plant, and *cochineal,* which is an animal substance, that affords a rich *carmine.* It is obtained from an insect which feeds on the leaves of certain species of the cactus plant. Its natural colour is crimson, but by adding the bi-tartrate of potash it yields a beautiful scarlet dye.

809. *Yellow* is obtained from the American *sumach,* from *turmeric,* the root of an East Indian plant, *saffron,*† *anotta,* the seeds of a plant which grows in Cayenne, and which is improperly called *otter,* and from some other substances.

810. *Black* dyes, like writing ink, are a compound of the *oxide of iron, gallic acid,* and *tannin;* *logwood* is also used. Every variety of shades of colour is produced by combining the different substances which have been mentioned.

811. *Tannin.* We have mentioned this principle, and will here observe, that, as its name would indicate, it is of important use in tanning leather. Those who have observed tanneries must have noticed that the vats contain large quantities of the ground bark of trees; oak, hemlock, or chestnut, are preferred, because the bark from these trees contain a large portion of *tannin.* This is an *astringent* principle, which has a great affinity for gelatine, a substance which is abundantly contained in the skins of animals, and with which it forms a tough, insoluble compound, called *leather.* Gall nuts, and the barks of most trees contain tannin; it exists in tea with gallic acid. With the peroxide of iron, tannin forms a dark-coloured compound, which, with the gallate of iron, forms black dyes and writing ink.

812. *Gluten* constitutes a large portion of wheat flour; after washing out the starch from flour, gluten remains in the form of a tough, adhesive paste. This substance is very nourishing, and renders wheat superior to other kinds of grain.—

* Pronounced *rojee,* the j soft.
† The saffron, so called commonly, among us, is a compound flower, and not the true saffron, which belongs to the genus *Crocus,* of the third class of Linnæus.

808. What are the principal red dyes?
809. What is yellow obtained from?
810. How are black dyes made?
811. What can you say respecting tannin, its use, properties, &c.
812. Give some account of gluten.

Yeast makes bread light on account of the gluten of the flour; the carbonic acid gas in its attempt to escape, becomes entangled in it, and this causes the little cavities which are so numerous in light bread ; they are filled with the gas. If yeast is put into Indian meal, very little effect is produced, because it contains little or no gluten. Potatoes contain a large quantity of *farina*, or starch, which is nourishing, and wheat flour a large quantity of gluten; they are therefore well adapted to each other, and good bread may be made by uniting them. Indian meal, which is sweet, and favourable in its tendency to promote digestion, may be added to wheat flour in a considerable quantity, and the gluten of the latter with a suitable portion of good yeast, will prove sufficient to make the mass light.

813. *Yeast*, or *emptins*, is produced during the *vinous fermentation of vegetable substances.* This is a very important article in domestic economy. Every housekeeper who does not live where she may procure yeast at the distillery, or brewery, should be careful to keep by her a quantity of this article. Its effect in raising bread has been already noticed, under the article gluten. In warm weather its operation is ● much more rapid than in cold ; the bread becomes light in a few hours, or goes through what is called the *vinous fermentation ;* it then proceeds to the *acid fermentation,* and the lazy housekeeper who made her bread at night finds her dough has soured while she was indulging in her morning nap. But there is for this misfortune a remedy. If a solution of pearlash, or the carbonate of potash be kneaded into the dough, the acetic acid will leave the dough, and unite with the potash, and carbonic acid (which, though possessing some properties in common with acids, is not sour) will diffuse itself in the meshes of the gluten, and help to make the bread lighter. But lest this knowledge should encourage carelessness, we will remark, that when dough has gone through this restorative process, although the bread may be lighter, and free from an acid taste, yet it will not be sweet and pleasant as that which has never been soured.

* So named from being left at the bottom of beer, and at first called *emptyings.*

---

813. How is yeast produced? What makes bread sour, and how can this be remedied?

CHAPTER XXIV.

Organic Chemistry.

ANIMAL CHEMISTRY.

814. ANIMAL Chemistry, though it affords much light upon the composition, and operations of living beings, is yet in its in fancy, and indeed, can never be so well understood as most oth er departments of chemical science. Physicians and anatomists search into the different substances which compose the animal frame; they tell us that blood is composed of *albumen, fibrin, water,* and some *mineral substances.* They examine the contents of the stomach, and find there a substance which they call the *gastric juice,* and whose office it is to dissolve the food that is introduced into its region; but the cause of the circulation of the blood, without which life ceases, and the manner in which the gastric juice performs its analysis, no physician or chemist can explain.

815. The animal system seems to present a wonderful laboratory, where, operating with only a few simple elements, a new and peculiar class of substances is composed; and decompositions are carried on upon principles wholly concealed from human observation. Should the great Creator condescend to reason with man, as with his servant of old, might he not say to him, "Behold the cumbrous machinery with which thy operations are performed, and then consider thine own frame! Canst thou tell how its breathing is carried on, how the heart has power at every instant to send forth the vital current, which, in ten thousand courses, rushes to every part of the system, and then in new avenues returns to its living fountain? Dost thou know how the lungs perform their part in the curious machinery, conveying to the blood the vital air, and conducting off that which is unfit for farther use?" Man, in the language of Job, must reply, "I am vile, what shall I answer thee? I *know* that *thou* canst *do every thing.*"

816. Ignorant as we are, and must be, respecting the complicated machinery of the living body, much may be learned respecting the action of different substances upon the animal

---

814. How far are physicians able to understand the animal frame?
815. What is remarked of the machinery of the animal system?
816. What is said of the difference between the experiments of the physician and the chemist?

system. (The physician observes the effect of different medicines; like the chemist, he makes his experiments; but while the chemist, in controlling inert matter, always produces the same effects, the physician often finds his efforts defeated and his most powerful medicines fail.

817. The human system, though partaking of a common nature with inorganic matter, is yet controlled by a power which that does not possess, and whose influence often defeats, or, in an unexpected manner, assists, the experiments of the physician. The *mind* is this power—if that is disturbed, the material organs are interrupted in their functions. The quick beating of the heart, the throbbing of the temples, the rush of blood to the mantling cheek, or the sudden paleness of the features, are often caused by mental excitement—and the mind, as was remarked in our introductory chapter, is no subject for chemical inquiries. It is when mind has left it, that this earthly tenement may be fully examined and analyzed by the chemist—but then he has nothing before him but matter, and matter hastening to blend with its native, inorganic elements.

818. We will now notice a few of the most important animal substances. The ultimate elements, you will recollect, are the same as those of vegetables, consisting chiefly of carbon, oxygen, and hydrogen—but in animal substances, *nitrogen*, which seldom exists in vegetables, is one of the constituents.

819. The *proximate principles* of animal matter are of a peculiar kind, differing from those of plants, not only in the circumstance of their containing nitrogen, but in their rapid decay and putrefaction, during which, they throw off offensive gases.

320. *Gelatine* is that soft, jelly-like substance which is abundant in the head and feet of calves. It is this which renders soup nourishing; it may be obtained from almost any kind of meat by boiling it a sufficient time, cooling it to remove the fat which rises at the top, and straining to separate it from the fibres of the meat. The skins of animals are mostly composed of gelatine. On account of the tough and hard compound which gelatine forms with tannin, skins are

---

817. What is said of the power which controls the inorganic matter of which the body is composed?
818. Are the ultimate elements of animal substances different from those of vegetables?
819. What is said of the proximate principles of animal matter?
820. What is gelatine, and what are its properties?

made into leather. Glue is made by boiling the skins and other parts of animals which abound in gelatine, and isinglass is made from fish gelatine.

821. *Fat* is an animal product which is used under various forms. *Lard* is the fat of swine, *tallow* of neat cattle; *spermaceti* is the fat found in the head of the whale, *lamp oil* is from the body of the whale. United to potash and other alkalies, all kinds of fat may be converted into soap.

822. *Fibrin* forms most of the flesh and muscles of animals. It exists in blood. If with a bundle of twigs, or a little brush from a broom, some fresh blood be beaten, long reddish filaments will be found adhering to the twigs; this is fibrin, which, on being washed in cold water, becomes colourless. Its ultimate elements are thus stated by a French chemist.

Carbon	50	parts
Nitrogen	20	"
Oxygen	20	"
Hydrogen	10	"
	100	

823. *Albumen* is found in its purest state in the whites of eggs, where it exists with water and a little soda. It is also found in a solid state in some parts of the body, and liquid in milk and other animal substances. The facility with which albumen coagulates or hardens, is apparent from the quickness with which the white of an egg cooks in boiling water.

824. *Blood* is composed of water, albumen, fibrin, and some salts, and oxides. Its colour is supposed to be owing to the oxide of iron. It is a deep purple until oxygen gives it a lively red colour. In breathing or respiration there are two processes, the drawing in of the breath, called *inspiration*, and the throwing out of the breath, called *expiration;* in the former, the air, which contains oxygen, is inhaled, this, mingling with the blood, changes it from a dark, to a bright red colour, and is carried from the lungs to the heart; in the latter process carbonic acid is thrown from the lungs. You have only to breathe through a tube into a tumbler of lime water, and you will see the evidence that you throw off car-

---

821. What are the different kinds of animal fat?
822. Where does fibrin exist, and what are the proportions of its elements?
823. Where does albumen exist, and for what property is it remarkable?
824. Give some account of blood, its composition, the effect of oxygen upon it, the process of breathing, &c.

bonic acid, in the fact that the lime water acquires a milky
appearance as if chalk had been mixed with it; this is in consequence of carbonate of lime being formed by the carbonic
acid, from the breath uniting with the lime. Blood, on being
taken from the veins, if suffered to stand for a short time, separates into two parts, one thick and dark-coloured, called the
cruor, and the upper portion light-coloured and watery, called
the *serum*.

825. *Milk* consists of three parts—the *cream*, which, being
lighter, rises to the surface, the *caseous* or cheesy substance,
and the *serum* or *whey;* the caseous particles are separated
from the serum by means of *rennet*. This is obtained from
the stomach of calves, which affords a peculiar substance capable of curdling milk ; in which process the cheesy or caseous part is separated from the whey or serum.

826. *Butter* is made by agitating cream, this is done by
churning, or stirring, during which operations the particles
of butter unite, and the cream is transformed into *butter* and
buttermilk; the latter is serum, containing caseous or cheesy
particles. Butter has been found to consist of an acid called
butyric acid, and two substances, called *stearine* and *elaine*,
which form the basis of all kinds of fat.

827. It is the province of animal Chemistry to explain the
nature and constituents of *bones, teeth, hair, wool, silk, feathers, &c.*, in short of every substance which either enters into
the animal organization, or which is the product of this organization during its active state. Under the latter head are,
saliva, tears, bile, gastric juice, &c. By referring to larger
works, these subjects may be examined by the pupil, who
comprehending what has been explained to him, feels a desire for farther information.

828. We have now, as far as science has penetrated into
the composition of the material things which compose the
globe, explained to you of *what they are made, and how they
are put together.* We have taught you the alphabet of nature, or her simple elements ; and shown you that by different combinations of them, all the various substances which
the earth presents are formed. You have now learned to understand chemical language. The Beginner in Chemistry
who has carefully studied the *great laws of affinity, the pow-*

825. Of what parts does milk consist?
826. How is butter made?
827. What subjects properly belong to animal chemistry?
828. Repeat the concuding remarks.

erful agency of caloric and electricity in uniting and disuniting substances, the wonderful properties of that all-pervading element, *oxygen*, and the relation of other substances to it; who has traced the *combinations of supporters of combustion* with *combustible bodies*, and observed the regular *proportions in which they are united*, is now prepared to understand chemical books and lectures, and to make his own researches into the great volume of nature!

... forms air ...
... people ... water

... Egyptian
... Egypt

CPSIA information can be obtained at www.ICGtesting.com
Printed in the USA
BVOW06*0028160216

436759BV00025B/133/P

9 781296 695965